PENGUIN (

# A NIETZSCHE READER

FRIEDRICH NIETZSCHE was born near Leipzig in 1844, the son of a Lutheran clergyman. He attended the famous Pforta School, then went to university at Bonn and at Leipzig, where he studied philology and read Schopenhauer. When he was only twenty-four he was appointed to the chair of classical philology at Basle University; he stayed there until his health forced him into retirement in 1879. While at Basle he made and broke his friendship with Wagner, participated as an ambulance orderly in the Franco-Prussian War, and published *The Birth of Tragedy* (1872), *Untimely Meditations* (1873–6) and the first part of *Human, All Too Human* (1878; two supplements entitled *Assorted Opinions and Maxims* and *The Wanderer and his Shadow* followed in 1879 and 1880 respectively). From 1880 until his final collapse in 1889, except for brief interludes, he divorced himself from everyday life and, supported by his university pension, he lived mainly in France, Italy and Switzerland. *The Dawn* appeared in 1881 followed by *The Gay Science* in the autumn of 1882. *Thus Spoke Zarathustra* was written between 1883 and 1885, and his last completed books were *Ecce Homo*, an autobiography, and *Nietzsche contra Wagner*. He became insane in 1889 and remained in a condition of mental and physical paralysis until his death in 1900.

R. J. HOLLINGDALE translated eleven of Nietzsche's books and published two books about him; he also translated works by, among others, Schopenhauer, Goethe, E. T. A. Hoffman, Lichtenberg and Theodor Fontane, many of these for Penguin Classics. He was the honorary president of the British Nietzsche Society. R. J. Hollingdale died on 28 September 2001. In its obituary *The Times* described him as 'Britain's foremost postwar Nietzsche specialist' and the *Guardian* paid tribute to his 'inspired gift for German translation'. Richard Gott wrote that he 'brought fresh generations – through fluent and intelligent translation – to read and relish Nietzsche's inestimable thought'.

Professor Richard Schacht, Executive Director of the North American Nietzsche Society, said that 'Hollingdale and Walter Kaufmann, his sometime collaborator, deserve much of the credit for Nietzsche's rehabilitation during the third quarter of the twentieth century. It is hard to imagine what Nietzsche's fate in the English-speaking world would have been without them. All of us in Nietzsche studies today are in Hollingdale's debt'.

# A Nietzsche Reader

*Selected and translated with an*
*Introduction by* R. J. HOLLINGDALE

PENGUIN BOOKS

PENGUIN BOOKS

Published by the Penguin Group
Penguin Books Ltd, 80 Strand, London WC2R ORL, England
Penguin Putnam Inc., 375 Hudson Street, New York, New York 10014, USA
Penguin Books Australia Ltd, 250 Camberwell Road, Camberwell, Victoria 3124, Australia
Penguin Books Canada Ltd, 10 Alcorn Avenue, Toronto, Ontario, Canada M4V 3B2
Penguin Books India (P) Ltd, 11 Community Centre, Panchsheel Park, New Delhi – 110 017, India
Penguin Books (NZ) Ltd, Cnr Rosedale and Airborne Roads, Albany, Auckland, New Zealand
Penguin Books (South Africa) (Pty) Ltd, 24 Sturdee Avenue, Rosebank 2196, South Africa

Penguin Books Ltd, Registered Offices: 80 Strand, London WC2R ORL, England

www.penguin.com

This translation first published in 1977
Reprinted with a new Chronology and Further Reading 2003
35

Introduction, selection and translation copyright © R. J. Hollingdale, 1977
All rights reserved

Printed in England by Clays Ltd, St Ives plc
Set in Monotype Garamond

Except in the United States of America, this book is sold subject
to the condition that it shall not, by way of trade or otherwise, be lent,
re-sold, hired out, or otherwise circulated without the publisher's
prior consent in any form of binding or cover other than that in
which it is published and without a similar condition including this
condition being imposed on the subsequent purchaser

ISBN-13: 978-0-140-44329-5
ISBN-10: 0-140-44329-0

www.greenpenguin.co.uk

Penguin Books is committed to a sustainable future
for our business, our readers and our planet.
The book in your hands is made from paper
certified by the Forest Stewardship Council.

# CONTENTS

# INTRODUCTION

*A Nietzsche Reader* is a compendium of Nietzsche's philosophizing; it offers the reader an overview of that terrain in the hope that he/she will afterwards want to explore it. I have selected from Nietzsche's writings passages which I think essential for an understanding of him – in the knowledge that no selection can do justice to the work as a whole, and that any selection must to a greater or less extent be a simplification and thus to some extent a falsification of it. This selection from Nietzsche is not presented as a substitute for studying all of Nietzsche: its ambition is to lure on to that undertaking.

A generalizing introduction is, I hope, unnecessary: the compendium ought to explain itself. A passage-by-passage commentary ought likewise to be unnecessary: it ought to be its own commentary – Nietzsche commenting on himself. But two kinds of explanation are called for: explanation of the method of selection and of the principle of selection. The method first.

Selection is made from *Nietzsche's philosophical works*: that is, from the series *Human, All Too Human* (1878) to *The Anti-Christ* (1888), plus the autobiography *Ecce Homo* (1888). The works published before *Human*, the *Nachlass* and all other writings are excluded. The grounds for this limitation seem to me compelling and to reinforce one another. Firstly: the chief purpose of the *Nietzsche Reader* is to present Nietzsche as a philosopher, and it is in the series of books referred to that his philosophical opinions are primarily to be discovered. Secondly: a subsidiary purpose is to present Nietzsche as a stylist, and again it is in the series referred to that he so appears – these are the mature compositions upon which he in a stylistic sense *worked*. Third: the present book is intended to be readable straight through: if the selection has been made correctly it is only by reading it straight through that you will derive the maximum benefit from it: but the intrusion of any material other than Nietzsche's mature writings would act against this intention (the *Nachlass* especially, being stylistically no more than notes and jottings, would cause the reader constantly to stumble). Fourth: limitation of space makes rigorous selection a necessity, and in this process the writings of the second rank select themselves out. Fifth: I agree with Karl Schlechta that it is 'a demand of intellectual tact to understand an author *primarily* as he wanted himself to be publicly understood' and in the present context this means limiting oneself to those works Nietzsche published or intended for publication. Sixth and last: the works from *Human* to *Ecce Homo* lend themselves well to excerpting; the immature works before *Human* do not. A volume of 'representative extracts' would presumably have to include something from *The Birth of Tragedy*: the purpose of the present volume does not require it.

The construction of the book is as slight as the presuppositions behind it permit. In Part One Nietzsche is seen as for a great part of the time he ought to be seen: as a 'problem philosopher' within the Western philosophical tradition treating of the conventional subjects of Western philosophy and speculation. Part Three presents the development and enunciation of his specific philosophy of 'will to power' and its consequences and ramifications. The short Part Two is the mid-point of his thought: the overcoming of the consequences of nihilistic and destructive speculation through a resolve to find a new mode of transcendence. Within each of the sections into which the parts are divided the selections are ordered strictly chronologically. The reasons for this are, firstly, that Nietzsche's philosophy is not a series of conclusions but essentially a developing body of thought (and a chronological presentation preserves this development); secondly, that a chronological presentation also preserves the development of his style, the final phase of which is so vastly different from the first that their juxtaposition is not to be thought of except for the purpose (not pursued here) of demonstrating this difference. As a natural consequence of the development of his thinking the proportion of later to earlier work within each section gradually increases: so that, although not explicitly ordered chronologically, the book as a whole possesses a chronological movement.

The Preface offers a selection of Nietzsche's dicta on how his work should be read; the Postscripts offer a selection of opinions and maxims on miscellaneous topics excluded from the three main parts. These too are ordered chronologically.

Three points in squared brackets indicate an omission; three points without brackets are Nietzsche's own punctuation and do not indicate an omission.

The construction of Nietzsche upon which the selection and arrangement of the present anthology are based is – within the briefest possible compass – as follows. I see his distinctive contribution to European thought to lie in his perception that Western man was facing a radical change in his relationship with 'truth': a change that would come about when he recognized that the metaphysical, religious, moral and rational truths which were formerly both backbone and substance of the Western tradition were in fact errors. This conclusion is, or will be, a consequence of the pretension of such truths to absoluteness, a pretension which is being undercut by the evolutionism of Hegel and Darwin. Modern man is acquiring the idea of 'becoming' as his ruling idea: and if everything evolves, then 'truth', too, evolves – so that, if 'truth' is synonymous with absolute truth true for all time and for everybody, a loss of belief in the truth of truth is on the way. 'Everything evolves' will come to mean 'nothing is true'.

In place of this paradoxical formulation Nietzsche proposes

to say that truth is a matter of perspective. A metaphysical, religious, moral or rational statement can be called true only for the perspective of the mind which views it: viewed absolutely, any statement of this sort is false.

The truths subverted by evolutionism are being replaced by scientific truth: the experimentally verifiable statements of empirical science. But of these Nietzsche says, firstly, that they are not, as they pretend to be, objective – that is, discoveries about the world – but a human arrangement (*Zurechtmachung*) and interpretation of an essentially structureless and irrational universe so that it can be 'understood' and lived in; secondly, that scientific statements are statements only of fact (or alleged fact) and never judgemental, value and meaning being outside the sphere of science – so that one effect of the substitution of scientific truth for other kinds of truth is to deprive the world of meaning. Science answers the question Why? only as if it meant 'from what cause': when it means 'to what end?' the question Why? now remains unanswered.

The consciousness that 'life' is a phenomenon that cannot be explained, and the world and mankind facts without meaning, is coming: and Nietzsche undertakes the experiment of an anticipatory account of this nihilist state of mind.

The subsequently most notorious part of this account is his delineation of *moral* nihilism. There is no 'moral law', no 'moral world-order': 'moral meaning', being a value, eludes scientific investigation, since science cannot establish values. Empirical method can discover why morality exists (what causes it), but thus demonstrates that moral 'truths' are true only from a particular perspective: that 'there are moralities but no morality'. But this disintegration of the moral order is only an aspect of Nietzsche's elimination of all order.

The corollary to 'nothing is true' is 'everything is permitted', and in describing this state of things Nietzsche becomes the 'prophet of great wars' and herald of convulsions and disasters: his prognostications of decline, of a collapse of morale through a consciousness of purposelessness, also belong here.

The delineation of the nihilist world is a necessary preliminary to transcending it: but if the metaphysical is recognized as illusory and our world as the only world, a new mode of transcendence of this world will have to be non-metaphysical. Is a non-metaphysical transcendence possible? Nietzsche answers with his theory of 'will to power'. He sought to explain the admired attributes and achievements of mankind as products of 'sublimated will to power' – of the capacity to transform the drive to power over the world and other men into power over oneself: he was thus compelled to advocate 'strong will to power' and to see in conflict and the aggressive instincts an essential component of the human psychical economy. He embodied this conception of a non-metaphysical transcendence in the *Übermensch*: the 'superman' who is at once the actuality and symbol of sublimated will to power and thus the supreme advocate of life-affirmation through acceptance of the totality of life, and especially of the suffering entailed in living, in which aspect he is also described as 'the Dionysian man'. Dionysian acceptance of life is then put to the hardest test through the postulation of 'the eternal recurrence of the same events'.

The continuing tension between the nihilist and the transcendent aspects of what had now become 'Nietzsche's philosophy' prevent it, however, from hardening into a dogmatic doctrine – it remains to the end an experiment in reorientating oneself within a world of total uncertainty.

# FURTHER READING

David B. Allison, *Reading the New Nietzsche* (2001)

MaudeMarie Clark, *Nietzsche on Truth and Morality* (1990)

R. J. Hollingdale, *Nietzsche: The Man and His Philosophy* (1965; 1999)

Brian Leiter, *Nietzsche on Morality* (2002)

Bernd Magnus and Kathleen Higgins (eds.), *The Cambridge Companion to Nietzsche* (1996)

Alexander Nehemas, *Nietzsche: Life as Literature* (1985)

F. Nietzsche, *Daybreak: Thoughts on the Prejudices of Morality*, trans. R. J. Hollingdale, introduction by M. Tanner (1982)

——, *Dithyrambs of Dionysus*, trans. with introduction and notes R. J. Hollingdale (1984; 2001)

——, *Untimely Meditations*, trans. R. J. Hollingdale, introduction by J. P. Stern (1983)

John Richardson and Brian Leiter (eds.), *Nietzsche* (2001)

Rudiger Safranski, *Nietzsche: A Philosophical Biography*, trans. Shelley Frisch (2002)

Henry Staten, *Nietzsche's Voice* (1990)

Tracy Strong, *Friedrich Nietzsche and the Politics of Transfiguration* (1988)

# KEY TO TITLE INITIALS

*A*   *The Anti-Christ.* Written in September 1888, published in 1895.

*AOM*   *Assorted Opinions and Maxims.* Published in 1879 as the First Supplement to *Human, All Too Human*; 2nd edition published in 1886.

*BGE*   *Beyond Good and Evil.* Published in 1886.

*D*   *Daybreak.* Published in 1881, 2nd edition published in 1886.

*EH*   *Ecce Homo.* Written in the autumn of 1888, published in 1908.

*GM*   *On the Genealogy of Morals.* Published in 1887.

*GS*   *The Gay Science.* Published in 1882, 2nd, expanded edition published in 1887.

*HA*   *Human, All Too Human.* Published in 1878, 2nd edition published in 1886.

*T*   *Twilight of the Idols.* Written in the summer of 1888, published in 1889.

*W*   *The Wagner Case.* Published in 1888.

*WS*   *The Wanderer and his Shadow.* Published in 1880 as the Second Supplement to *Human, All Too Human*; 2nd edition published in 1886.

*Z*   *Thus Spoke Zarathustra.* Parts I and II published in 1883, Part III published in 1884, Part IV written in 1885, published in 1892.

The numbers after the initials at the foot of each extract refer to the section of the book from which the extract is taken in each case.

# PREFACE

## I

*Dangerous books.* – Somebody remarked: 'I can tell by my own reaction to it that this book is harmful.' But let him only wait and perhaps one day he will admit to himself that this same book has done him a great service by bringing out the hidden sickness of his heart and making it visible. – Altered opinions do not alter a man's character (or do so very little); but they do illuminate individual aspects of the constellation of his personality which with a different constellation of opinions had hitherto remained dark and unrecognizable.

[*AOM* 58]

## 2

*Against the censurers of brevity.* – Something said briefly can be the fruit of much long thought: but the reader who is a novice in this field, and has as yet reflected on it not at all, sees in everything said briefly something embryonic, not without censuring the author for having served him up such immature and unripened fare.

[*AOM* 127]

## 3

*The worst readers.* – The worst readers are those who behave like plundering troops: they take away a few things they can use, dirty and confound the remainder, and revile the whole.

[*AOM* 137]

## 4

*Marks of the good writer.* – Good writers have two things in common; they prefer to be understood rather than admired; and they do not write for knowing and over-acute readers.

[*AOM* 138]

## 5

Of all that is written I love only that which is written with blood. Write with blood: and you will discover that blood is spirit.

It is not easy to understand the blood of another: I hate the reading idler.

He who knows the reader does nothing further for the reader. Another century of readers – and spirit itself will stink.

That everyone is allowed to learn to read will in the long run ruin not only writing but thinking, too.

Once spirit was God, then it became man, and now it is even becoming mob.

He who writes in blood and aphorisms does not want to be read, he wants to be learned by heart.

In the mountains the shortest route is from peak to peak: but for that you must have long legs. Aphorisms should be peaks: and those to whom they are addressed should be big and tall of stature.

The air thin and pure, danger near and the spirit full of a joyful wickedness: these things go well together.

I want hobgoblins around me, for I am courageous. Courage which scares away phantoms creates hobgoblins for itself – courage wants to laugh.

I no longer feel as you do: this cloud which I see under me, this blackness and heaviness I laugh at – precisely this is your thundercloud.

You look up when you desire to be exalted. And I look down because I am exalted.

Who of you can at once laugh and be exalted?

He who climbs upon the highest mountains laughs at all tragedies, real or imaginary.

Courageous, untroubled, mocking, violent – that is what wisdom wants us to be: wisdom is a woman and loves only a warrior. [. . .]

[Z I *Of Reading and Writing*]

# 6

[. . .] It is not for nothing that one has been a philologist, perhaps one is a philologist still, that is to say, a teacher of slow reading: – in the end one also writes slowly. Nowadays it is not only my habit, it is also to my taste – a malicious taste, perhaps? – no longer to write anything which does not reduce to despair every sort of man who is 'in a hurry'. For philology is that venerable art which demands of its votaries one thing above all: to go aside, to take time, to become still, to become slow – it is a goldsmith's art and connoisseurship of the *word* which has nothing but delicate, cautious work to do and achieves nothing if it does not achieve it *lento*. But for precisely this reason it is more necessary than ever today, by precisely this means does it entice and enchant us the most, in the midst of an age of 'work', that is to say, of hurry, of indecent and perspiring haste, which wants to 'get everything done' at once, including every old or new book: – this art does not so easily get anything done, it teaches to read *well*, that is to say, to read slowly, deeply, looking cautiously before and aft, with reservations, with doors left open, with delicate eyes and fingers . . . My patient friends, this book desires for itself only perfect readers and philologists: *learn* to read me well! –

[*D* Preface (1886)]

*On the question of intelligibility.* – One does not want only to be
understood when one writes but just as surely *not* to be understood. It is absolutely no objection to a book if anyone finds
it unintelligible: perhaps that was part of its author's intention
– he did not *want* to be understood by 'anyone'. When it
wants to communicate itself, every nobler spirit and taste also
selects its audience; in selecting them it also debars 'the
others'. All the more subtle rules of style have their origin
here: they hold at arm's length, they create distance, they forbid 'admission', understanding – while at the same time they
alert the ears of those who are related to us through their ears.
But between ourselves and with reference to my own case –
I want neither my ignorance nor the ebullience of my tem-
perament to hinder my being intelligible to *you*, my friends:
however much my ebullience may compel me to get hold of
a thing quickly if I am to get hold of it at all. For I regard
profound problems as I do a cold bath – quick in, quick out.
That one thereby fails to get down deep enough, fails to reach
the depths, is the superstition of hydrophobics, of the enemies
of cold water; they speak without experience. Oh! Great cold
makes one quick! – And by the way: does a thing really remain
unintelligible and unrecognized if it is touched, viewed, illumined simply in passing? Does one absolutely have to sit
down on it first? to have brooded on it as on an egg? [...]
There are, at the very least, truths of a peculiar timidity and
ticklishness which one can seize hold of only suddenly – which
one must *surprise* or leave alone ... My brevity has finally
another value: within such questions as engage my attention
I have to say many things briefly so that they may be heard
even more briefly. For as an immoralist one must guard
against corrupting innocence – I mean the asses and old maids
of both sexes who have got nothing from life except their
innocence; more, my writings ought to inspire and uplift
them and encourage them to virtue. [...] So much as regards
brevity; my ignorance, of which I make no secret even to

myself, is a worse matter. There are times when I am ashamed of it; also, to be sure, times when I am ashamed of being ashamed. Perhaps we philosophers are all of us ill-equipped when it comes to knowledge: science is expanding, the most scholarly of us are on the point of discovering that they know too little. Still, it would be even worse if things were otherwise – if we knew *too much*; our task is and remains above all not to take ourselves for what we are not. We *are* something other than scholars; though the fact cannot be got round that, among other things, we are also scholarly. We have other requirements, another way of growing, another way of digesting: we need more, we also need less. For how much nourishment a spirit requires there is no formula; but if its taste is for independence, for rapid coming and going, for wandering, perhaps for adventures to which only the swiftest are equal, then it prefers to live free on a light diet than unfree and stuffed. Not fat, but the greatest suppleness and strength is what a good dancer wants from his food – and I do not know what the spirit of a philosopher could more wish to be than a good dancer. For the dance is his ideal, also his art, finally also the only kind of piety he knows, his 'divine service' . . .

[*GS* 381 (1887)]

## 8

If this writing is unintelligible to anyone and jars on his ears the fault is, it seems to me, not necessarily mine. It is clear enough, assuming, as I do assume, that one has read my earlier writings and has not spared some effort in doing so: for they are not easily accessible. As regards my *Zarathustra*, for example, I count no one as being familiar with it who has not at some time been profoundly wounded and at some time profoundly enraptured by every word in it: for only then may he enjoy the privilege of reverentially participating in the halcyon element out of which that work was born, in its sunlit brightness, remoteness, breadth and certainty. In other cases the aphoristic form creates difficulty: it arises from the fact that today this form is not taken *sufficiently seriously*. An aphorism, properly stamped and moulded, has not been 'deciphered' when it has simply been read; one has then rather to begin its *exegesis*, for which is required an art of exegesis. [. . .] To be sure, to practise reading as an *art* in this fashion one thing above all is needed, precisely the thing which has nowadays been most thoroughly unlearned – and that is why it wiil be some time before my writings are 'readable' – a thing for which one must be almost a cow and in any event *not* a 'modern man': *rumination* . . .

[*GM* Preface 8]

# 9

[. . .] I am often asked why I really write in German: nowhere am I read worse than in the Fatherland. But who knows, after all, whether I even *wish* to be read today? – To create things upon which time tries its teeth in vain; in form and *in substance* to strive for a little immortality – I have never been modest enough to demand less of myself. The aphorism, the apophthegm, are the forms of 'eternity'; my ambition is to say in ten sentences what everyone else says in a book – what everyone else *does not* say in a book. [. . .]

[*T Expeditions of an Untimely Man* 51]

# 10

[. . .] The conditions under which one understands me and then *necessarily* understands – I know them all too well. One must be honest in intellectual matters to the point of harshness to so much as endure my seriousness, my passion. One must be accustomed to living on mountains – to seeing the wretched ephemeral chatter of politics and national egoism *beneath* one. One must have become indifferent, one must never ask whether

truth is useful or whether it is a fatality . . . A preference, born
of strength, for questions for which no one today has the
courage; courage for the *forbidden*; predestination for the
labyrinth. An experience out of seven solitudes. New ears for
new music. New eyes for the most distant things. A new conscience for truths which have hitherto remained dumb. *And*
the will to economy in the grand style; to keeping one's force,
one's *enthusiasm* in bounds . . . Reverence for oneself; love for
oneself; unconditional freedom with respect to oneself . . .

Very well! These alone are my readers, my rightful readers,
my predestined readers: what do the *rest* matter? – The rest
are merely mankind. – One must be superior to mankind in
force, in *loftiness* of soul – in contempt . . .

[*A* Foreword]


## II

I am one thing, my writings are another. – Here, before I speak
of these writings themselves, I shall touch on the question of
their being understood or *not* being understood. I shall do so
as perfunctorily as is fitting: for the time for this question has
certainly not yet come. My time has not yet come, some are
born posthumously. – One day or other institutions will be
needed in which people live and teach as I understand living
and teaching: perhaps even chairs for the interpretation of
Zarathustra will then be established. But it would be a complete contradiction of myself if I expected ears *and hands* for
*my* truths already today: that I am not heard today, that no
one today knows how to take from me, is not only compre-
hensible, it even seems to me right. I do not want to be taken
for what I am not – and that requires that I do not take myself
for what I am not [. . .] It seems to me that to take a book of
mine into his hands is one of the rarest distinctions anyone
can confer upon himself – I even assume he removes his shoes
when he does so – not to speak of boots . . . When Doctor
Heinrich von Stein once honestly complained that he under-

stood not one word of my Zarathustra, I told him that was quite in order: to have understood, that is to say *experienced*, six sentences of that book would raise one to a higher level of mortals than 'modern' man could attain to. How *could* I, with *this* feeling of distance, even want the 'modern men' I know – to read me! [. . .] Not that I should like to underestimate the pleasure which the *innocence* in the rejection of my writings has given me. This very summer just gone, at a time when, with my own weighty, too heavily weighty literature, I was perhaps throwing all the rest of literature off its balance, a professor of Berlin University kindly gave me to understand that I ought really to avail myself of a different form: no one read stuff like mine. – In the end it was not Germany but Switzerland which offered the two extreme cases. An essay of Dr V. Widmann in the *Bund* on *Beyond Good and Evil* under the title 'Nietzsche's Dangerous Book', and a general report on my books as a whole on the part of Herr Karl Spitteler, also in the *Bund*, constitute a maximum in my life – of what I take care not to say . . . The latter, for example, dealt with my Zarathustra as an *advanced exercise in style*, with the request that I might later try to provide some content; Dr Widmann expressed his respect for the courage with which I strive to abolish all decent feelings. – Through a little trick of chance every sentence here was, with a consistency I had to admire, a truth stood on its head: remarkably enough, all one had to do was to 'revalue all values' in order to hit the nail on the head with regard to me – instead of hitting my head with a nail . . . All the more reason for me to attempt an explanation. – Ultimately, no one can extract from things, books included, more than he already knows. What one has no access to through experience one has no ear for. Now let us imagine an extreme case: that a book speaks of nothing but events which lie outside the possibility of general or even of rare experience – that it is the *first* language for a new range of experiences. In this case simply nothing will be heard, with the acoustical illusion that where nothing is heard there *is* nothing . . . This is in fact my average experience and, if you like,

the *originality* of my experience. Whoever believed he had understood something of me had dressed up something out of me
after his own image – not uncommonly an antithesis of me,
for instance an 'idealist'; whoever had understood nothing
of me denied that I came into consideration at all. [. . .]

[*EH Why I Write Such Excellent Books* 1]


## 12

I know my privileges as a writer to some extent: in individual
cases it has also been put to me how greatly habituation to
my writings 'ruins' taste. One can simply no longer endure
other books, philosophical ones least of all. To enter this
noble and delicate world is an incomparable distinction – to
do so one absolutely must not be a German; it is in the end a
distinction one has to have earned. But he who is related to
me through *loftiness* of will experiences when he reads me real
ecstasies of learning: for I come from heights no bird has ever
soared to, I know abysses into which no foot has ever yet
strayed. I have been told it is impossible to put a book of
mine down – I even disturb the night's rest . . . There is altogether no prouder and at the same time more exquisite kind
of book than my books – they attain here and there the highest
thing that can be attained on earth, cynicism; one needs the
most delicate fingers as well as the bravest fists if one is to
master them. Any infirmity of soul excludes one from them
once and for all, any dyspepsia, even, does so: one must have
no nerves, one must have a joyful belly. Not only does the
poverty, the hole-and-corner air of a soul exclude it from
them – cowardice, uncleanliness, secret revengefulness in the
entrails does so far more: a word from me drives all bad instincts into the face. I have among my acquaintances several
experimental animals on whom I bring home to myself the
various, very instructively various reactions to my writings.
Those who want to have nothing to do with their contents,
my so-called friends for example, become 'impersonal': they

congratulate me on having 'done it' again – progress is apparent, too, in a greater cheerfulness of tone . . . The completely vicious 'spirits', the 'beautiful souls', the thoroughly and utterly mendacious have no idea at all what to do with these books – consequently they see the same as *beneath* them, the beautiful consistency of all 'beautiful souls'. The horned cattle among my acquaintances, mere Germans if I may say so, give me to understand they are not always of my opinion, though they are sometimes . . . I have heard this said even of Zarathustra . . . Any 'feminism' in a person, or in a man, likewise closes the gates on me: one will never be able to enter this labyrinth of daring knowledge. One must never have spared oneself, *harshness* must be among one's habits, if one is to be happy and cheerful among nothing but hard truths. When I picture a perfect reader, I always picture a monster of courage and curiosity, also something supple, cunning, cautious, a born adventurer and discoverer. [. . .]

[*EH Why I Write Such Excellent Books* 3]

## 13

I know my fate. One day there will be associated with my name the recollection of something frightful – of a crisis like no other before on earth, of the profoundest collision of conscience, of a decision evoked *against* everything that until then had been believed in, demanded, sanctified. I am not a man, I am dynamite. – And with all that there is nothing in me of a founder of a religion – religions are affairs of the rabble, I have need of washing my hands after contact with religious people . . . I do not *want* 'believers', I think I am too malicious to believe in myself, I never speak to masses . . . I have a terrible fear I shall one day be pronounced *holy*: one will guess why I bring out this book *beforehand*, it is intended to prevent people from making mischief with me . . . I do not want to be a saint, rather even a buffoon . . . Perhaps I am a buffoon . . . And nonetheless, or rather *not* nonetheless – for there has hitherto been nothing more mendacious than saints – the truth speaks out of me. – But my truth is *dreadful*: for hitherto the *lie* has been called truth. – *Revaluation of all values*: that is my formula for an act of supreme coming-to-oneself on the part of mankind which in me has become flesh and genius. It is my fate to have to be the first *decent* human being, to know myself in opposition to the mendaciousness of millennia ... I was the first to *discover* the truth, in that I was the first to sense – *smell* – the lie as lie ... My genius is in my nostrils ... I contradict as has never been contradicted and am nonetheless the opposite of a negative spirit. I am a *bringer of good tidings* such as there has never been, I know tasks from such a height that any conception of them has hitherto been lacking; only after me is it possible to hope again. With all that I am necessarily a man of fatality. For when truth steps into battle with the lie of millennia we shall have convulsions, an earthquake spasm, a transposition of valley and mountain such as has never been dreamed of. The concept politics has then become completely absorbed into a war of spirits, all the power-structures of the old society have been blown into the air – they one and all reposed on the lie: there will be wars such as there have never yet been on earth. Only after me will there be *grand politics* on earth. –

[*EH Why I am a Destiny* 1]

# PART ONE

# PHILOSOPHY AND PHILOSOPHERS

## I

*Family failing of philosophers.* – All philosophers have the common failing of starting out from man as he is now and thinking they can reach their goal through an analysis of him. They involuntarily think of 'man' as an *aeterna veritas*, as something that remains constant in the midst of all flux, as a sure measure of things. Everything the philosopher has declared about man is, however, at bottom no more than a testimony as to the man of a *very limited* period of time. Lack of historical sense is the family failing of all philosophers; many, without being aware of it, even take the most recent manifestation of man, such as has arisen under the impress of certain religions, even certain political events, as the fixed form from which one has to start out. They will not learn that man has become, that the faculty of cognition has become; while some of them would have it that the whole world is spun out of this faculty of cognition. Now, everything *essential* in the development of mankind took place in primeval times, long before the 4,000 years we more or less know about; during these years mankind may well not have altered very much. But the philosopher here sees 'instincts' in man as he now is and assumes that these belong to the unalterable facts of mankind, and to that extent could provide a key to the understanding of the world in general: the whole of teleology is constructed by speaking of the man of the last four millennia as of an *eternal* man towards whom all things in the world have had a natural relationship from the time he began. But everything has become: there are *no eternal facts*, just as there are no absolute truths. Consequently what is needed from now on is *historical philosophizing*, and with it the virtue of modesty.

[*HA* 2]

## 2

*Private and public morality.* – Since belief has ceased that a God broadly directs the destinies of the world and that, all the apparent twists and turns in its path notwithstanding, is leading mankind gloriously upward, man has to set himself ecumenical goals embracing the whole earth. The former morality, namely Kant's, demanded of the individual actions which one desired of all men: that was a very naive thing; as if everyone knew without further ado what mode of action would benefit the whole of mankind, that is, what actions at all are desirable; it is a theory like that of free trade, presupposing that universal harmony *must* result of itself in accordance with innate laws of progress. Perhaps some future survey of the requirements of mankind will show that it is absolutely not desirable that all men should act in the same way, but rather that in the interest of ecumenical goals whole tracts of mankind ought to have special, perhaps under certain circumstances even evil tasks imposed upon them. – In any event, if mankind is not to destroy itself through such conscious universal rule, it must first of all attain to a hitherto altogether unprecedented *knowledge of the preconditions of culture* as a scientific standard for ecumenical goals. Herein lies the tremendous task facing the great spirits of the coming century.

[*HA* 25]

## 3

*From the thinker's innermost experience.* – Nothing is more difficult for man than to apprehend a thing impersonally: I mean to see it as a thing, *not as a person*: one might question, indeed, whether it is at all possible for him to suspend the clockwork of his person-constructing, person-inventing drive even for a moment. He traffics even with *ideas*, though they be the most abstract, as if they were individuals with whom one has to struggle, to whom one has to ally oneself, whom one has to tend, protect and nourish. We have only to spy on ourselves at that moment when we hear or discover a proposition new to us. Perhaps it displeases us because of its defiant and autocratic bearing; we unconsciously ask ourselves whether we shall not set a counter-proposition as an enemy beside it, whether we can append to it a 'perhaps', a 'sometimes'; even the little word 'probably' does us good, because it breaks the personally burdensome tyranny of the unconditional. If, on the other hand, this new proposition approaches in a milder shape, nice and tolerant, humble, and sinking as it were into the arms of contradiction, we try another way of testing our autocracy: what, can we not come to the assistance of this weak creature, stroke and feed it, give it strength and fullness, indeed truth and even unconditionality? Can we possibly be parental or knightly or pitying towards it? – Then again, we behold a judgement here and a judgement there, separated from one another, not regarding one another, making no impression one upon the other: and we are tickled by the thought of whether here a marriage might not be arranged, a *conclusion* drawn, in the presentiment that, if a consequence should proceed from this conclusion, the honour of it will fall not only to the two married judgements but also to those who arranged the marriage. If, however, one can get hold of that idea neither by means of defiance and ill-will nor by means of good-will (if one holds it for *true* – ), then one yields and pays it homage as a prince and leader, accords it a seat of honour and speaks of it with pomp and pride: for in *its* glitter one glitters too. Woe to him who seeks to darken it; unless it itself should one day become suspicious to us: – then, unwearying king-makers in the history of the spirit that we are, we hurl it from the throne and immediately raise its opponent in its place. Let one ponder this and then think on a little further: certainly no one will then speak of a 'drive to knowledge in and for itself'! – Why then does man prefer the true to the untrue in this *secret* struggle with idea-persons [. . .]? For the same reason as he practises justice in traffic with real persons: *now* out of habit, heredity and training, *originally* because the true – as also the fair and just – is *more useful* and *more productive of honour* than the untrue. For in the realm of thought, *power* and *fame* are hard to maintain if erected on the basis of error or lies: the feeling that such a building could at some time or other fall down is *humiliating* to the self-conceit of its architect; he is ashamed of the fragility of his material and, because he takes *himself more seriously* than he does the rest of the world, wants to do nothing that is not *more enduring* than the rest of the world. [. . .] It is his immeasurable pride which wants to employ only the finest, hardest stones for its work, that is to say truths or what it takes for truths. [. . .] That we are *afraid* of our own ideas, concepts, words, but also *honour* ourselves in them and involuntarily ascribe to them the capacity to instruct, despise, praise and censure us, that we thus traffic with them as with free intelligent persons, with independent powers, as equals with equals – it is in this that the strange phenomenon I have called 'intellectual conscience' has its roots. [. . .]

[*AOM* 26]

## 4

*In the desert of science.* – To the man of science on his unassuming and laborious travels, which must often enough be journeys through the desert, there appear those glittering mirages called 'philosophical systems': with bewitching, deceptive power they show the solution of all enigmas and the freshest draught of the true water of life to be near at hand; his heart rejoices, and it seems to the weary traveller that his lips already touch the goal of all the perseverance and sorrows of the scientific life, so that he involuntarily presses forward.

There are other natures, to be sure, which stand still, as if bewildered by the fair illusion: the desert swallows them up and they are dead to science. Other natures again, which have often before experienced this subjective solace, may well grow exceedingly ill-humoured and curse the salty taste which these apparitions leave behind in the mouth and from which arises a raging thirst – without one's having been brought so much as a single step nearer to any kind of spring.

[*AOM* 31]

5

*Error of philosophers*. – The philosopher believes that the value of his philosophy lies in the whole, in the building: posterity discovers it in the bricks with which he built and which are then often used again for better building: in the fact, that is to say, that that building can be destroyed and *nonetheless* possess value as material.

[*AOM* 201]

6

*The tyrants of the spirit*. – The march of science is now no longer crossed by the accidental fact that men live for about seventy years, as was for all too long the case. Formerly, a man wanted to reach the far end of knowledge during this period of time and the methods of acquiring knowledge were evaluated in accordance with this universal longing. The small single questions and experiments were counted contemptible: one wanted the shortest route; one believed that, because everything in the world seemed to be *accommodated to man*, the knowability of things was also accommodated to a human time-span. To solve everything at a stroke, with a single word – that was the secret desire. [. . .] 'There is a *riddle* to be solved': thus did the goal of life appear to the eye of the philosopher; the first thing to do was to find the riddle and to compress the problem of the world into the simplest riddle-form. The boundless ambition and exultation of being the 'unriddler of the world' constituted the thinker's dreams: nothing seemed worth-while if it was not the means of bringing everything to a conclusion *for him*! Philosophy was thus a kind of supreme struggle to possess the tyrannical rule of the spirit – that some such very fortunate, subtle, inventive, bold and mighty man was in reserve – one only! – was doubted by none, and several, most recently Schopenhauer, fancied themselves to be that one. – From this it follows that by and large the sciences have hitherto been kept back by the *moral narrowness* of their disciples and that henceforth they must be carried on with a higher and *more magnanimous* basic feeling. 'What do I matter!' – stands over the door of the thinker of the future.

[*D* 547]


7

*Intellectual conscience.* – Again and again I am brought up against it, and again and again I resist it: I don't want to believe it, even though it is almost palpable: *the vast majority lack an intellectual conscience*; indeed, it often seems to me that to demand such a thing is to be in the most populous cities as solitary as in the desert. Everyone looks at you strangely and goes on working his scales, calling this good, that evil; nobody blushes for shame when you remark that the weights he is using are giving short weight – but nobody is annoyed with you either: perhaps they laugh at your doubts. What I mean to say is: the *vast majority* do not find it contemptible to believe this or that, and to live in accordance with this belief *without* first being aware of the ultimate and securest reasons for and against it and without afterwards even taking the trouble to discover such reasons – the most gifted men and the noblest women are still among this 'vast majority'. But what is good-heartedness, refinement and genius to me if the person possessing these virtues tolerates in himself slack feelings with respect to

34

belief and judgement, if *the demand for certainty* is not his inner-most desire and profoundest need – as that which divides the higher men from the lower! Among certain pious people I have lit upon a hatred of reason and I was grateful to them for it: at least the bad intellectual conscience thus betrayed itself! But to stand in the midst of this *rerum concordia discors* and the whole marvellous uncertainty of existence *and not to question*, not to tremble with the desire and joy of questioning, not even to hate him who does ask questions, perhaps even to be thoroughly entertained by him – that is what I feel to be *contemptible*, and it is this feeling I seek first of all in everyone I meet – some folly or other again and again persuades me that every man possesses this feeling, as man. It is my kind of injustice.

[*GS* 2]

## 8

*Unwelcome disciples*. – What shall I do with these two little dis-ciples! – ill-humouredly exclaimed a philosopher who 'cor- · rupted' youth as Socrates had once corrupted them – they are pupils I do not want. This one cannot say no, and the other says to everything: 'half and half'. Supposing they grasped my teaching, the former would *suffer* too much, for my way of thinking calls for a warlike soul, a desire to hurt, a joy in denial, a hard hide – he would sicken and die of open and inner wounds. And the other will make for himself out of every cause he espouses something mediocre and will thus make the cause itself into something mediocre – such a dis-ciple I wish to my enemy!

[*GS* 32]

## 9

*Sense for truth*. – Give me any kind of sceptical proposal to which I am permitted to reply: 'Let's try it!' But I want to hear nothing more of any thing or question which does not admit of experimentation. This is the limit of my 'sense for truth': for there bravery has lost its rights.

[*GS* 51]

## 10

*Ability to contradict.* – Everyone now knows that the ability to endure contradiction is a high sign of culture. Some even know that the higher man wants and evokes contradiction so as to acquire a guidepost to his own acts of injustice hitherto unknown to him. But that the *ability* to contradict calls for a *good* conscience in enmity towards the customary, the traditional, the sanctified – that it is more than the other two and what is actually great, new, astonishing in our culture, the step of steps for the liberated spirit: who knows that?

[*GS* 297]

## 11

*As interpreters of our experiences.* – One kind of honesty has been unknown to all founders of religions and their like – they have never made of their experiences a matter of conscience for knowledge. 'What did I really experience? What happened in me and around me then? Was my mind sufficiently alert? Was my will bent against fantasy?' – none of them has asked such questions, none of our dear religious people asks such questions even now: they feel, rather, a thirst for things which are *contrary to reason* and do not put too many difficulties in the way of satisfying it – thus they experience 'miracles' and 're-births' and hear the voices of angels! But we, we others, thirsty for reason, want to look our experiences as fixedly in the eye as a scientific experiment, hour by hour, day after day. We ourselves want to be our own experiments and vivi-sectional animals!

[*GS* 319]

## 12

I name you three metamorphoses of the spirit: how the spirit shall become a camel, and the camel a lion, and the lion at last a child.

There are many heavy things for the spirit, for the strong, weight-bearing spirit in which dwell respect and awe: its strength longs for the heavy, for the heaviest.

What is heavy? thus asks the weight-bearing spirit thus it kneels down like the camel and wants to be well laden.

What is the heaviest thing, you heroes? so asks the weight-bearing spirit, that I may take it upon me and rejoice in my strength.

Is it not this: to debase yourself in order to injure your pride? To let your folly shine out in order to mock your wisdom?

Or is it this: to desert our cause when it is celebrating its victory? To climb high mountains in order to tempt the tempter?

Or is it this: to feed upon the acorns and grass of knowledge and for the sake of truth to suffer hunger of the soul?

Or is it this: to be sick and to send away comforters and make friends with the deaf, who never hear what you ask?

Or is it this: to wade into dirty water when it is the water of truth, and not to disdain cold frogs and hot toads?

Or is it this: to love those who despise us and to offer our hand to the ghost when it wants to frighten us?

The weight-bearing spirit takes upon itself all these heaviest things: like a camel hurrying laden into the desert, thus it hurries into its desert.

But in the loneliest desert the second metamorphosis occurs: the spirit here becomes a lion; it wants to capture freedom and be lord in its own desert.

It seeks here its ultimate lord: it will be an enemy to him and to its ultimate god, it will struggle for victory with the great dragon.

What is the great dragon which the spirit no longer wants

to call lord and god? The great dragon is called 'You shall'. But the spirit of the lion says 'I will!'

'You shall' lies in its path, sparkling with gold, a scale-covered beast, and on every scale glitters golden 'You shall'.

Values of a thousand years glitter on the scales, and thus speaks the mightiest of all dragons: 'All the values of things – glitter on me.

'All values have already been created, and all created values – are in me. Truly, there shall be no more "I will"!' Thus speaks the dragon.

My brothers, why is the lion needed in the spirit? Why does the beast of burden, that renounces and is reverent, not suffice?

To create new values – even the lion is incapable of that: but to create itself freedom for new creation – that the might of the lion can do.

To create freedom for itself and a sacred No even to duty: the lion is needed for that, my brothers.

To seize the right to new values – that is the most terrible proceeding for a weight-bearing and reverential spirit. Truly, to this spirit it is a theft and a work for an animal of prey.

Once it loved this 'You shall' as its holiest thing: now it has to find illusion and caprice even in the holiest, that it may steal freedom from its love: the lion is needed for this theft.

But tell me, my brothers, what can the child do that even the lion cannot? Why must the preying lion still become a child?

The child is innocence and forgetfulness, a new beginning, a sport, a self-propelling wheel, a first motion, a sacred Yes.

Yes, a sacred Yes is needed, my brothers, for the sport of creation: the spirit now wills *its own* will, the spirit sundered from the world now wins *its own* world.

I have named you three metamorphoses of the spirit: how the spirit became a camel, and the camel a lion, and the lion at last a child.

[*Z* 1 *Of the Three Metamorphoses*]

## 13

It has gradually become clear to me what every great philosophy has hitherto been: a confession on the part of its author
and a kind of involuntary memoir; moreover, that the moral
(or immoral) intentions in every philosophy have every time
constituted the real germ of life out of which the entire plant
has grown. To explain how a philosopher's most remote metaphysical assertions have actually been arrived at, it is always
well (and wise) to ask oneself first: what morality does this
(does *he* – ) aim at? I accordingly do not believe a 'drive to
knowledge' to be the father of philosophy but that another
drive has, here as elsewhere, only employed knowledge (and
false knowledge!) as a tool. But anyone who looks at the basic
drives of mankind to see to what extent they may in precisely
this connection have come into play as *inspirational* spirits (or
demons and kobolds –) will discover that they have all at some
time or other practised philosophy – and that each one of
them would be only too glad to present *itself* as the ultimate
goal of existence and as the legitimate *master* of all the other
drives. For every drive is tyrannical: and it is as *such* that it
tries to philosophize. [. . .] In the philosopher [. . .] there is
nothing whatever impersonal; and, above all, his morality
bears decided and decisive testimony to *who he is* – that is to
say, to the order of rank in which the innermost drives of his
nature stand in relation to one another.

[*BGE* 6]

## 14

A new species of philosopher is appearing: I venture to bap-
tize these philosophers with a name not without danger in it.
As I divine them, as they let themselves be divined – for it
pertains to their nature to *want* to remain a riddle in some
respects – these philosophers of the future might rightly, but
perhaps also wrongly, be described as *attempters*. This name

itself is in the end only an attempt and, if you will, a temptation.

Are they new friends of 'truth', these coming philosophers? In all probability: for all philosophers have hitherto loved their truths. But certainly they will not be dogmatists. It must offend their pride, and also their taste, if their truth is supposed . to be a truth for everyman, which has hitherto been the secret desire and hidden sense of all dogmatic endeavours. [. . .] One has to get rid of the bad taste of wanting to be in agreement with many. 'Good' is no longer good when your neighbour takes it into his mouth. And how could there exist a 'common good'! The expression is a self-contradiction: what can be common has ever but little value. In the end it must be as it is and has always been: great things are for the great, abysses for the profound, shudders and delicacies for the refined, and, in sum, all rare things for the rare. –

[*BGE* 42–3]

## 15

At the risk that moralizing will here too prove to be what it has always been – namely an undismayed *montrer ses plaies*, as Balzac says – I should like to venture to combat a harmful and improper displacement of the order of rank between science and philosophy which is today, quite unnoticed and as if with a perfect good conscience, threatening to become established. [. . .] The Declaration of Independence of the man of science, his emancipation from philosophy, is one of the more subtle after-effects of the democratic form and formlessness of life: the self-glorification and presumption of the scholar now stands everywhere in full bloom and in its finest springtime [. . .] My memory – the memory of a man of science, if I may say so! – is full of arrogant naiveties I have heard about philosophy and philosophers from young scientists and old physicians [. . .] Now it was the specialist and jobbing workman who instinctively opposed synthetic undertakings and capacities in general; now the industrious labourer who had got a scent of the *otium* and noble luxury in the philosopher's psychical economy and felt wronged and diminished by it. Now it was that colour blindness of the utility man who sees in philosophy nothing but a series of *refuted* systems and a wasteful expenditure which 'benefits' nobody. Now a fear of disguised mysticism and a rectification of the frontiers of knowledge leaped out; now a disrespect for an individual philosopher which had involuntarily generalized itself into a disrespect for philosophy. Finally, what I found most frequently among young scholars was that behind the arrogant disdain for philosophy there lay the evil after-effect of a philosopher himself, from whom they had, to be sure, withdrawn their allegiance, without, however, having got free from the spell of his disparaging evaluation of other philosophers – the result being a feeling of ill-humour towards philosophy in general. [. . .] In general and broadly speaking, it may have been above all the human, all too human element, in short the poverty of the most recent philosophy itself, which has been most thoroughly prejudicial to respect for philosophy and has opened the gates to the instinct of the plebeian. For one must admit how completely the whole species of a Heraclitus, a Plato, an Empedocles, and whatever else these royal and splendid hermits of the spirit were called, is lacking in our modern world; and to what degree, in face of such representatives of philosophy as are, thanks to fashion, at present as completely on top as they are completely abysmal [. . .] a worthy man of science is *justified* in feeling he is of a better species and descent. It is, in particular, the sight of those hotchpotch-philosophers who call themselves 'philosophers of reality' or 'positivists' which is capable of implanting a perilous mistrust in the soul of the ambitious young scholar: these gentlemen are at best scholars and specialists themselves, that fact is palpable! – they are one and all defeated men *brought back* under the sway of science, who at some time or other demanded *more* of themselves without having the right to this 'more' and the responsibility that goes with it – and who now honourably, wrathfully, revengefully represent by word and deed the *unbelief* in the lordly task and lordliness of philosophy. Finally: how could things be otherwise! Science is flourishing today and its good conscience shines in its face, while that to which the whole of modern philosophy has gradually sunk, this remnant of philosophy, arouses distrust and displeasure when it does not arouse mockery and pity. Philosophy reduced to 'theory of knowledge', actually no more than a timid epochism and abstinence doctrine: a philosophy that does not even get over the threshold and painfully *denies* itself the right of entry – that is philosophy at its last gasp, an end, an agony, something that arouses pity. How could such a philosophy – *rule*!

[*BGE* 204]

# 16

I insist that philosophical labourers and men of science in general should once and for all cease to be confused with philosophers [. . .] It may be required for the education of a philosopher that he himself has also once stood on all those steps on which his servants, the scientific labourers of philosophy, remain standing – *have* to remain standing; he himself must perhaps have been critic and sceptic and dogmatist and historian and, in addition, poet and collector and traveller and reader of riddles and moralist and seer and 'free spirit' and practically everything, so as to traverse the whole range of human values and value-feelings and be *able* to gaze from the heights into every distance, from the depths into every height, from the nook-and-corner into every broad expanse with manifold eyes and a manifold conscience. But all these are only preconditions of his task: this task itself demands something different – it demands that he *create values*. [. . .] *Actual philosophers* [. . .] *are commanders and law-givers*: they say 'thus it *shall* be!', it is they who determine the Wherefore and Whither of mankind, and they possess for this task the preliminary work of all the philosophical labourers, of all those who have subdued the past – they reach for the future with creative hand, and everything that is or has been becomes for them a means, an instrument, a hammer. Their 'knowing' is *creating*, their creating is a lawgiving, their will to truth is – *will to power*. – Are there such philosophers today? Have there been such philosophers? *Must* there not be such philosophers? ...

[*BGE* 211]

## 17

One may conjecture that a spirit in whom the type 'free spirit' will one day become ripe and sweet to the point of perfection has had its decisive experience in a *great liberation* and that previously it was all the more a fettered spirit and seemed to be chained for ever to its pillar and corner. What fetters the fastest? What bonds are all but unbreakable? In the case of men of a high and select kind they will be their duties: that reverence proper to youth, that reserve and delicacy before all that is honoured and revered from of old, that gratitude for the soil out of which they have grown, for the hand which led them, for the holy place where they learned to worship – their supreme moments themselves will fetter them the fastest, lay upon them the most enduring obligation. The great liberation comes for those who are thus fettered suddenly, like the shock of an earthquake: the youthful soul is all at once convulsed, torn loose, torn away – it itself does not know what is happening. A drive and impulse rules and masters it like a command; a will and desire awakens to go off, anywhere, at any cost; a vehement dangerous curiosity for an undiscovered world flames and flickers in all its senses. 'Better to die than to go on living *here*' – thus resounds the imperious voice and temptation: and this 'here', this 'at home' is everything it had hitherto loved! A sudden terror and suspicion of what it loved, a lightning-bolt of contempt for what it called 'duty', a rebellious, arbitrary, volcanically erupting desire for travel, strange places, estrangement, coldness, soberness, frost, a hatred for love, perhaps a desecrating blow and glance *backwards* to where it formerly loved and worshipped, perhaps a hot blush of shame at what it has just done and at the same time an exultation *that* it has done it, a drunken, inwardly exultant shudder which betrays that a victory has been won – a victory? over what? over whom? an enigmatic, question-packed, questionable victory, but the *first* victory nonetheless: such bad and painful things are part of the history of the great liberation. It is at the same time a sickness that can destroy the man who has it, this first outbreak of strength and will to self-determination, to evaluating on one's own account, this will to *free* will: and how much sickness is expressed in the wild experiments and singularities through which the liberated prisoner now seeks to demonstrate his mastery over things! He prowls cruelly around with an unslaked lasciviousness; what he captures has to expiate the perilous tension of his pride; what excites him he tears apart. With a wicked laugh he turns round whatever he finds veiled and through some sense of shame or other spared and pampered: he puts to the test what these things look like *when* they are reversed. [. . .] Behind all his toiling and weaving – for he is restlessly and aimlessly on his way as if in a desert – stands the question-mark of a more and more perilous curiosity. 'Can *all* values not be turned round? and is good perhaps evil? and God only an invention and finesse of the Devil? Is everything perhaps in the last resort false? And if we are deceived, are we not for that very reason also deceivers? *must* we not be deceivers?' – such thoughts as these tempt him and lead him on, ever further away, ever further down. Solitude encircles and embraces him, ever more threatening, suffocating, heart-tightening, that terrible goddess and *mater saeva cupidinum* – but who today knows what *solitude* is? . . .

From this morbid isolation, from the desert of these years of temptation and experiment, it is still a long road to that tremendous overflowing certainty and health which may not dispense even with sickness, as a means and fish-hook of knowledge, to that *mature* freedom of spirit which is equally self-mastery and discipline of the heart and permits access to many and contradictory modes of thought – to that inner spaciousness and indulgence of superabundance which excludes the danger that the spirit may even on its own road perhaps lose itself and become infatuated and remain seated intoxicated in some corner or other, to that superfluity of formative, curative, moulding and restorative forces which is precisely the sign of *great* health, that superfluity which grants to the free spirit the dangerous privilege of living *experimentally* and of being allowed to offer itself to adventure: the master's privilege of the free spirit! In between there may lie long years of convalescence, years full of variegated, painfully magical transformations ruled and led along by a tenacious *will to health* which often ventures to clothe and disguise itself as health already achieved. There is a midway condition which a man of such a destiny will not be able to recall without emotion: it is characterized by a pale, subtle happiness of light and sunshine, a feeling of bird-like freedom, bird-like altitude, bird-like exuberance, and a third thing in which curiosity is united with a tender contempt. A 'free spirit' – this cool expression does one good in every condition, it is almost warming. One lives no longer in the fetters of love and hatred, without yes, without no, near or far as one wishes, preferably slipping away, evading, fluttering off, gone again, again flying aloft; one is spoiled, as everyone is who has at some time seen a tremendous number of things *beneath* him – and one becomes the opposite of those who concern themselves with things which have nothing to do with them. Indeed, the free spirit henceforth has to do only with things – and how many things! – with which he is no longer *concerned* ...

A step further in convalescence: and the free spirit again draws near to life – slowly, to be sure, almost reluctantly, almost mistrustfully. It again grows warmer around him, yellower, as it were; feeling and feeling for others acquire depth, warm breezes of all kinds blow across him. It seems to him as if his eyes are only now open to what is *close at hand*. He is astonished and sits silent: where *had* he been? These close and closest things: how changed they seem! what bloom and magic they have acquired! He looks back gratefully – grateful to his wandering, to his hardness and self-alienation, to his viewing of far distances and bird-like flights in cold heights. What a good thing he had not always stayed 'at home', stayed 'under his own roof' like a delicate apathetic loafer! He had been *beside* himself: no doubt of that. Only now does he see himself – and what surprises he experiences as he does so! What unprecedented shudders! What happiness even in the weariness, the old sickness, the relapses of the convalescent! How he loves to sit sadly still, to spin out patience, to lie in the sun! Who understands as he does the happiness that comes in winter, the spots of sunlight on the wall! They are the most grateful animals in the world, also the most modest, these convalescents and lizards again half turned towards life: – there are some among them who allow no day to pass without hanging a little song of praise on the hem of its departing robe. [. . .]

At that time it may finally happen that, under the sudden illumination of a still stressful, still changeable health, the free, ever freer spirit begins to unveil the riddle of that great liberation which had until then waited dark, questionable, almost untouchable in his memory. If he has for long hardly dared to ask himself: 'why so apart? so alone? renouncing everything I once reverenced? renouncing reverence itself? why this hardness, this suspiciousness, this hatred for your own virtues?' – now he dares to ask it aloud and hears in reply something like an answer. 'You shall become master over yourself, master also over your virtues. Formerly *they* were your masters; but they must be only your instruments beside other instruments. You shall get control over your For and Against and learn how to display first one and then the other in accordance with your higher goal. You shall learn to grasp the sense of perspective in every value judgement [. . .] You shall learn to grasp the *necessary* injustice in every For and Against,

46

injustice as inseparable from life, life itself as *conditioned* by the sense of perspective and its injustice. You shall above all see with your own eyes where injustice is always at its greatest: where life has developed at its smallest, narrowest, neediest, most incipient and yet cannot avoid taking *itself* as the goal and measure of things and for the sake of its own preservation secretly and meanly and ceaselessly crumbling away and calling into question the higher, greater, richer – you shall see with your own eyes the problem of *order of rank*, and how power and right and spaciousness of perspective grow into the heights together. You shall' – enough: from now on the free spirit *knows* what 'you shall' he has obeyed, and he also knows what he now *can*, what only now he – *may* do ...

[*HA* Preface 3–6 (1886)]

## 18

[...] A philosopher who has made his way through many forms of health, and continues to make it, has also made his way through just as many philosophies: he *can* do nothing other than transpose his condition each time into the most spiritual form and distance – this art of transfiguration *is* precisely philosophy. We philosophers are not free to divide soul from body as the people does, we are even less free to divide soul from spirit. We are not thinking frogs, not observing and recording apparatus with disconnected intestines – we have continually to bear our thoughts out of our pain and, like mothers, share with them what we have in us of blood, heart, fire, joy, passion, torment, conscience, destiny, fatality. To live – that means for us continually to transform everything we are into light and fire; also everything that encounters us, we *can* do absolutely nothing other. And as for sickness: would we not almost be tempted to ask whether we can in any way do without it? Only great pain is, as the teacher of *great suspicion*, the ultimate liberator of the spirit. [...] It is only great pain, that slow protracted pain which takes its time and in

47

which we are as it were burned with green wood, that compels us philosophers to descend into our ultimate depths and to put from us all trust, all that is good-hearted, palliated, gentle, average, wherein perhaps our humanity previously reposed. I doubt whether such pain 'improves' –; but I do know it *deepens* us [. . .]

[*GS* Preface 3 (1887)]


## 19

[. . .] It makes all the difference whether a thinker stands in a personal relationship to his problems, so that he possesses in them his destiny, his necessity and also his greatest happiness, or whether this relationship is 'impersonal': that is, he knows how to feel and grasp them only with the tentacles of cold, inquisitive thought. In the latter case nothing will result, so much is certain: for the grand problems, even if they let themselves be grasped, refuse to let themselves be *retained* by frogs and weaklings, that has been their taste from all eternity [. . .]

[*GS* 345 (1887)]


## 20

*In honour of priestly natures.* – Of that which the people understands by wisdom (and who today is not 'people'?), I think of that prudent, cow-like composure, piety and country parson gentleness which lies in the meadow and earnestly and ruminatively *looks on* at life – it is precisely the philosophers who have always felt themselves furthest removed from this, probably because they were insufficiently 'people', insufficiently country parson for it. No doubt, too, they will be the last to learn to believe that the people can be *permitted* to understand anything of what lies furthest removed from it, of the grand *passion* of the man of knowledge who lives and has to live constantly in the storm-cloud of the highest problems and the heaviest responsibilities (therefore absolutely not looking on, outside, indifferent, safe, objective . . .) The people reveres quite another kind of man when it makes for itself an ideal of the 'wise man', and it is a thousand times right to do homage to precisely this kind of man with its finest honours and phrases: the mild, earnestly simple, chaste, priestly natures and what is related to them – it is they to whom the praise is given in that people's reverence before wisdom. And to whom should the people have more reason to show itself grateful than to these men, who belong to the people, and emerge from it, but as consecrated and select men *sacrificed* for the people's good – they themselves believe they are sacrificed to God – before whom it can pour out its heart with impunity, on whom it can *get free of* its secrets, its cares and crimes ( – for the man who 'communicates' gets free of himself; and he who has 'confessed' forgets). Here a great necessity commands: for the refuse of the soul, too, needs drainaways and the clear purifying waters in them, impetuous streams of love and strong, pure and humble hearts are needed which prepare themselves for such a non-public hygiene service and sacrifice themselves to it – for it *is* a sacrifice, a priest is and remains a human sacrifice . . . The people feels such sacrificed, quiet, earnest men of 'faith' as *wise*, that is, as men who have come to know, as 'certain' men in contrast to its own uncertainty: who would want to deprive it of this word and this reverence? – But, as is on the other hand only reasonable, among philosophers the priest too still counts as 'people' and *not* as 'one who knows', above all because philosophers do not believe in the existence of 'those who know' and already smell 'people' in precisely this belief and superstition. It was *modesty* which in Greece invented the word 'philosopher' and left the splendid arrogance of calling oneself wise to the actors of the spirit – the modesty of such monsters of pride and self-glorification as Pythagoras, as Plato.–

[*GS* 351 (1887)]

*Revenge on the spirit and other backgrounds of morality.* – Morality
– where would you think it has its most dangerous and malicious advocates? ... Here is a man who has turned out a
failure, a man who possesses too little spirit to be able to enjoy
it and just enough culture to realize that fact; bored, weary,
a self-despiser; through some inherited capacity unfortunately
deprived even of the last consolation, the 'blessing of work',
self-forgetfulness in the 'daily round'; such a one as is fundamentally ashamed of his existence – perhaps he harbours a
couple of little vices as well – and on the other hand cannot
help over-indulging himself and exacerbating his vanity worse
and worse with books to which he has no right or more intelligent company than he can digest: such a man poisoned
through and through [. . .] falls finally into an habitual condition of revengefulness, of the will to revenge ... *What* do
you think he needs, absolutely must have, to create for himself in his own eyes the appearance of superiority over more
spiritual men, to enjoy, at least in his imagination, the delight
of *consummate revenge*? Always *morality*, on that you may wager,
always the grand moral words, always the thump-thump of
justice, wisdom, holiness, virtue, always the stoicism of bearing ( – how well stoicism conceals what one does *not* have! ...),
always the cloak of prudent silence, of geniality, of mildness
and whatever else all those idealist-cloaks are called under
which the incurable self-despisers, likewise the incurably vain,
go about. Do not misunderstand me: out of such born *enemies
of the spirit* there sometimes arises that rare piece of humanity
which the people honours under the name of saint and wise
man; out of such men there come those monsters of morality
which make a great noise in the world, which make history –
Saint Augustine is one of them. Fear of the spirit, revenge on
the spirit – oh how often have these dynamic vices already
become the root of virtues! Become, indeed, virtue itself! –
And, between ourselves, even that philosophers' pretension
to *wisdom* which has been advanced here and there on earth

from time to time, the maddest and most immodest of all pre-
tensions – has it not always hitherto been, in India as in Greece,
*before all a hiding-place*? Sometimes, perhaps, from the viewpoint of education, which sanctifies so many lies, a tender regard for the young and developing, for disciples who often
have to be defended against themselves by belief in a person
(by an error) . . . Most frequently, however, a hiding-place of
the philosopher into which from weariness, age, coldness,
hardening he escapes, the feeling that the end is near, the prudence of that instinct which the animals have before death –
they go aside, become still, choose solitude, crawl away into
caves, become *wise* . . . What? Wisdom a hiding-place of the
philosopher in face of – the spirit?

[*GS* 359 (1887)]


## 22

To live alone one must be an animal or a god – says Aristotle.
There is yet a third case: one must be both – a *philosopher*.

[*T Maxims and Arrows* 3]


## 23

– He who knows how to breathe the air of my writings knows
that it is an air of the heights, a *robust* air. One has to be made
for it, otherwise there is no small danger one will catch cold.
The ice is near, the solitude is terrible – but how peacefully
all things lie in the light! how freely one breathes! how much
one feels *beneath* one! – Philosophy, as I have hitherto understood and lived it, is a voluntary living in ice and high mountains – a seeking after everything strange and questionable in
existence, all that has hitherto been excommunicated by
morality. From the lengthy experience afforded by such a
wandering in the *forbidden* I learned to view the origins of
moralizing and idealizing very differently from what might be

desirable: the *hidden* history of the philosophers, the psychology of their great names came to light for me. – How much truth can a spirit *bear*, how much truth can a spirit *dare*? that became for me more and more the real measure of value. Error ( – belief in the ideal – ) is not blindness, error is *cowardice* . . . Every acquisition, every step forward in knowledge, is the *result* of courage, of severity towards oneself, of cleanliness with respect to oneself . . . *Nitimur in vetitum*: in this sign my philosophy will one day conquer, for fundamentally what has hitherto been forbidden has never been anything but the truth. –

[*EH* Foreword 3]

# LOGIC, EPISTEMOLOGY,
# METAPHYSICS

## 24

*Chemistry of concepts and sensations.* – Almost all the problems of
philosophy once again pose the same form of question as they
did 2,000 years ago: how can something originate in its opposite, for example rationality in irrationality, the sentient in the
dead, logic in illogic, disinterested contemplation in covetous
desire, living for others in egoism, truth in errors? Metaphysical philosophy has hitherto surmounted this difficulty
by denying that the one originates in the other and assuming
for the more highly valued thing a miraculous source in the
very kernel and being of the 'thing in itself'. Historical philosophy, on the other hand, which can no longer be separated
from natural science, the youngest of all philosophical
methods, has discovered in individual cases (and this will
probably be the result in every case) that there are no opposites, except in the customary exaggeration of popular or
metaphysical interpretations, and that a mistake in reasoning
lies at the bottom of this antithesis: according to this explanation there exists, strictly speaking, neither an unegoistic
action nor completely disinterested contemplation; both are
only sublimations, in which the basic element seems almost
to have dispersed and reveals itself only under the most pains-
taking observation. All we require, and what can be given us
only now that the individual sciences have attained their present level, is a chemistry of the moral, religious, and aesthetic
conceptions and sensations, likewise of all the agitations we
experience within ourselves in cultural and social intercourse
and indeed even when we are alone: what if this chemistry

would end up by revealing that in this domain, too, the most glorious colours are derived from base, indeed from despised materials? Will there be many who desire to pursue such researches? Mankind likes to put questions of origin and beginnings out of its mind: must one not be almost inhuman to detect in oneself a contrary inclination? –

[*HA* 1]


## 25

*Estimation of unpretentious truths.* – It is the mark of a higher culture to value the little unpretentious truths which have been discovered by means of rigorous method more highly than the errors handed down by metaphysical ages and men, which blind us and make us happy. [. . .]

[*HA* 3]


## 26

*Misunderstanding of the dream.* – The man of the ages of barbarous primordial culture believed that in the dream he was getting to know a *second real world*: here is the origin of all metaphysics. Without the dream, one would have had no occasion to divide the world into two. The dissection into soul and body is also connected with the oldest idea of the dream, likewise the postulation of a life of the soul, thus the origin of all belief in spirits and probably also of the belief in gods. 'The dead live on, *for* they appear to the living in dreams': that was the conclusion one formerly drew, throughout many millennia.

[*HA* 5]


## 27

*Metaphysical world.* – It is true, there could be a metaphysical world; the absolute possibility of it is hardly to be disputed.

We behold all things through the human head and cannot cut off this head; while the question nonetheless remains what of the world would still be there if one had cut it off. This is a purely scientific problem and one not very well calculated to bother people overmuch; but all that has hitherto made metaphysical assumptions *valuable, terrible, delightful* to them, all that has begotten these assumptions, is passion, error and self-deception; the worst of all methods of acquiring knowledge, not the best of all, have taught belief in them. When one has disclosed these methods as the foundation of all extant religions and metaphysical systems one has refuted them! Then that possibility still remains over; but one can do absolutely nothing with it, not to speak of letting happiness, salvation and life depend on the gossamer of such a possibility. – For one could assert nothing at all of the metaphysical world except that it was a being-other, an inaccessible, incomprehensible being-other; it would be a thing with negative qualities. – Even if the existence of such a world were never so well demonstrated, it is certain that knowledge of it would be the most useless of all knowledge: more useless even than knowledge of the chemical composition of water must be to the sailor in danger of shipwreck.

[*HA* 9]

## 28

*Language as putative science.* – The significance of language for the evolution of culture lies in this, that mankind set up in language a separate world beside the other world, a place it took to be so firmly set that, standing upon it, it could lift the rest of the world off its hinges and make itself master of it. To the extent that man has for long ages believed in the concepts and names of things as in *aeternae veritates* he has appropriated to himself that pride by which he raised himself above the animal: he really thought that in language he possessed knowledge of the world. The sculptor of language

was not so modest as to believe that he was only giving
things designations, he conceived rather that with words he
was expressing supreme knowledge of things; language is, in
fact, the first stage of the occupation with science. Here, too,
it is the *belief that the truth has been found* out of which the
mightiest sources of energy have flowed. Very much subsequently – only now – it dawns on men that in their belief in
language they have propagated a tremendous error. Happily,
it is too late for the evolution of reason, which depends on
this belief, to be again put back. – *Logic* too depends on presuppositions with which nothing in the real world corresponds, for example on the presupposition that there are
identical things, that the same thing is identical at different
points of time: but this science came into existence through
the opposite belief (that such conditions do obtain in the real
world). It is the same with *mathematics*, which would certainly
not have come into existence if one had known from the beginning that there was in nature no exactly straight line, no
real circle, no absolute magnitude.

[*HA* 11]

## 29

*Number*. – The invention of the laws of numbers was made
on the basis of the error, dominant even from the earliest
times, that there are identical things (but in fact nothing is
identical with anything else); at least that there are things
(but there is no 'thing'). The assumption of plurality always
presupposes the existence of *something* that occurs more than
once: but precisely here error already holds sway, here already
we are fabricating beings, unities which do not exist. – Our
sensations of space and time are false, for tested consistently
they lead to logical contradictions. [. . .] When Kant says 'the
understanding does not draw its laws from nature, it pre-
scribes them to nature', this is wholly true with regard to the
*concept of nature* which we are obliged to attach to nature

(nature = world as idea, that is as error), but which is the summation of a host of errors of the understanding. – To a world which is *not* our idea the laws of numbers are wholly inapplicable: these are valid only in the human world.

[*HA* 19]

## 30

*Where the theory of freedom of will originated.* – Over one man *necessity* stands in the shape of his passions, over another as the habit of hearing and obeying, over a third as a logical conscience, over a fourth as caprice and a mischievous pleasure in escapades. These four will, however, seek the *freedom* of their will precisely where each of them is most firmly fettered: it is as if the silkworm sought the freedom of its will in spinning. How does this happen? Evidently because each considers himself most free where his *feeling of living* is greatest; thus, as we have said, in passion, in duty, in knowledge, in mischievousness respectively. That through which the individual human being is strong, wherein he feels himself animated, he involuntarily thinks must also always be the element of his freedom: he accounts dependence and dullness, independence and the feeling of living as necessarily coupled. – Here an experience in the social-political domain has been falsely transferred to the farthest metaphysical domain: in the former the strong man is also the free man; the lively feeling of joy and sorrow, high hope, boldness in desire, powerfulness in hatred is the property of the rulers and the independent, while the subjected man, the slave, lives dull and oppressed. – The theory of freedom of will is an invention of *ruling* classes.

[*WS* 9]

## 31

*Freedom of will and isolation of facts.* – Our usual imprecise mode of observation takes a group of phenomena as one and calls it a fact: between this fact and another fact it imagines in addition an empty space, it *isolates* every fact. In reality, however, all our doing and knowing is not a succession of facts and empty spaces but a continuous flux. Now, belief in freedom of will is incompatible precisely with the idea of a continuous, homogeneous, undivided, indivisible flowing: it presupposes that *every individual action is isolate and indivisible*; it is an *atomism* in the domain of willing and knowing. – Just as we understand characters only imprecisely, so do we also facts: we speak of identical characters, identical facts: *neither exists*. Now, we praise and censure, however, only under this false presupposition that there are *identical* facts, that there exists a graduated order of *classes* of facts which corresponds to a graduated world-order: thus we *isolate*, not only the individual fact, but also again groups of supposedly identical facts (good, evil, sympathetic, envious actions, etc.) – in both cases erroneously. – The word and the concept are the most manifest ground for our belief in this isolation of groups of actions: we do not only *designate* things with them, we think originally that through them we grasp the *true* in things. Through words and concepts we are still continually misled into imagining things as simpler than they are, separate from one another, indivisible, each existing in and for itself. A philosophical mythology lies concealed in *language* which breaks out again every moment, however careful one may be otherwise. Belief in freedom of will – that is to say in *identical* facts and in *isolated* facts – has in language its constant evangelist and advocate.

[*WS* 11]

### 32

*Source of knowledge.* – Throughout tremendous periods of time the intellect begot nothing but errors; some of them proved useful and preservative of the species: he who came upon them or inherited them fought his fight for himself and his posterity with greater good fortune. These articles of belief, which have been repeatedly handed down and have finally become almost a basic component of the human species, are for example the following: that there are enduring things, that there are identical things, that there are things, material, bodies, that a thing is what it appears to be, that our willing is free, that what is good for me is good in itself. Deniers and doubters of these propositions appeared only very late – truth, as the feeblest form of knowledge, appeared only very late. It seemed one was incapable of living with truth, our organism was adapted to the opposite; all its higher functions, the perceptions of the senses and every kind of sensation in general worked in concert with those primevally incorporated fundamental errors. More: those propositions became even within the domain of knowledge the norms according to which one meted out 'true' and 'untrue' – right into the remotest regions of pure logic. Thus the *strength* of items of knowledge lies, not in their degree of truth, but in their age, their incorporatedness, their character as a condition of life. Where life and knowledge seem to come into contradiction there is never any serious contest; doubt and denial here count as madness. Those exceptions as thinkers, the Eleatics, who nonetheless advanced and maintained the antithesis of these natural errors, believed it was possible to *live* this opposite, too: they invented the sage as the man of unchangeability, impersonality, universality of perception, as one and at the same time all, with a special capacity for that inverted knowledge; they held the belief that their knowledge was at the same time the principle of *life*. [. . .] The evolution of honesty and scepticism in greater refinement at length rendered these people, too, impossible. [. . .] This more refined honesty and scepticism everywhere had its origin when two antithetical propositions seemed to be *applicable* to life because both were compatible with those fundamental errors, when, that is to say, there could be dispute as to the greater or less degree of *utility* for life of these propositions; likewise wherever novel propositions, though not useful to life, were at any rate not harmful to it, being expressions of an intellectual instinct for play, at the same time innocent and happy, like all play. Gradually the human brain was filled with such judgements and convictions; fermentation, struggle and lust for power arose within this throng. Not only utility and pleasure, every kind of drive took sides in the struggle over 'truth'; the intellectual struggle became an occupation, excitement, profession, duty, dignity: knowledge and the striving after the true finally ordered itself as a need among the other needs. From then on not only belief and conviction, but examination, denial, mistrust, contradiction, too, were a *power*, all the 'evil' instincts were subordinated to knowledge and placed in its service and acquired the lustre of the permitted, honoured, useful and finally the eye and innocence of the *good*. Knowledge thus becomes a piece of life itself and, as life, a perpetually increasing power: until at last knowledge and those primeval fundamental errors come into collision, both as life, both as power, both in the same man. The thinker: this is now the being within whom the drive to truth and those life-preservative errors fight their first fight, after which the drive to truth, too, has proved itself a life-preservative power. In comparison with the importance of this fight everything else is a matter of indifference: the ultimate question as to the conditions of life is posed here, and the first attempt to answer this question by experiment is made here. To what extent can truth endure incorporation? – that is the question, that is the experiment.

[*GS* 110]

### 33

*Origin of the logical*. – Whence did logic come into existence in the human head? Certainly out of illogic, whose realm must initially have been tremendous. But countless creatures who reasoned differently from the way we now reason have perished: they could always have been better reasoners. He, for example, who did not know how to discover the 'identical' sufficiently often in regard to food or to animals hostile to him, he who was thus too slow to subsume, too cautious in subsuming, had a smaller probability of survival than he who in every case of similarity at once conjectured identity. But it was the prevailing tendency to treat the similar at once as identical, an illogical tendency – for nothing is identical – which first created all the foundations of logic. Likewise, for the concept of substance to arise – a concept indispensable to logic, though again there is in the strictest sense nothing real which corresponds to it – the changing in things must for a long time not have been seen or sensed; the creatures who did not see accurately had an advantage over those who saw everything 'in flux'. In and for itself, every high degree of caution in reasoning, every sceptical tendency is a great danger for life. No living creatures would have been preserved if the opposite tendency rather to affirm than to defer judgement, rather to err and invent than to watch and attend, rather to assent than to deny, rather to judge than to be just – had not been cultivated with extraordinary vigour. – The course of logical thinking and concluding in our present brain corresponds to a process and struggle of drives which in themselves individually are all very illogical and unjust; we usually experience only the outcome of that struggle: so rapidly and secretly does that primeval mechanism now work in us.

[*GS* 111]

34

*Cause and effect*. – We call it 'explanation', but it is 'description' which distinguishes us from earlier stages of knowledge and science. We describe better – we explain just as little as any who came before us. We have revealed a plural succession where the naive man and investigator of earlier cultures saw only two things, 'cause' and 'effect' as they were called; we have perfected an image of how things become, but we have not got past an image or behind it. In every case the row of 'causes' stands before us much more completely; we conclude: this must first happen if that is to follow – but we have therewith *understood* nothing. Quality, in any chemical change for example, appears as it has always done as a 'miracle'; likewise all locomotion; no one has 'explained' thrust. How could we explain them! We operate with nothing but things which do not exist, with lines, planes, bodies, atoms, divisible time, divisible space – how should explanation even be possible when we first make everything into an *image*, into our own image! It is sufficient to regard science as the most fruitful possible humanization of things, we learn to describe ourselves more and more exactly by describing things and the succession of things. Cause and effect: such a duality probably never occurs – in reality there stands before us a continuum of which we isolate a couple of pieces; just as we always perceive a movement only as isolated points, therefore do not really see it but infer it. The suddenness with which many events rise up leads us astray; but it happens suddenly only for us. There is an infinite host of occurrences in this sudden second which elude us. An intellect which saw cause and effect as a continuum and not, as we do, as a capricious division and fragmentation, which saw the flux of events – would reject the concept cause and effect and deny all conditionality.

[*GS* 112]

## 35

Having kept a close eye on philosophers and read between their lines for a sufficient length of time, I tell myself: the greater part of conscious thinking must still be counted among the instinctive activities, and this is so even in the case of philosophical thinking [. . .] Just as the act of being born plays no part in the procedure and progress of heredity, so 'being conscious' is in no decisive sense the *opposite* of the instinctive – most of a philosopher's conscious thinking is secretly directed and compelled into definite channels by his instincts. Behind all logic, too, and its apparent autonomy there stand evaluations, in plainer terms physiological demands for the preservation of a certain species of life. For example, that the definite shall be of greater value than the indefinite, appearance of less value than 'truth': but such valuations as these could, their regulatory importance for *us* notwithstanding, be no more than foreground valuations, a certain species of *niaiserie* which may be necessary precisely for the preservation of beings such as us. Assuming, that is to say, that it is not precisely man who is the 'measure of things'. . .

[*BGE* 3]

## 36

The falseness of a judgement is to us not necessarily an objection to a judgement [. . .] The question is to what extent it is life-advancing, life-preserving, species-preserving, perhaps even species-breeding; and our fundamental tendency is to assert that the falsest judgements (to which synthetic *a priori* judgements belong) are the most indispensable to us, that without granting as true the fictions of logic, without measuring reality against the purely invented world of the unconditional and self-identical, without a continual falsification of the world by means of numbers, mankind could not live – that to renounce false judgements would be to renounce life, would be to deny life [. . .]

[*BGE* 4]

## 37

It is perhaps just dawning on five or six minds that physics too is only an interpretation and arrangement of the world [. . .] and *not* an explanation of the world: but insofar as it is

founded on belief in the senses it passes for more than that
and must continue to do so for a long time to come. It has
the eyes and ears on its side, it has ocular evidence and palp-
ability on its side: and this has the effect of fascinating, per-
suading, *convincing* an age with fundamentally plebeian tastes
[. . .] What is obvious, what has been 'explained'? Only that
which can be seen and felt – thus far has every problem been
scrutinized. Obversely: it was precisely in opposition to palp-
ability that the charm of the Platonic mode of thinking,
which was a *noble* mode of thinking, consisted [. . .] 'Where
man has nothing more to see or grasp he has nothing more
to do' – that is certainly a different imperative from the Platonic, but for an uncouth industrious race of machinists and
bridge-builders of the future, which has nothing but *course*
work to get through, it may well be the right one.

[*BGE* 14]

## 38

That individual philosophical concepts are not something
arbitrary, something growing up autonomously, but on the
contrary grow up connected and related to one another; that,
however suddenly and arbitrarily they appear to emerge in
the history of thought, they nonetheless belong just as much
to a system as do the members of the fauna of a continent:
that fact is in the end also shown in the fact that the most
diverse philosophers unfailingly fill out again and again a certain basic scheme of *possible* philosophies. Under an invisible
spell they always trace once more the identical orbit: however
independent of one another they may feel, with their will to
criticism or systematism, something in them leads them, something drives them in a definite order one after another: it is
precisely that innate systematism and relationship of concepts.
[. . .] The singular family resemblance between all Indian,
Greek and German philosophizing is easy enough to explain.
Where there exists a language affinity it is quite impossible,

thanks to the common philosophy of grammar – I mean thanks to unconscious domination and directing by similar grammatical functions – to avoid everything being prepared in advance for a similar evolution and succession of philosophical systems: just as the road seems to be barred to certain other possibilities of world interpretation. [. . .]

[*BGE* 20]

## 39

*Of the 'genius of the species'.* – The problem of consciousness (more correctly: of becoming conscious of oneself) steps before us only when we begin to understand to what extent we could do without it: and we are now placed at this beginning of understanding by physiology and the natural history of the animals [. . .] For we could think, feel, will, recollect, we could likewise 'act' in every sense of the word: and yet none of this would need to 'enter our consciousness' (as one says in a metaphor). The whole of life would be possible without, as it were, regarding itself in a mirror: as indeed in our case by far the greater part of this life even now does pass without this reflection – including our thinking, feeling, willing life, however offensive it may sound to a philosopher of earlier days. *To what end* consciousness at all, if it is in the main *superfluous*? – Now it seems to me [. . .] that refinement and strength of consciousness always stands in proportion to the *capacity for communication* of a human being (or animal), capacity for communication in turn in proportion to *need for communication* [. . .] Supposing this observation to be correct, I may then go on to conjecture that *consciousness evolved at all only under the pressure of need for communication* – that it was from the very first necessary and useful only between man and man (between commanders and obeyers in particular) and also evolved only in proportion to the degree of this usefulness. Consciousness is really only a connecting network between man and man – only as such did it have to evolve: the solitary and predatory man would not have needed it. That our actions, thoughts, feelings, movements come into our consciousness – at least a part of them – is the consequence of a fearfully protracted compulsion which lay over man: as the most endangered animal he *required* help, protection, he required his own kind, he had to express his needs, know how to make himself understood – and for all that he first had need of 'consciousness', that is to say, himself needs to 'know' what he lacks, to 'know' how he feels, to 'know' what he is thinking. For, to say it again: man, like every living creature, thinks continually but does not know it; thinking which has become *conscious* is only the smallest part of it, let us say the most superficial part, the worst part – for only this conscious thinking *takes place in words, that is to say in communication-signs*, by which the origin of consciousness reveals itself. In short, the evolution of language and the evolution of consciousness (*not* of reason but only of reason's becoming conscious of itself) go hand in hand. Add to this the fact that it is not only language which serves as a bridge between man and man, but that the glance, the clasp, the bearing do so, too; our becoming-conscious of our own sense-impressions, the power of fixing them and, as it were, setting them outside ourselves, has increased in the measure that the constraint grew to transmit them *to others* by signs. The sign-inventing man is at the same time the man who is ever more sharply conscious of himself; only as a social animal did man learn to become conscious of himself – he does it still, he does it more and more. – My idea, as one can see, is that consciousness does not really belong to the existence of man as an individual but rather to that in him which is community and herd; that, as follows from this, it has also evolved in refinement only with regard to usefulness for community and herd, and that consequently each of us, even with the best will to *understand* himself in as individual a way as possible, 'to know himself', will nonetheless bring into his consciousness only what is not individual in him, his 'average' – that our thought itself is continually, as it were, *outvoted* by the character of consciousness – by the 'genius of the species' which rules in it – and translated back into the perspective of the herd. Our actions are fundamentally one and all in an incomparable way personal, unique, boundlessly individual, there is no doubt about that; but as soon as we translate them into consciousness *they no longer seem to be* . . . This is real phenomenalism and application of the principle of perspectives as *I* understand it: the nature of *animal consciousness* brings it about that the world of which we can become conscious is only a surface- and sign-world, a world made universal and common – that everything which becomes conscious thereby *becomes* shallow, thin, relatively stupid, general, sign, characteristic of the herd, that with all becoming conscious there is united a great fundamental corruption, falsification, superficializing and generalization. Finally, increasing consciousness is a danger; and he who lives among the most conscious Europeans knows that it is even an illness. It is, as one will have divined, not the antithesis of subject and object which concerns me here: I leave this distinction to the epistemologists, who have got caught in the coils of grammar (the metaphysics of the people). It is not really even the antithesis of 'thing in itself' and appearance: for we do not 'know' nearly enough even to be allowed to *distinguish* in this way. For we have no organ at all for *knowledge*, for 'truth': we 'know' (or believe or imagine) precisely as much as may be *useful* in the interest of the human herd, the species: and even what is here called 'usefulness' is in the end only a belief, something imagined and perhaps precisely that most fatal piece of stupidity by which we shall one day perish.

[*GS* 354 (1887)]


40

*The source of our concept 'knowledge'.* – I take this explanation from the street; I heard someone of the people say 'he knew me' – : I asked myself: what does the people really understand by knowledge? what does it want when it wants 'knowledge'? Nothing more than this: something strange shall be traced back to something *familiar*.* And we philosophers – have we really understood anything *more* by knowledge? The familiar, that is to say: that to which we are accustomed, so that we are no longer surprised at it, the everyday, some rule or other to which we stick, each and every thing with which we feel ourselves at home. what? is our need to know not precisely this – need for the familiar, the will to discover among all that is strange, unaccustomed, questionable something which no longer disturbs us? Is it not the *instinct of fear* which bids us know? Is the rejoicing of the man of knowledge not precisely the rejoicing of the feeling of security re-attained? ... This philosopher supposed the world 'known' when he had traced it back to the 'idea': was it not, alas, because the 'idea' was so familiar to him, because he was so accustomed to it and now had so little to fear from the 'idea'? – Oh this complacency of men of knowledge! just consider their *principia* and their solutions of the universal enigma in this light! Whenever they re-discover something in things, under things, behind things which is unfortunately very familiar to us, for example our one-times table or our logic or our willing and desiring, how happy they immediately are! For 'what is familiar is known': over that they are of one accord. Even the most cautious among them think at any rate that the familiar is *easier to know* than the strange; it is, for example, a law of method to start out from the 'inner world', from the 'facts of consciousness', because they are the world *more familiar to us*! Error of errors! The familiar is that to which we are accustomed; and that to which we are accustomed is hardest to 'know', that is to see as a problem, that is to see as strange, as distant, as 'outside us' ... The great assurance of the natural sciences in comparison with psychology and critique of the elements of consciousness – *unnatural* sciences, one might almost say – rests

---

*  *Bekannt* = known by the senses (here translated *familiar*), *erkannt* = known by the mind (here translated *known*). The distinction is the same as that between *connaître* and *savoir, conoscere* and *sapere*.

precisely on the fact that they take the *strange* as their object: while it is something almost contradictory and contrary to sense to *want* to take the non-strange as object at all . . .

[*GS* 355 (1887)]

## 41

*Our new 'infinity'*. – How far the perspectival character of existence extends or whether it has any other character at all, whether an existence without interpretation, without 'meaning' would not become 'meaninglessness', whether on the other hand all existence is not an *interpreting* existence – this, as is only reasonable, cannot be determined even by the most assiduous and painfully conscientious analysis and self-examination of the intellect: since in the course of this analysis the human intellect cannot avoid viewing itself in its perspectival forms and *only* in them. We cannot see round our own corner: it is a hopeless piece of curiosity to want to know what *could* exist for other species of intellect and perspective: for example, whether any kind of being could experience time in a reverse direction or alternately forwards and backwards (which would posit a different direction of life and a different conception of cause and effect). But I think that today we are at least far from the ludicrous immodesty of decreeing from out of our corner that perspectives are *permissible* only from out of this corner. The world has rather once again become for us 'infinite': insofar as we cannot reject the possibility that it *contains in itself infinite interpretations*. [. . .]

[*GS* 374 (1887)]

## 42

[. . .] Change, mutation, becoming in general were formerly taken as proof of appearance, as a sign of the presence of something which led us astray. Today, on the contrary, we see ourselves as it were entangled in error, *necessitated* to error, to precisely the extent that our prejudice in favour of reason compels us to posit unity, identity, duration, substance, cause, materiality, being; however sure we may be, on the basis of a strict reckoning, *that* error is to be found here. The situation is the same as with the motions of the sun: in that case error has our eyes, in the present case our *language* as a perpetual advocate. Language belongs in its origin to the age of the most rudimentary form of psychology: we find ourselves in the midst of a rude fetishism when we call to mind the basic presuppositions of the metaphysics of language – which is to say, of *reason*. It is *this* which sees everywhere deed and doer; this which believes in will as cause in general; this which believes in the 'ego' as being, in the ego as substance, and which *projects* its belief in the ego-substance on to all things – only thus does it *create* the concept 'thing' . . . Being is everywhere thought in, *foisted on*, as cause; it is only from the conception 'ego' that there follows, derivatively, the concept 'being' . . . At the beginning stands the great fateful error that the will is something which *produces an effect* – what will is a *faculty* . . . Today we know it is merely a word [. . .]

[*T* '*Reason*' *in Philosophy* 5]

# MORALITY

## 43

*The fable of intelligible freedom.* – The principal stages in the history of the sensations by virtue of which we make anyone accountable for his actions, that is to say, of the moral sensations, are as follows. First of all, one calls individual actions good or bad quite irrespective of their motives but solely on account of their useful or harmful consequences. Soon, however, one forgets the origin of these designations and believes that the quality 'good' and 'evil' is inherent in the actions themselves, irrespective of their consequences: thus committing the same error as that by which language designates the stone itself as hard, the tree itself as green – that is to say, by taking for cause that which is effect. Then one consigns the being good or being evil to the motives and regards the deeds in themselves as morally ambiguous. One goes further and accords the predicate good or evil no longer to the individual motive but to the whole nature of a man out of whom the motive grows as the plant does from the soil. Thus one successively makes men accountable for the effects they produce, then for their actions, then for their motives, and finally for their nature. Now one finally discovers that this nature, too, cannot be accountable, in as much as it is altogether a necessary consequence and assembled from the elements and influences of things past and present: that is to say, that man can be made accountable for nothing, not for his nature, nor for his motives, nor for his actions, nor for the effects he produces. One has thereby attained to the knowledge that the history of the moral sensations is the history of an error, the error of accountability, which rests on the error of freedom of will. [. . .] No one is accountable for his deeds, no one for his nature; to judge is the same thing as to be unjust. This applies when the individual judges himself. The proposition is as clear as daylight, and yet here everyone prefers to retreat back into the shadows and untruth: from fear of the consequences.

[*HA* 39]

## 44

*Gratitude and revenge.* – The reason the man of power is grateful is this. His benefactor has, through the help he has given him, as it were laid hands on the sphere of the man of power and intruded into it: now, by way of requital, the man of power in turn lays hands on the sphere of his benefactor through the act of gratitude. It is a milder form of revenge. If he did not have the compensation of gratitude, the man of power would have appeared unpowerful and thenceforth counted as such. That is why every community of the good, that is to say originally the powerful, places gratitude among its first duties. Swift suggested that men are grateful in the same degree as they are revengeful.

[*HA* 44]

## 45

*Twofold prehistory of good and evil.* – The concept good and evil has a twofold prehistory: *firstly* in the soul of the ruling tribes and castes. He who has the power to requite, good with good, evil with evil, and also actually practises requital – is, that is to say, grateful and revengeful – is called good; he who is powerless and cannot requite counts as bad. As a good man one belongs to the 'good', a community which has a sense of belonging together because all the individuals in it are combined with one another through the capacity for requital. As a bad man one belongs to the 'bad', to a swarm of subject, powerless people who have no sense of belonging together. The good are a caste, the bad a mass like grains of sand. Good and bad is for a long time the same thing as noble and base, master and slave. On the other hand, one does not regard the enemy as evil: he can requite. In Homer the Trojan and the Greek are both good. It is not he who does us harm but he who is contemptible who counts as bad. [. . .] *Then* in the soul of the subjected, the powerless. Here every *other* man, whether he be noble or base, counts as inimical, ruthless, cruel, cunning, ready to take advantage. Evil is the characterizing expression for man, indeed for every living being one supposes to exist, for a god, for example; human, divine mean the same thing as diabolical, evil. Signs of goodness, benevolence, sympathy are received fearfully as a trick, a prelude with a dreadful termination, a means of confusing and outwitting, in short as refined wickedness. When this disposition exists in the individual a community can hardly arise, at best the most rudimentary form of community: so that wherever this conception of good and evil reigns the downfall of such individuals, of their tribes and races, is near. – Our present morality has grown up in the soil of the *ruling* tribes and castes.

[*HA* 45]

## 46

*Morality as the self-division of man.* – A good author whose heart is really in his subject wishes that someone would come and annihilate him by presenting the same subject with greater clarity and resolving all the questions contained in it. A girl in love wishes the faithfulness and devotion of her love could be tested by the faithlessness of the man she loves. A soldier wishes he could fall on the battlefield for his victorious fatherland: for his supreme desire is victor in the victory of his fatherland. A mother gives to her child that of which she deprives herself, sleep, the best food, if need be her health, her strength. – But are these all unegoistic states? Are these deeds of morality *miracles* because they are, in Schopenhauer's words, 'impossible and yet real'? Is it not clear that in all these instances man loves *something of himself*, an idea, a desire, an offspring, more than *something else of himself*, that he thus *divides* his nature and sacrifices one part of it to the other? Is it something *essentially* different from when some obstinate man says: 'I would rather be shot down than move an inch out of that fellow's way'? – The *inclination for something* (wish, impulse, desire) is present in all the above-mentioned instances; to give in to it, with all the consequences, is in any event not 'unegoistic'. – In morality man treats himself not as *individuum* but as *dividuum*.

[HA 57]

47

*Origin of iustice*. – Justice (fairness) originates between parties of approximately *equal power*, as Thucydides correctly grasped (in the terrible colloquy between the Athenian and Melian ambassadors): where there is no clearly recognizable superiority of force and a contest would result in mutual injury producing no decisive outcome the idea arises of coming to an understanding and negotiating over one another's demands: the characteristic of *exchange* is the original characteristic of justice. Each satisfies the other [. . .] Justice is thus requital and exchange under the presupposition of an approximately equal power position: revenge therefore belongs originally within the domain of justice, it is an exchange. Gratitude likewise. – Justice goes back naturally to the viewpoint of an enlightened self-preservation, thus to the egoism of the reflection: 'to what end should I injure myself uselessly and perhaps even then not achieve my goal?' – So much for the *origin* of justice. Since, in accordance with their intellectual habit, men have *for-*

*gotten* the original purpose of so-called just and fair actions, and especially because children have for millennia been trained to admire and imitate such actions, it has gradually come to appear that a just action is an unegoistic one: but it is on this appearance that the high value accorded it depends; and this high value is, moreover, continually increasing, as all valuations do: for something highly valued is striven for, imitated, multiplied through sacrifice, and grows as the worth of the toil and zeal expended by each individual is added to the worth of the valued thing. – How little moral would the world appear without forgetfulness! A poet could say that God has placed forgetfulness as a doorkeeper on the threshold of the temple of human dignity.

[*HA* 92]

## 48

*Custom and what is in accordance with it.* – To be moral, to act in accordance with custom, to be ethical means to practise obedience towards a law or tradition established from of old. Whether one subjects oneself with effort or gladly and willingly makes no difference, it is enough that one does it. He is called 'good' who does what is customary as if by nature, as a result of a long inheritance, that is to say easily and gladly, and this is so whatever what is customary may be (exacts revenge, for example, when exacting revenge is part of good custom, as it was with the ancient Greeks). He is called good because he is good 'for something'; since, however, benevolence, sympathy and the like have throughout all the changes in customs always been seen as 'good for something', as useful, it is now above all the benevolent, the helpful who are called 'good'. To be evil is 'not to act in accordance with custom', to practise things not sanctioned by custom, to resist tradition, however rational or stupid that tradition may be; in all the laws of custom of all times, however, doing injury to one's neighbour has been seen as injurious above all else, so that now at the word 'evil' we think especially of voluntarily doing injury to one's neighbour. 'Egoistic' and 'unegoistic' is not the fundamental antithesis which has led men to make the distinction between 'in accordance with custom' and 'in defiance of custom', between good and evil, but adherence to a tradition, a law, and severance from it. How the tradition has *arisen* is here a matter of indifference, and has in any event nothing to do with good and evil or with any kind of immanent categorical imperative; it is above all directed at the preservation of a *community*, a people; every superstitious usage which has arisen on the basis of some chance event mistakenly interpreted enforces a tradition which it is in accordance with custom to follow; for to sever oneself from it is dangerous, and even more injurious to the *community* than to the individual (because the gods punish the community for misdeeds and for every violation of their privileges and only to that extent punish the individual). Every tradition now continually grows more venerable the farther away its origin lies and the more this origin is forgotten; the respect paid to it increases from generation to generation, the tradition at last becomes holy and evokes awe and reverence; and thus the morality of piety is in any event a much older morality than that which demands unegoistic actions.

[*HA* 96]

# 49

*The innocent element in so-called evil acts.* – All 'evil' acts are motivated by the drive to preservation or, more exactly, by the individual's intention of procuring pleasure and avoiding displeasure; so motivated, however, they are not evil. 'Procuring pain as such' *does not exist*, except in the brain of philosophers neither does 'procuring pleasure as such' (pity in the Schopenhauerian sense). [. . .] The evil acts at which we are now most indignant rest on the error that he who perpetrates them against us possesses free will, that is to say, that he could have *chosen* not to cause us this harm. It is this belief in choice that engenders hatred, revengefulness, deceitfulness, complete degradation of the imagination, while we are far less censorious towards an animal because we regard it as unaccountable. To do injury not from the drive to preservation but as requital – is the consequence of a mistaken judgement and therefore likewise innocent. [. . .]

[*HA* 99]

## 50

'*Man's actions are always good*'. – We do not accuse nature of immorality when it sends us a thunderstorm and makes us wet: why do we call the harmful man immoral? Because in the latter case we assume a voluntarily commanding free-will, in the former necessity. But this distinction is an error. And then: we do not call even intentional harming immoral under all circumstances; one unhesitatingly kills a fly intentionally, for example, merely because one does not like its buzzing, one punishes the criminal intentionally and does him harm so as to protect ourselves and society. [. . .] All morality allows the intentional causing of harm in the case of self-defence: that is, when it is a matter of *self-preservation*. But these two points of view *suffice* to explain all evil acts perpetrated by men against men: one desires pleasure or to ward off displeasure; it is always in some sense a matter of self-preservation. Socrates and Plato are right: whatever man does he always does the good, that is to say: that which seems to him good (useful) according to the relative degree of his intellect, the measure of his rationality.

[*HA* 102]

## 51

*Unaccountability and innocence.* – The complete unaccountability of man for his actions and his nature is the bitterest draught the man of knowledge has to swallow if he has been accustomed to seeing in accountability and duty the patent of his humanity. All his evaluations, all his feelings of respect and antipathy have thereby become disvalued and false: his profoundest sentiment, which he accorded to the sufferer, the hero, rested upon an error; he may no longer praise, no longer censure, for it is absurd to praise and censure nature and necessity. As he loves a fine work of art but does not praise it since it can do nothing for itself, as he stands before the plants, so must he stand before the actions of men and before his own. He can admire their strength, beauty, fullness, but he may not find any merit in them: the chemical process and the strife of the elements, the torment of the sick man who yearns for an end to his sickness, are as little merits as are those states of distress and psychic convulsions which arise when we are torn back and forth by conflicting motives until we finally choose the most powerful of them – as we put it (in truth, however, until the most powerful motive chooses us). But all these motives, whatever exalted names we may give them, have grown up out of the same roots as those we believe evilly poisoned; between good and evil actions there is no difference in kind, but at the most one of degree. Good actions are sublimated evil ones; evil actions are coarsened, brutalized good ones. It is the individual's sole desire for self-enjoyment (together with the fear of losing it) which gratifies itself in every instance, let a man act as he can, that is to say as he must: whether his deeds be those of vanity, revenge, pleasure, utility, malice, cunning, or those of sacrifice, sympathy, knowledge. Degrees of intelligent judgement decide whither each person will let his desire draw him; every society, every individual always has present an order of rank of things considered good, according to which he determines his own actions and judges those of others. But this standard is continually changing, many actions are called evil but are only stupid, because the degree of intelligence which decided for them was very low. Indeed, in a certain sense *all* present actions are stupid, for the highest degree of human intelligence which can now be attained will certainly be exceeded in the future: and then all our actions and judgements will seem in retrospect as circumscribed and precipitate as the actions and judgements of still existing primitive peoples now appear to us. To perceive all this can be very painful, but then comes a consolation: such pains are birth-pangs. The butterfly wants to get out of its cocoon, it tears at it, it breaks it open: then it is blinded and confused by the unfamiliar light, the realm of freedom. It is in such men as are *capable* of that suffering – how few they will be! – that the first attempt will be made to see whether mankind could *transform itself from a moral to a wise mankind.* [. . .] Everything is necessity – thus says the new knowledge; and this knowledge itself is necessity. Everything is innocence: and knowledge is the path to insight into this innocence. If pleasure, egoism, vanity are *necessary* for the pro-duction of the moral phenomena and their finest flower, the sense for truth and justice in knowledge; if error and aber-ration of the imagination was the only means by which man-kind was able gradually to raise itself to this degree of self-enlightenment and self-redemption – who could venture to denigrate those means? Who could be despondent when he becomes aware of the goal to which those paths lead? It is true that everything in the domain of morality has become and is changeable, unsteady, everything is in flux: but *every-thing is also flooding forward,* and towards *one* goal. Even if the inherited habit of erroneous evaluation, loving, hating does continue to rule in us, under the influence of increasing know-ledge it will grow weaker: a new habit, that of comprehending, not-loving, not-hating, surveying is gradually implanting it-self in us on the same soil and will in thousands of years' time perhaps be strong enough to bestow on mankind the power of bringing forth the wise, innocent (conscious of innocence) man as regularly as it now brings forth – *not his antithesis but necessary preliminary* – the unwise, unjust, guilt-conscious man.

[*HA* 107]

## 52

*The cyclops of culture.* – When we behold those deeply-furrowed
hollows in which glaciers have lain, we think it hardly possible
that a time will come when a wooded, grassy valley, watered
by streams, will spread itself out upon the same spot. So it is,
too, in the history of mankind: the most savage forces beat a
path, and are mainly destructive; but their work was nonetheless necessary, in order that later a gentler civilization might
raise its house. The frightful energies – those which are called
evil – are the cyclopean architects and road-makers of humanity.

[*HA* 246]

## 53

*The desire to be just and the desire to be a judge.* – Schopenhauer
[. . .] makes that striking distinction which is very much more
justified than he really dared to admit to himself: 'the insight
into the strict necessity of human actions is the boundary line
which divides *philosophical* heads from *the others*'. This mighty
insight, which from time to time he publicly avowed, he nonetheless counteracted in his own mind with that prejudice
which he still had in common with moral men (*not* with the
moralists) and which, quite innocuously and credulously, he
expressed as: 'the ultimate and true elucidation of the inner
nature of the whole of things must necessarily hang closely
together with that of the ethical significance of human behaviour' – which is absolutely not 'necessary' but, on the contrary, has been rejected by precisely that proposition of the
strict necessity of human actions, that is to say, the unconditional unfreedom and unaccountability of the will. Philosophical heads will thus distinguish themselves from the others
through their unbelief in the metaphysical significance of
morality: and that may establish a gulf between them of whose
depth and unbridgeableness the so much lamented gulf be-

tween the 'cultured' and the 'uncultured', as it now exists, gives hardly any idea. Many more back-doors, to be sure, which 'philosophical heads' have, like Schopenhauer himself, left open must be recognized as useless: *none* leads outside, into the air of free will; *every one* which has hitherto been slipped through reveals behind it every time a brazen wall of fate: we *are* in prison, we can only *dream* ourselves free, not make ourselves free. That this knowledge cannot for very much longer be resisted is indicated by the despairing and incredible postures and contortions of those who assail it, who still continue to wrestle with it. – This, approximately, is how they go on: 'What, is no man accountable? And is everything full of guilt and feeling of guilt? But someone or other has to be the sinner, if it is impossible and no longer permissible to accuse and to judge the individual, the poor wave in the necessary wave-play of becoming – very well: then let the wave-play itself, becoming, be the sinner: here is free-will, here there can be accusing, condemning, atonement and expiation: then let *God be the sinner and man his redeemer*: then let world history be guilt, self-condemnation and suicide; thus will the offender become his own judge, the judge his own executioner.' – This *Christianity stood on its head* – for what else is it? – is the final lunge in the struggle of the theory of unconditional morality with that of unconditional unfreedom – a horrible thing if it were anything *more* than a *logical grimace*, more than an ugly gesture on the part of the defeated idea – perhaps the death-throes of the despairing and salvation-thirsty heart to which madness whispers: 'Behold, thou art the lamb that beareth the sins of God.' – The error lies not only in the feeling 'I am accountable', but equally in that antithesis 'I am not, but somebody has to be.' – This is, in fact, not true: the philosopher thus has to say, as Christ did, 'judge not!' and the ultimate distinction between philosophical heads and the others would be that the former desire *to be just*, the others *to be a judge*.

[*AOM* 33]

## 54

*Custom and its sacrifices.* – The origin of custom lies in two ideas: 'the community is worth more than the individual' and 'an enduring advantage is to be preferred to a transient one'; from which it follows that the enduring advantage of the community is to take unconditional precedence over the advantage of the individual, especially over his momentary well-being but also over his enduring advantage and even over his survival. Even if the individual suffers from an arrangement which benefits the whole, even if he languishes under it, perishes by it – the custom must be maintained, the sacrifice offered [. . .]

[*AOM* 89]

## 55

*The good and the good conscience.* – Do you think that every good thing has always had a good conscience? – Science, which is certainly something good, entered the world without one, and quite destitute of pathos, but did so rather in secret, by crooked and indirect paths, hooded or masked like a criminal and at least always with the *feeling* of dealing in contraband. The good conscience has as a preliminary stage the bad conscience – the latter is not its opposite: for everything good was once new, consequently unfamiliar, contrary to custom, *immoral*, and gnawed at the heart of its fortunate inventor like a worm.

[*AOM* 90]

## 56

*Have the adherents of the theory of free-will the right to punish?* – People who judge and punish as a profession try to establish in each case whether an ill-doer is at all accountable for his deed, whether he was *able* to employ his intelligence, whether he acted for *reasons* and not unconsciously or under compulsion. If he is punished, he is punished for having preferred the worse reasons to the better: which he must therefore have *known*. Where this knowledge is lacking a man is, according to the prevailing view, unfree and not responsible: except if his lack of knowledge, his *ignorantia legis* for example, is a result of an intentional neglect to learn; in which case, when he failed to learn what he should have learned he had already preferred the worse reasons to the better and must now suffer the consequences of his bad choice. If, on the other hand, he did not see the better reasons, perhaps from dull-wittedness or weakness of mind, it is not usual to punish him: he lacked, one says, the capacity to choose, he acted as an animal would. For an offence to be punishable presupposes that its perpetrator intentionally acted contrary to the better dictates of his intelligence. But how can anyone intentionally be less intelligent than he has to be? Whence comes the decision when the scales are weighted with good and bad motives? Not from error, from blindness, not from an external nor from an internal compulsion? (Consider, moreover, that every so-called 'external compulsion' is nothing more than the internal compulsion of fear and pain.) Whence? one asks again and again. The *intelligence* is not the cause, because it could not decide against the better reasons? And here one calls 'free-will' to one's aid: it is *pure wilfulness* which is supposed to decide, an impulse is supposed to enter within which motive plays no part, in which the deed, arising out of nothing, occurs as a miracle. It is this supposed *wilfulness*, in a case in which wilfulness ought not to reign, which is punished: the rational intelligence, which knows law, prohibition and command, ought to have permitted no choice, and to have had the effect of compulsion and a higher power. Thus the offender is punished because he employs 'free-will', that is to say, because he acted without a reason where he ought to have acted in accordance with reasons. Why did he do this? But it is precisely this question that can no longer even be *asked*: it was a deed without a 'for that reason', without motive, without origin, something purposeless and non-rational. – *But such a deed too ought*, in accordance with the first condition of all punishability laid down above, *not to be punished*! It is not as if something had *not* been done here, something omitted, the intelligence had *not* been employed: for the omission is under all circumstances *unintentional*! and only the intentional omission to perform what the law commands counts as punishable. The offender certainly preferred the worse reasons to the better, but *without* reason or intention: he certainly failed to employ his intelligence, but not *for the purpose* of not employing it. The presupposition that for an offence to be punishable its perpetrator must have intentionally acted contrary to his intelligence – it is precisely this presupposition which is annulled by the assumption of 'free will'. You adherents of the theory of 'free will' *have no right* to punish, your own principles deny you that right! [. . .]

[*WS* 23]

## 57

*The significance of forgetting for the moral sensation.* – The same actions as within primitive society appear to have been performed first with a view to common *utility* have been performed by later generations for other motives: out of fear of or reverence for those who demanded and recommended them, or out of habit because one had seen them done all around one from childhood on, or from benevolence because their performance everywhere produced joy and concurring faces, or from vanity because they were commended. Such actions, whose basic motive, that of utility, has been *forgotten*, are then called *moral* actions: not because, for instance, they are performed out of those *other* motives, but because they are *not* performed from any conscious reason of utility. – Where does it come from, this *hatred* of utility which becomes visible *here*, where all praiseworthy behaviour formally excludes behaviour with a view to utility? – It is plain that society, the hearth of all morality and all eulogy of moral behaviour, has had to struggle too long and too hard against the self-interest and self-will of the individual not at last to rate *any other* motive morally higher than utility. Thus it comes to appear that morality has *not* grown out of utility; while it is originally social utility, which had great difficulty in asserting itself against all the individual private utilities and making itself more highly respected.

[*WS* 40]

## 58

*Prohibition without reasons*. – A prohibition whose reason we do not understand or admit is not only for the obstinate man but also for the man thirsty for knowledge almost the injunction: let us put it to the test, so as to learn *why* this prohibition exists. Moral prohibitions such as those of the Decalogue are suitable only for ages when reason is subjugated: nowadays a prohibition 'thou shalt not kill', 'thou shalt not commit adultery', presented without reasons, would produce a harmful rather than a beneficial effect.

[*WS* 48]

## 59

*Content of the conscience*. – The content of our conscience is everything that was during the years of our childhood regularly *demanded* of us without reason by people we honoured or feared. It is thus the conscience that excites that feeling of compulsion ('I must do this, not do that') which does not ask: *why* must I? – In every case in which a thing is done with 'because' and 'why' man acts *without* conscience; but not yet for that reason against it. – The belief in authorities is the source of the conscience: it is therefore not the voice of God in the heart of man but the voice of some men in man.

[*WS* 52]

## 60

*Habit of seeing opposites.* – The general imprecise way of observing sees everywhere in nature opposites (as, e.g., 'warm and cold') where there are, not opposites, but differences of degree. This bad habit has led us into wanting to comprehend and analyse the inner world, too, the spiritual-moral world, in terms of such opposites. An unspeakable amount of painfulness, arrogance, harshness, estrangement, frigidity has entered into human feelings because we think we see opposites instead of transitions.

[*WS* 67]

## 61

*Prejudice of the learned.* – The learned judge correctly that people of all ages have believed they *know* what is good and evil, praise- and blameworthy. But it is a prejudice of the learned that *we now know better* than any other age.

[*D* 2]

## 62

*Everything has its day.* – When man gave all things a sex he thought, not that he was playing, but that he had gained a profound insight: – it was only very late that he confessed to himself what an enormous error this was, and perhaps even now he has not confessed it completely. – In the same way man has ascribed to all that exists a connection with morality and laid an *ethical significance* on the world's back. One day this will have as much value, and no more, as the belief in the masculinity or femininity of the sun has today.

[*D* 3]

## 63

*Concept of morality of custom.* – In comparison with the mode of life of whole millennia of mankind we present-day men live in a very immoral [*unsittlich*] age: the power of custom [*Sitte*] is astonishingly enfeebled and the moral sense [*Gefühl der Sittlichkeit*] so rarefied and lofty it may be described as having more or less evaporated. That is why the fundamental insights into the origin of morality [*Moral*] are so difficult for us late-comers, and even when we have acquired them we find it impossible to enunciate them, because they sound so uncouth or because they seem to slander morality [*Sittlichkeit*]! This is, for example, already the case with the *chief proposition*: morality [*Sittlichkeit*] is nothing other (therefore *no more!*) than obedience to customs [*Sitten*], of whatever kind they may be; customs, however, are the *traditional* way of behaving and evaluating. In things in which no tradition commands there is no morality [*Sittlichkeit*]; and the less life is determined by tradition, the smaller the circle of morality. The free human being is immoral [*unsittlich*] because in all things he is *determined* to depend upon himself and not upon a tradition: in all the original conditions of mankind, 'evil' signifies the same as 'individual', 'free', 'capricious', 'unusual', 'unforeseen', 'incalculable'. Judged by the standard of these conditions, if an action is performed *not* because tradition commands it but for other motives (because of its usefulness to the individual, for example), even indeed for precisely the motives which once founded the tradition, it is called immoral [*unsittlich*] and is felt to be so by him who performed it: for it was not performed in obedience to tradition. What is tradition? A higher authority which one obeys, not because it commands what is *useful* to us, but because it *commands*. – What distinguishes this feeling in the presence of tradition from the feeling of fear in general? It is fear in the presence of a higher intellect which here commands, of an incomprehensible, indefinite power, of something more than personal – there is *superstition* in this fear. – Originally all education and care of health, marriage, cure of sickness, agriculture, war, speech and silence, traffic with one another and with the gods belonged within the domain of morality [*Sittlichkeit*]: they demanded one observe prescriptions *without thinking of oneself* as an individual. Originally, therefore, everything was custom [*Sitte*], and whoever wanted to elevate himself above it had to become lawgiver and medicine man and a kind of demi-god: that is to say, he had to *make customs* – a dreadful, mortally dangerous thing! [. . .] Those moralists who, following in the footsteps of *Socrates*, offer the *individual* a morality of self-control and temperance as a means to his own *advantage*, as his personal key to happiness, *are the exceptions* – and if it seems otherwise to us that is because we have been brought up in their after-effect: they all take a new path under the highest disapprobation of all advocates of the morality of custom [*Sittlichkeit der Sitte*] – they cut themselves off from the community, as immoral men [*Unsittliche*], and are in the profoundest sense evil. Thus to a virtuous Roman of the old stamp every *Christian* who 'considered first of all his *own* salvation' appeared – evil. [. . .] Every individual action, every individual mode of thought arouses dread; it is impossible to compute what precisely the rarer, choicer, more original spirits in the whole course of history have had to suffer through being felt as evil and dangerous, indeed through *feeling themselves to be so*. Under the dominion of the morality of custom, originality of every kind has acquired a bad conscience; the sky above the best men is for this reason to this very moment gloomier than it need be.

[*D* 9]

## 64

*Significance of madness in the history of morality.* – When in spite of that fearful pressure of 'morality of custom' [. . .] new and deviate ideas, evaluations, drives again and again broke out, they did so accompanied by a dreadful attendant: almost everywhere it was madness which prepared the way for the

new idea, which broke the spell of a venerated usage and
superstition. Do you understand why it had to be madness
which did this? Something in voice and bearing as uncanny
and incalculable as the demonic moods of the weather and the
sea and therefore worthy of a similar awe and observation?
Something that bore so visibly the sign of total unfreedom as
the convulsions and froth of the epileptic, that seemed to
mark the madman as the mask and speaking-trumpet of a
divinity? Something that awoke in the bearer of a new idea
himself reverence for and dread of himself and no longer
pangs of conscience and drove him to become the prophet and
martyr of his idea? – While it is constantly suggested to us today
that, instead of a grain of salt, a grain of the spice of madness
is joined to genius, all earlier people found it much more
likely that wherever there is madness there is also a grain of
genius and wisdom – something 'divine', as one whispered
to oneself. Or rather: as one said aloud forcefully enough. 'It
is through madness that the greatest good things have come
to Greece,' Plato said, in concert with all ancient mankind.
Let us go a step further: all superior men who were irresistibly
drawn to throw off the yoke of any kind of morality and to
frame new laws had, *if they were not actually mad*, no alternative
but to make themselves or pretend to be mad – and this indeed
applies to innovators in every domain and not only in the domain of priestly and political dogma: – even the innovator of
poetical metre had to establish his credentials by madness.
[. . .] 'How can one make oneself mad when one is not mad
and does not dare to appear so?' – almost all the significant
men of ancient civilization have pursued this train of thought;
a secret teaching of artifices and dietetic hints was propagated
on this subject, together with the feeling that such reflections
and purposes were innocent, indeed holy. The recipes for becoming a medicine-man among the Indians, a saint among the
Christians of the Middle Ages, an angekok among Green-
landers, a pajee among Brazilians are essentially the same:
senseless fasting, perpetual sexual abstinence, going into the
desert or ascending a mountain or a pillar, or 'sitting in an

aged willow tree which looks upon a lake' and thinking of nothing at all except what might bring on an ecstasy and mental disorder. Who would venture to take a look into the wilderness of bitterest and most superfluous agonies of soul in which probably the most fruitful men of all times have languished! To listen to the sighs of these solitary and agitated minds: 'Ah, give me madness, you heavenly powers! Madness, that I may at last believe in myself! Give deliriums and convulsions, sudden lights and darkness, terrify me with frost and fire such as no mortal has ever felt, with deafening din and prowling figures, make me howl and whine and crawl like a beast: so that I may only come to believe in myself! I am consumed by doubt, I have killed the law, the law anguishes me as a corpse does a living man: if I am not *more* than the law I am the vilest of all men. The new spirit which is in me, whence is it if it is not from you? Prove to me that I am yours; madness alone can prove it.' And only too often this fervour achieved its goal all too well: in that age in which Christianity proved most fruitful in saints and desert solitaries, and thought it was proving itself by this fruitfulness, there were in Jerusalem vast madhouses for abortive saints, for those who had surrendered to it their last grain of salt.

[*D* 14]

## 65

*First proposition of civilization.* – Among barbarous peoples there exists a species of customs whose purpose appears to be custom in general: minute and fundamentally superfluous stipulations [. . .] which, however, keep continually in the consciousness the constant proximity of custom, the perpetual compulsion to practise customs: so as to strengthen the mighty proposition with which civilization begins: any custom is better than no custom.

[*D* 16]

# 66

*Free-doers and freethinkers.* – Free-doers are at a disadvantage compared with freethinkers because people suffer more obviously from the consequences of deeds than from those of thoughts. If one considers, however, that both the one and the other are in search of gratification, and that in the case of the freethinker the mere thinking through and enunciation of forbidden things provides this gratification, both are on an equal footing with regard to motive: and with regard to consequences the decision will even go against the freethinker, provided one does not judge – as all the world does – by what is most immediately and crassly obvious. One has to take back much of the defamation which people have cast upon all those who broke through the spell of a custom by means of a *deed* – in general, they are called criminals. Whoever has overthrown an existing law of custom has hitherto always first been accounted a *bad man*: but when, as did happen, the law could not afterwards be reinstated and this fact was accepted the predicate gradually changed; – history treats almost exclusively of these *bad men* who subsequently became *good men*!

[*D* 20]

# 67

*Animals and morality.* – The practices demanded in polite society: careful avoidance of the ridiculous, the offensive, the presumptuous, the suppression of one's virtues as well as of one's strongest inclinations, self-adaptation, self-deprecation, submission to orders of rank – all this is to be found as social morality in a crude form everywhere, even in the depths of the animal world – and only at this depth do we see the purpose of all these amiable precautions: one wishes to elude one's pursuers and be favoured in the pursuit of one's prey. For this reason the animals learn to master themselves and alter their form, so that many, for example, adapt their colouring to the colouring of their surroundings (by virtue of the so-called 'chromatic function'), pretend to be dead or assume the forms and colours of another animal or of sand, leaves, lichen, fungus (what English researchers designate 'mimicry'). Thus the individual hides himself in the general concept 'man', or in society, or adapts himself to princes, classes, parties, opinions of his time or place: and all the subtle ways we have of appearing fortunate, grateful, powerful, enamoured have their easily discoverable parallels in the animal world. [. . .] The beginnings of justice, as of prudence, moderation, bravery – in short, of all we designate as the *Socratic virtues*, are *animal*: a consequence of that drive which teaches us to seek food and elude enemies. Now if we consider that even the highest human being has only become more elevated and subtle in the nature of his food and in his conception of what is inimical to him, it is not improper to describe the entire phenomenon of morality as animal.

[*D* 26]

## 68

*Mutation of morality.* – There is a continual moiling and toiling going on in morality – the effect of *successful crimes* (among which, for example, are included all innovations in moral thinking).

[*D* 98]

## 69

*The oldest moral judgements.* – What really are our reactions to the behaviour of someone in our presence? – First of all, we see what there is in it *for us* – we regard it only from this point of view. We take *this* effect as the *intention* behind the behaviour – and finally we ascribe the harbouring of such intentions as a *permanent* quality of the person whose behaviour we are observing and thenceforth call him for instance 'a harmful person'. Threefold error! Threefold primeval blunder! Perhaps inherited from the animals and their power of judgement! Is the *origin of all morality* not to be sought in the detestable petty conclusions: 'what harms *me* is something *evil* (harmful in itself); what is useful *to me* is something *good* (beneficent and advantageous in itself); what harms me *once or several times* is the inimical as such and in itself; what is useful to me *once or several times* is the friendly as such and in itself.' *O pudenda origo!* [. . .]

[*D* 102]

## 70

*Fashions in morality.* – How the overall moral judgements have shifted! The great men of antique morality, Epictetus for instance, knew nothing of the now normal glorification of thinking of others, of living for others; in the light of our moral fashion they would have to be called downright immoral, for they strove with all their might *for* their *ego* and *against* feeling with others (that is to say, with the sufferings and moral frailties of others). Perhaps they would reply to us: 'If you are so boring or ugly an object to yourself, by all means think of others more than of yourself! It is right you should!'

[*D* 131]

## 71

*The echo of Christianity in morality.* – 'On n'est bon que par la pitie: il faut donc qu'il y ait quelque pitie dans tous nos sentiments' – thus says morality today! And why is that? – That man today feels the sympathetic, disinterested, generally useful, social actions to be the *moral* actions – this is perhaps the most general effect and conversion which Christianity has produced in Europe: although it was not its intention nor contained in its teaching. But it was the residuum of Christian states of mind left when the very much antithetical, strictly egoistic fundamental belief in the 'one thing needful', in the absolute importance of eternal *personal* salvation, together with the dogmas upon which it rested, gradually retreated and the subsidiary belief in 'love', in 'love of one's neighbour', in concert with the tremendous practical effect of ecclesiastical charity, was thereby pushed into the foreground. The more one liberated oneself from the dogmas, the more one sought as it were a *justification* of this liberation in a cult of philanthropy: not to fall short of the Christian ideal in this, but where possible to outdo it, was a secret spur with all French freethinkers from Voltaire up to Auguste Comte [. . .] In Germany it was Schopenhauer, in England John Stuart Mill who gave the widest currency to the teaching of the sympathetic affections and of pity or the advantage of others as the principle of behaviour: but they themselves were no more than an echo – those teachings have shot up with a mighty impetus everywhere and in the crudest and subtlest forms together from about the time of the French Revolution onwards, every socialist system has placed itself as if involuntarily on the common ground of these teachings. There is today perhaps no more firmly credited prejudice than this: that one *knows* what really constitutes the moral. Today it seems *to do everyone good* when they hear that society is on the way to *adapting* the individual to general requirements, and that *the happiness and at the same time the sacrifice of the individual* lies in feeling himself to be a useful member and instrument of the whole: except that one is at present very uncertain as to where this whole is to be sought, whether in an existing state or one still to be created, or in the nation, or in a brotherhood of peoples, or in new little economic communalities. [. . .] What is wanted – whether this is admitted or not – is nothing less than a fundamental remoulding, indeed weakening and abolition of the *individual*: one never tires of enumerating and indicting all that is evil and inimical, prodigal, costly, extravagant in the form individual existence has assumed hitherto, one hopes to manage more cheaply, more safely, more equitably, more uniformly if there exist only *large bodies and their members* [. . .]

[*D* 132]

## 72

*To what extent one has to guard against pity.* – Pity [*Mitleiden*], insofar as it really causes suffering [*Leiden*] – and this is here our only point of view – is a weakness, like every losing of oneself through a *harmful* affect. It *increases* the amount of suffering in the world: if suffering is here and there indirectly reduced or removed as a consequence of pity, this occasional and on the whole insignificant consequence must not be employed to justify its essential nature, which is, as I have said, harmful. Supposing it was dominant even for a single day, mankind would immediately perish of it. In itself, it has as little a good character as any other drive: only where it is demanded and commended – and this happens where one fails to grasp that it is harmful but discovers a *source of pleasure* in it – does a good conscience adhere to it, only then does one gladly succumb to it and not hesitate to demonstrate it. Under other conditions, where the fact of its harmfulness is grasped, it counts as weakness: or, as with the Greeks, as a morbid recurring affect the perilousness of which can be removed by periodical deliberate discharge. [. . .]

[*D* 134]

## 73

*Distant prospect.* – If only those actions are moral which are performed for the sake of another and only for his sake, as one definition has it, then there are no moral actions! If only those actions are moral which are performed out of freedom of will, as another definition says, then there are likewise no moral actions! – What is it then which is so *named* and which in any event exists and wants explaining? It is the effects of certain intellectual mistakes. – And supposing one freed oneself from these errors, what would become of 'moral actions'? – By virtue of these errors we have hitherto accorded certain actions a higher value than they possess: we have segregated them from the 'egoistic' and 'unfree' actions. If we now realign them with the latter, as we shall have to do, we shall certainly *reduce* their value (the value we feel they possess), and indeed shall do so to an unfair degree, because the 'egoistic' and 'unfree' actions were hitherto evaluated too low on account of their supposed profound and intrinsic difference. – Will they from then on be performed less often because they are now valued less highly? – Inevitably! At least for a good length of time, as long as the balance of value-feelings continues to be affected by the reaction of former errors! But our counter-reckoning is that we shall restore to men their goodwill towards the actions decried as egoistic and restore to these actions their *value – we shall deprive them of their bad conscience*! And since they have hitherto been by far the most frequent actions, and will continue to be so for all future time, we thus remove from the entire aspect of action and life its *evil appearance*! This is a very significant result! When man no longer regards himself as evil he ceases to be so!

[*D* 148]

# 74

*Moral fashion of a commercial society.* – Behind the basic principle of the current moral fashion: 'moral actions are actions performed out of sympathy for others', I see the social effect of timidity hiding behind an intellectual mask: it desires, first and foremost, that *all the dangers* which life once held should be removed from it, and that *everyone* should assist in this with all his might: hence only those actions which tend towards the common security and society's sense of security are to be accorded the predicate 'good'! [. . .]

[*D* 174]

## 75

*' Humanity'*. – We do not regard the animals as moral beings.
But do you suppose the animals regard us as moral beings? –
An animal which could speak said: 'Humanity is a prejudice
of which we animals at least are free.'

[*D* 333]

## 76

*A virtue in process of becoming.* – Such assertions and promises
as those of the antique philosophers concerning the unity of
virtue and happiness, or the Christian 'But seek ye first the
kingdom of God, and his righteousness; and all these things
shall be added unto you' have never been made with total
honesty and yet always without a bad conscience: one has
advanced such propositions, which one very much desires to
be true, boldly as the truth in the face of all appearance and
has felt in doing so no religious or moral pang of conscience
– for one had transcended reality *in honorem majorem* of virtue
or of God and without any selfish motive! Many worthy
people still stand at this *level of truthfulness*: when they *feel*
themselves selfless they think they are permitted to *trouble
themselves less* about truth. Notice, however, that *honesty* is
among neither the Socratic nor the Christian virtues: it is the
youngest virtue, still very immature, still often misjudged and
taken for something else, still hardly aware of itself – something in process of becoming which we can advance or ob-
struct as we think fit.

[*D* 456]

## 77

*Preserver of the species.* – It is the strongest and most evil spirits
who have up till now advanced mankind the most: they have

again and again re-ignited the slumbering passions – all
ordered society makes the passions drowsy – they have
awoken again and again the sense of comparison, of contradiction, of joy in the new, daring, untried, they have compelled men to set opinion against opinion, model against
model. Most of all by weapons, by overturning boundary
stones, by wounding piety: but also by new religions and
moralities! The same 'wickedness' is in every teacher and
preacher of the *new* as makes a conqueror infamous [. . .] The
new, however, is under all circumstances the *evil*, as that which
wants to conquer and overturn the old boundary stones and
the old pieties; and only the old is the good! The good men
of every age are those who bury the old ideas in the depths of
the earth and bear fruit with them, the agriculturalists of the
spirit. But that land will at length become exhausted, and the
ploughshare of evil must come again and again. – There is
nowadays a fundamentally false theory of morality which is
especially celebrated in England: according to this theory the
judgements 'good' and 'evil' are the summation of experiences of 'useful' and 'not useful'; that which is called 'good'
is that which preserves the species, that which is called 'evil'
is that which injures the species. In truth, however, the evil
impulses are just as useful, indispensable and preservative of
the species as the good: – only their function is different.

[*GS* 4]

## 78

*Unconditional duties.* – All those who feel in need of the most
powerful words and tones, the most eloquent gestures and
postures if they are to make any effect *at all*, revolutionary
politicians, socialists, Lenten preachers with and without
Christianity, none of whom dare risk a half-success: all these talk
of 'duties' and, indeed, always of duties of an unconditional
character – without them they would have no right to their
mighty pathos: they know that well enough! So they grasp

at philosophies of morals which preach some categorical imperative or other, or they take to themselves a large portion of religion, as Mazzini for example did. Because they want to be trusted unconditionally they first need to trust themselves unconditionally on the basis of some ultimate undiscussable and inherently exalted commandment as the servant and instrument of which they would like to feel and pass themselves off for. Here we have the most natural and usually very influential opponents of moral enlightenment and scepticism: but they are rare. On the other hand, there exists a very comprehensive class of such opponents wherever interest demands subjection while fame and honour seem to forbid subjection. Whoever feels himself degraded at the thought of being the *instrument* of a prince or a party and sect, or even of a money market, as, for example, the scion of a proud and ancient family may, but wants or has to be this instrument, both in his own eyes and those of the public, has need of pathetic principles which can be uttered at any time – principles of an unconditional obligation to which one can subject oneself and show oneself subjected without shame. All subtler servility cleaves to the categorical imperative and is the mortal enemy of those who want to divest duty of its unconditional character: their dignity demands it, and not only their dignity.

[*GS* 5]

# 79

*Something for the industrious.* – Whoever now wants to make a study of moral things opens up for himself an enormous field of work. Every sort of passion has to be thought through separately and followed separately through ages, peoples, great and little individuals; all the reason in them and all their evaluations and illuminations of things should be brought to light! All that which has given colour to existence has had no history hitherto: or where is there a history of love, avarice, envy, conscience, piety, cruelty? Even a comparative history of justice, or even only of punishment, is completely lacking. Have the various divisions of the day, the consequences of fixing a regular succession of work, play and rest been the object of research? Are the moral effects of food known? Is there a philosophy of nourishment? [. . .] Have the experiences of communal living, the experiences of the monastery for example, yet been assembled? Has the dialectic of marriage and friendship yet been presented? The morals of scholars, merchants, artists, craftsmen – have they yet found their thinker? There is so much in them to be thought over! [. . .] Observation alone of the different ways in which the human drives have developed and could still develop in accordance with differing moral climates provides too much work even for the most industrious; whole generations of scholars working in planned collaboration are needed to exhaust the material and points of view here. The same applies to the demonstration of the grounds for the differences in moral climate. [. . .] And it is again a separate labour to determine the erroneousness of all these grounds and the whole nature of moral judgement hitherto. Supposing all this work has been done, then the trickiest of all questions steps into the foreground: whether science is in a position to *provide* goals of behaviour, having proved it can take and destroy them – and then an experimentation would be in place in which every kind of heroism could gratify itself, a centuries-long experimentation which could put every great labour and sacrifice of history into the shade. Hitherto science has not yet built its cyclopean structures; the time will come for that too!

[*GS* 7]

## 80

*Evil.* – Examine the lives of the best and most fruitful men and peoples, and ask yourselves whether a tree, if it is to grow proudly into the sky, can do without bad weather and storms: whether unkindness and opposition from without, whether some sort of hatred, envy, obstinacy, mistrust, severity, greed and violence do not belong to the *favouring* circumstances without which a great increase even in virtue is hardly possible. The poison which destroys the weaker nature strengthens the stronger – and he does not call it poison, either.

[*GS* 19]

## 81

*To the teachers of selflessness.* – A person's virtues are called *good*, not with regard to the effects they produce for him himself, but with regard to the effects we suppose they will produce for us and for society – praise of virtue has always been very little 'selfless', very little 'unegoistic'! For otherwise it must have been seen that virtues (such as industriousness, obedience, chastity, piety, justness) are mostly *injurious* to their possessors, as drives which rule in them too fervently and demandingly and will in no way allow reason to hold them in equilibrium with the other drives. If you possess a virtue, a real whole virtue (and not merely a puny drive towards a virtue!) – you are its *victim*! But that precisely is why your neighbour praises your virtue! [. . .] Praise of the selfless, sacrificing, virtuous – that is to say, of those who do not expend all their strength and reason on *their own* preservation, evolution, elevation, advancement, amplification of their power, but who live modestly and thoughtlessly, perhaps even indifferently or ironically with regard to themselves – this praise is in any event not a product of the spirit of selflessness! One's 'neighbour' praises selflessness because *he derives advantage from it*! [. . .] Herewith is indicated the fundamental contradiction of that morality which is precisely today held in such high esteem: the *motives* for this morality stand in antithesis to its *principle*! That with which this morality wants to prove itself it refutes by its criterion of the moral! [. . .]

[*GS* 21]

## 82

*Where the good begins.* – Where weak eyesight is no longer capable of seeing the evil drive as such on account of its refinement, there mankind establishes the realm of the good, and the sensation of now having stepped over into the realm of the good also excites all those drives which were threatened and circumscribed by the evil drive, such as the feeling of security, of comfort, of benevolence. Thus: the duller the eye, the farther does the good extend! Hence the eternal cheerfulness of the people and of children! Hence the gloominess and the moroseness, related to the bad conscience, of the great thinker!

[*GS* 53]

## 83

*Herd instinct.* – Where we encounter a morality we find a valuation and order of rank of human drives and actions. These valuations and orders of rank are always the expression of the needs of a community and herd: that which is *its* first requirement – and second and third – is also the supreme standard for the value of every individual. With morality the individual is led into being a function of the herd and to ascribing value to himself only as a function. As the conditions for the preservation of one community have been very different from those of another community, there have been very different moralities; and considering the fundamental transformations of herds and communities, states and societies still to come, one can prophesy that there will be more very divergent moralities in the future. Morality is the herd instinct in the individual.

[*GS* 116]

## 84

*Belief makes blessed.* – Virtue brings happiness and a kind of blessedness only to those who have belief in their virtue – not, however, to those more subtle souls whose virtue consists in a profound mistrust of themselves and of all virtue. Thus here too it is in the end belief which 'makes blessed' – and, *nota bene*, *not* virtue!

[*GS* 214]

# 85

*Guilt.* – Although the most clear-sighted judges of witches and even the witches themselves were convinced the witches were guilty of witchcraft, no guilt in fact existed. So it is with all guilt.

[*GS* 250]

# 86

When I visited men, I found them sitting upon an old self-conceit. Each one thought he had long since known what was good and evil for man.

All talk of virtue seemed to them an ancient wearied affair; and he who wished to sleep well spoke of 'good' and 'evil' before retiring.

I disturbed this somnolence when I taught that *nobody yet knows* what is good and evil – unless it be the creator!

But he it is who creates a goal for mankind and gives the earth its meaning and its future: he it is who *creates* the quality of good and evil in things.

And I bade them overturn their old professional chairs, and wherever that old self-conceit had sat. I bade them laugh at their great masters of virtue and saints and poets and world-redeemers.

I bade them laugh at their gloomy sages, and whoever had sat as a black scarecrow, cautioning, on the tree of life.

I sat myself on their great grave-street, and even beside carrion and vultures – and I laughed over all their 'past' and its decayed expiring glory.

Truly, like Lenten preachers and fools did I cry anger and
shame over all their great and small things – their best is so
very small! Their worst is so very small! – thus I laughed.

Thus from out of me cried and laughed my wise desire,
which was born on the mountains, a wild wisdom, in truth!
– my great desire with rushing wings. [. . .]

[Z III *Of Old and New Law-Tables* 2]


# 87

There are no moral phenomena at all, only a moral interpretation of phenomena . . .

[*BGE* 108]


# 88

Moral sensibility is as subtle, late, manifold, sensitive and refined in Europe today as the 'science of morals' pertaining to
it is still young, inept, clumsy and coarse-fingered [. . .] Even
the expression 'science of morals' is, considering what is designated by it, far too proud, and contrary to *good* taste: which is
always accustomed to choose the more modest expressions.
One should, in all strictness, admit *what* will be needful here
for a long time to come, *what* alone is provisionally justified
here: assembly of material, conceptual comprehension and
arrangement of a vast domain of delicate value-feelings and
value-distinctions which live, grow, beget and perish – and
perhaps attempts to display the more frequent and recurring
forms of these living crystallizations – as preparation of a
*typology* of morals. To be sure: one has not been so modest
hitherto. Philosophers one and all have, with a strait-laced
seriousness that provokes laughter, demanded something
much higher, more pretentious, more solemn of themselves
as soon as they have concerned themselves with morality as a
science: they wanted to furnish the *rational ground* of morality

– and every philosopher hitherto has believed he has furnished this rational ground; morality itself, however, was taken as 'given'. [. . .] they did not so much as catch sight of the real problems of morality – for these come into view only if we compare *many* moralities. Strange though it may sound, in all 'science of morals' hitherto the problem of morality itself has been *lacking*: the suspicion was lacking that there was anything problematic here. [. . .]

[*BGE* 186]

## 89

Every morality is, as opposed to *laisser aller*, a piece of tyranny against 'nature', likewise against 'reason': but that can be no objection to it unless one is in possession of some other morality which decrees that any kind of tyranny and unreason is impermissible. The essential and invaluable element in every morality is that it is a protracted constraint: to understand Stoicism or Port-Royal or Puritanism one should recall the constraint under which every language has hitherto attained strength and freedom – the metrical constraint, the tyranny of rhyme and rhythm. How much trouble the poets and orators of every nation have given themselves! – not excluding a few present-day prose writers in whose ear there dwells an inexorable conscience – 'for the sake of foolishness', as the utilitarian fools say, thinking they are clever – 'from subjection to arbitrary laws', as the anarchists say, feeling themselves 'free', even free-spirited. But the strange fact is that all there is or has been on earth of freedom, subtlety, boldness, dance and masterly certainty, whether in thinking itself, or in ruling, or in speaking and persuasion, in the arts as in morals, has evolved only by virtue of the 'tyranny of such arbitrary laws'; and, in all seriousness, there is no small probability that precisely this is 'nature' and 'natural' – and *not* that *laisser aller*! [. . .] The essential thing 'in heaven and upon earth' seems, to say it again, to be a protracted *obedience* in *one* direction:

from out of that there always emerges and has always emerged
in the long run something for the sake of which it is worth-
while to live on earth, for example virtue, art, music, reason,
spirituality – something transfiguring, refined, mad and divine.
[. . .] 'Thou shalt obey someone and for a long time: *otherwise*
thou shalt perish and lose all respect for thyself' – this seems
to me to be nature's imperative, which is, to be sure, neither
'categorical', as old Kant demanded it should be (hence the
'otherwise' – ), nor addressed to the individual (what do individuals matter to nature), but to peoples, races, ages, classes,
and above all to the entire animal 'man', to *mankind*.

[*BGE* 188]

## 90

In a tour of the many finer and coarser moralities which have
ruled or still rule on earth I found certain traits regularly recurring together and bound up with one another: until at
length two basic types were revealed and a basic distinction
emerged. There is *master morality* and *slave morality* – I add at
once that in all higher and mixed cultures attempts at medi-
ation between the two are apparent and more frequently confusion and mutual misunderstanding between them, indeed
sometimes their harsh juxtaposition – even within the same
man, within *one* soul. The moral value-distinctions have
arisen either among a ruling order which was pleasurably conscious of its distinction from the ruled – or among the ruled,
the slaves and dependants of every degree. In the former case,
when it is the rulers who determine the concept 'good', it is
the exalted, proud states of soul which are considered distinguishing and determine the order or rank. The noble human
being separates from himself those natures in which the opposite of such exalted proud states finds expression: he despises
them. It should be noted at once that in this first type of
morality the antithesis 'good' and 'bad' means the same
thing as 'noble' and 'despicable' – the antithesis 'good' and

'*evil*' originates elsewhere. The cowardly, the timid, the petty, and those who think only of narrow utility are despised; as are the mistrustful with their constricted glance, those who abase themselves, the dog-like type of man who lets himself be maltreated, the fawning flatterer, above all the liar – it is a fundamental belief of all aristocrats that the common people are liars. [. . .] It is immediately obvious that designations of moral value were everywhere first applied to *human beings*, and only later and derivatively to *actions*: which is why it is a grave error when moral historians start from such questions as 'why has the compassionate action been praised?' The noble type of man feels *himself* to be the determiner of values, he does not need to be approved of, he judges 'what harms me is harmful in itself', he knows himself to be that which in general first accords to honour things, he *creates values*. Everything he knows to be part of himself, he honours: such a morality is self-glorification. In the foreground stands the feeling of plenitude, of power which seeks to overflow, the happiness of high tension, the consciousness of a wealth which would like to give away and bestow – the noble human being, too, aids the unfortunate but not, or almost not, from pity, but more from an urge begotten by superfluity of power. The noble human being honours in himself the man of power, also the man who has power over himself, who understands how to speak and how to keep silent, who enjoys practising severity and harshness upon himself and feels reverence for all that is severe and harsh. [. . .] Deep reverence for age and the traditional – all law rests on this twofold reverence – belief in and prejudice in favour of ancestors and against descendants, is typical of the morality of the powerful; and when, conversely, men of 'modern ideas' believe almost instinctively in 'progress' and 'the future' and show an increasing lack of respect for age, this reveals clearly enough the ignoble origin of these 'ideas'. A morality of the rulers is, however, most alien and painful to contemporary taste in the severity of its principle that one has duties only towards one's equals; that towards beings of a lower rank, towards everything alien, one may act as one wishes or 'as the heart dictates' and in any case 'beyond good and evil': it is here that pity and the like can have a place. The capacity for and the duty of protracted gratitude and protracted revenge – both only among one's equals – subtlety in requital, a refined conception of friendship, a certain need to have enemies (as conduit systems, as it were, for the emotions of envy, quarrelsomeness, arrogance – fundamentally so as to be able to be a good *friend*): all these are typical marks of noble morality [. . .] It is otherwise with the second type of morality, *slave morality*. Suppose the abused, oppressed, suffering, unfree, those uncertain of themselves and weary should moralize: what would their moral evaluations have in common? Probably a pessimistic mistrust of the entire situation of man will find expression, perhaps a condemnation of man together with his situation. The slave is suspicious of the virtues of the powerful: he is sceptical and mistrustful, *keenly* mistrustful, of everything 'good' that is honoured among them – he would like to convince himself that happiness itself is not genuine among them. On the other hand, those qualities which serve to make easier the existence of the suffering will be brought into prominence and flooded with light: here it is that pity, the kind and helping hand, the warm heart, patience, industriousness, humility, friendliness come into honour – for here these are the most useful qualities and virtually the only means of enduring the burden of existence. Slave morality is essentially the morality of utility. Here is the source of the famous antithesis 'good' and '*evil*' – power and danger were felt to exist in evil, a certain dreadfulness, subtlety and strength which could not admit of contempt. Thus, according to slave morality the 'evil' inspire fear; according to master morality it is precisely the 'good' who inspire fear and want to inspire it, while the 'bad' man is judged contemptible. The antithesis reaches its height when, consistently with slave morality, a breath of disdain finally also comes to be attached to the 'good' of this morality – it may be a slight and benevolent disdain – because within the slaves' way of thinking the good man has in any event to be a *harmless* man: he is good-natured, easy to deceive, perhaps a bit stupid, *un bonhomme*. Wherever slave morality comes to predominate, language exhibits a tendency to bring the words 'good' and 'stupid' closer to each other. – A final fundamental distinction: the longing for *freedom*, the instinct for the happiness and the refinements of the feeling of freedom, belong just as necessarily to slave morality and morals as the art of reverence and devotion and the enthusiasm for them are the regular symptom of an aristocratic mode of thinking and valuating. – This makes it clear without further ado why love *as passion* – it is our European speciality – absolutely must be of aristocratic origin: it was, as is well known, invented by the poet-knights of Provence, those splendid, inventive men of the '*gai saber*' to whom Europe owes so much and, indeed, almost itself. –

[*BGE* 260]

## 91

[. . .] the judgement 'good' does *not* originate with those to whom 'goodness' is shown! It was rather 'the good' themselves, that is to say the noble, powerful, higher placed and high-minded, who felt and posited themselves and their actions as good, namely as of the first rank, in antithesis to everything low, low-minded, common and plebeian. It was out of this *pathos of distance* that they assumed the right to create values, to coin the names of values: what concern did they have with utility! The utilitarian point of view is with regard to such a fiery eruption of supreme rank-distinguishing value judgements as foreign and inappropriate as it possibly could be: for here the feeling is the exact opposite of that tepid degree of heat which every kind of calculating prudence, every calculus of utility presupposes – and not for a single instance, not for an exceptional hour, but permanently. The pathos of nobility and distance, as I have said, the permanent and domineering collective fundamental feeling of a higher ruling type in relation to a lower type, to a 'beneath' – *that* is

the origin of the antithesis 'good' and 'bad'. [...] It is because of this origin that the word 'good' was from the very
first absolutely *not* necessarily connected with 'unegoistic'
actions [...] It is rather only with a *decline* in aristocratic value
judgements that this whole antithesis 'egoistic' 'unegoistic'
obtrudes itself more and more on the human conscience – it
is, to employ my own language, *the herd instinct* which with
this antithesis at length finds speech (and words to speak
with). And even then it is a long time before this instinct becomes sufficiently master for moral evaluation to be caught
and fixed to that antithesis (as is, for example, the case in contemporary Europe: the prejudice which takes 'moral', 'unegoistic', '*désintéressé*' as equivalent concepts rules already
today with the force of a 'fixed idea' and brainsickness).

\*

The signpost to the *right* track [to the discovery of the origin
of the value judgement 'good'] was the question: what was
the real etymological significance of the symbols for 'good'
which have been coined in the various languages? I found they
all led back to the *same conceptual transformation* – that everywhere 'noble', 'aristocratic' in the social sense is the basic
concept from which 'good' in the sense of 'with aristocratic
soul', 'noble', 'with a soul of a high order', 'with a privileged
soul' necessarily developed: a development which always runs
parallel with that other in which 'common', 'plebeian', 'low'
are finally transformed into the concept 'bad'. The most convincing instance of the latter is the German word *schlecht* [bad]
itself: which is identical with *schlicht* [plain] [...] and originally
designated the plain, common man, as yet without any in-
culpatory side-glance but simply in antithesis to the nobleman.
About the time of the Thirty Years War – recently enough,
that is – this sense shifted to the one now current. – With respect to the genealogy of morals this seems to me an *essential*
insight: that it was arrived at only so late is to be attributed
to the retarding influence exercised by the democratic prejudice within the modern world in regard to all questions of

origin. And this extends even into the apparently most objective domain of natural science and physiology [. . .]

*

In regard to *our* problem [. . .] it is of no small interest to establish that many of the chief traits by virtue of which the noble felt themselves to be human beings of a higher rank still shine through those words and roots which designate 'good'. To be sure, they name themselves in perhaps the most frequent cases simply after their superiority in power (as 'the powerful', 'the masters', 'the commanders') or after the most obvious mark of this superiority, as 'the rich', for example, or 'the owners' (this is the meaning of *arya*, and correspondingly in Iranian and Slavic). But they also do so after a *typical characteristic*: and this is the case with which we are concerned. They call themselves, for example, 'the truthful'; the Greek nobility above all, whose mouthpiece is the Megarian poet Theognis. The word coined for this, *esthlos*, signifies in its root one who *is*, who possesses reality, who is real, who is true; then, with a subjective change, the true men as the truthful men: at this phase of conceptual transformation it becomes the motto and slogan of the nobility and passes over wholly into the sense 'noble' in distinction from the *lying* common man, as Theognis takes him to be and describes him – until, after the decline of the nobility, the word is finally left to designate *noblesse* of soul and becomes, as it were, ripe and sweet. In the word *kakos*, as in *deilos* (the plebeian in antithesis to the *agathos*), it is cowardice which is underlined [. . .] The Latin *malus* (which I set beside *melas*) may characterize the common man as the dark-coloured, above all as the black-haired man ('*hic niger est* –'), as the pre-Aryan inhabitant of Italy most clearly distinguished from the blond, Aryan conquering race by his colour; in any event, the Gaelic language offers me an exactly corresponding case – *fin* (in the name *Fin-Gal*, for example), the distinguishing word for the nobility, ultimately the good, clean, originally the blond-headed in antithesis to the dark, black-haired aboriginals.

[. . .] I believe I may explicate the Latin *bonus* as 'the warrior': supposing I am right to trace *bonus* back to an earlier *duonus* (compare *bellum = duellum = duen-lum*, which seems to me to contain *duonus*). *Bonus*, therefore, as the man of discord, of dissension (*duo*), as the man of war: one sees what constituted 'the good' to a man of ancient Rome. Our German *gut* [good] itself: does it not signify *den Göttlichen* [the god-like], the man of *göttlichen Geschlechts* [god-like race]? And is it not identical with the national name (originally the nobility's name) of the Goths? [. . .]

\*

The slave revolt in morality begins when *ressentiment* itself becomes creative and gives birth to values: the *ressentiment* of creatures to whom the real reaction, that of the deed, is denied and who can indemnify themselves only through an imaginary revenge. While every noble morality develops from a triumphant affirmation of itself, slave morality from the outset says No to what is 'outside', what is 'different', what is 'not itself': and *this* No is its creative act. This reversal of the value-creating view – this *necessary* directing of the eye outwards instead of back to oneself – pertains precisely to *ressentiment*: in order to come into existence, slave morality always first requires a contrary and outer world, it requires, in the language of physiology, an external stimulus in order to act at all – its action is from the very bottom reaction. The opposite is the case with the noble mode of valuation: it acts and grows spontaneously, it seeks its antithesis only so as to affirm itself more gratefully and joyously – its negative concept 'low', 'common', 'bad' is only a subsequently produced pale contrasting image in comparison with its positive basic concept, saturated through and through with life and passion, 'we noble, we good, we beautiful, we happy!' [. . .] The 'well born' *feel* themselves to be the 'happy'; they do not first have to construct their happiness artificially, or if need be convince themselves of it, *lie* themselves into it (as all men of *ressentiment* are accustomed to do), by gazing on their enemies; and as whole men, overcharged with strength and therefore *necessarily* active, they likewise do not know how to sever themselves from the happiness of acting – to be active is with them necessarily a part of happiness (whence *eu prattein* takes its origin) – all this very much in contrast to 'happiness' on the level of the powerless, the oppressed, those festering with poisonous and inimical feelings, with whom it appears essentially as narcosis, stupefaction, rest, peace, 'Sabbath', relaxation of the heart and stretching of the limbs, in short *passively*. While the noble man lives in trust and openness with himself (*gennaios*, 'nobly born', underlines the nuance 'upright' and probably also 'naive'), the man of *ressentiment* is neither upright nor naive, or honest and straightforward with himself. His soul *squints*: his spirit loves hiding-places, secret paths and back doors, everything covert strikes him as *his* world, *his* security, *his* refreshment; he knows how to keep silent, how not to forget, how to wait, how to make himself provisionally small and humble. A race of such men of *ressentiment* will necessarily end up *cleverer* than any noble race, it will also hold cleverness in an altogether higher degree of honour: namely, as a condition of its existence of the first order; while with noble men cleverness can easily acquire a slight flavour of luxury and *raffinement* – here it is not nearly so essential as the perfect functioning of the regulatory *unconscious* instincts or even a certain lack of cleverness, perhaps a brave recklessness in face of danger or in face of the enemy, or that enthusiastic impetuosity in anger, love, reverence, gratitude and revenge by which noble souls have in all ages recognized one another. When the noble man does feel *ressentiment* it consummates and exhausts itself in an immediate reaction, it therefore does not *poison*: on the other hand, it simply fails to appear in countless instances in which it would inevitably do so with the weak and powerless. An inability to take their enemies, their misfortunes, even their *misdeeds* seriously for long – that is a sign of strong, full natures in which there is an excess of plastic, formative, curative power, and also the power of forgetting. [. . .] Such a man shakes from himself with a *single* shrug much vermin which would bore its way into others; here alone, too, is there possible, if it is possible on earth at all – actual 'love of one's enemies'. How much respect for his enemies does a noble man already feel! – and such respect is already a bridge to love . . . For he wants his enemy for himself, as his distinction, he can indeed endure no enemy but one in whom there is nothing to despise and *very much* to honour! Picture, on the other hand, 'the enemy' as the man of *ressentiment* conceives him – and here precisely is his deed, his creation: he has conceived 'the evil enemy', '*the Evil One*', and this indeed is his basic conception from which he then evolves, as a corresponding and opposing figure, a 'good one' – himself! . . .

This is, then, quite the contrary of what the noble man does, who conceives the basic conception 'good' spontaneously, out of himself, and only then creates from that an idea of 'bad'! This 'bad' of noble origin and that 'evil' out of the cauldron of unsatisfied hatred, [. . .] how different these words 'bad' and 'evil' are, although they are both apparently the opposite of the same concept 'good'. But it is *not* the same concept 'good': one should ask rather precisely *who* is 'evil' in the sense of the morality of *ressentiment*. The answer is, in all strictness: *precisely* the 'good man' of the other morality, precisely the noble, powerful man, the ruler, only recoloured, reinterpreted and seen differently by the poisoned eye of *ressentiment*. Let us here deny one thing least of all: he who gets to know these 'good men' only as enemies gets to know only *evil enemies*, and the same men who are held so strictly in bounds *inter pares* by custom, respect, usage, gratitude, even more by mutual watchfulness, by jealousy, and who on the other hand show themselves so inventive in consideration, self-control, sensitivity, loyalty, pride and friendship in their relations with one another – with respect to what lies outside, where the strange and the stranger begin, these men are not much better than beasts of prey let loose. There they enjoy a freedom from all social constraint; they indemnify themselves in the wilderness for the tension which a protracted imprisonment and enclosure within the peace of the community pro-

duces; they *go back* to the innocence of the beast-of-prey conscience, as rejoicing monsters who perhaps make off from a
hideous succession of murders, conflagrations, rapes and tor-
turings in high spirits and equanimity of soul as if they had
been engaged in nothing more than a student prank, and convinced that the poets now again have something to sing about
and praise for a long time to come. One cannot fail to see at
the core of all these noble races the animal of prey, the splendid
*blond beast* prowling about avidly in search of spoil and victory;
this hidden core needs to erupt from time to time, the animal
has to get out again and go back to the wilderness: the
Roman, Arabian, Germanic, Japanese nobility, the Homeric
heroes, the Scandinavian Vikings – they all shared this need.
It is the noble races which have left behind them the concept
'barbarian' wherever they have gone [. . .]

*

[. . .] To require of strength that it should *not* express itself as
strength, that it should *not* be a desire to conquer, a desire to
subdue, a desire to become master, a thirst for enemies and
resistances and triumphs, is just as absurd as to require of
weakness that it should express itself as strength. A quantum
of force is an equivalent quantum of drive, will, operation –
or, rather, it is nothing whatever other than this driving, willing, operating itself, and only under the misleading influence
of language (and the fundamental errors of reason fossilized
in it), which understands and misunderstands all operation as
conditioned by an operator, by a 'subject', can it seem otherwise. For just as the people separates the lightning from its
flash and takes the latter as an *action*, as an operation on the
part of a subject called lightning, so popular morality separates
strength from expressions of strength, as if there were a neutral
substratum behind the strong man which was *free* to express
strength or not to do so. But there is no such substratum;
there is no 'being' behind doing, operating, becoming; 'the
doer' is merely added to the deed – the deed is everything.
[. . .] When the oppressed, downtrodden, despoiled say to

themselves in the revengeful cunning of impotence: 'let us be different from the evil, namely good! and good is everyone who does not despoil, who injures no one, who does not attack, who does not requite, who leaves vengeance to God, who lives in obscurity as we do, who avoids everything evil and demands little from life in general, like us, the patient, humble and just' – this, heard coldly and without prepossession, really means nothing more than: 'we weak are after all weak; it would be a good thing to do nothing *for which we are insufficiently strong*'; but this austere fact, this prudence of the lowest sort which even insects possess (who, when there is danger, pretend to be dead so as not to do 'too much') has, thanks to that false-coinage and self-deluding of impotence, clothed itself in the finery of the virtue of renunciation and silent waiting, as if the weakness of the weak man itself – and that means his *essence*, his actions, his whole, sole, inevitable, irredeemable actuality – were a voluntary achievement, something willed, chosen, a *deed*, *meritorious*. [. . .]

[*G M 'Good and Evil', 'Good and Bad'* 2, 4, 5, 10, 11, 13]

## 92

[. . .] I regard the bad conscience as the serious illness which man was bound to contract under the stress of the most fundamental change he had ever experienced – that change which occurred when he found himself finally enclosed within the walls of society and of peace. The situation that must have faced the sea animals when they were compelled either to become land animals or perish was the same as faced these semi-animals which were well adapted to the wilderness, to war, to prowling about, to adventure – suddenly all their instincts were deprived of value and 'suspended'. [. . .] They felt incapable of the simplest undertakings, in this new unfamiliar world their former guides, the regulating and unconsciously certain drives, deserted them – these unhappy creatures were reduced to thinking, inferring, reckoning, co-ordinating cause and effect, to their 'consciousness', to their poorest and most fallible organ! I believe there has never been such a feeling of misery, such leaden discomfort on earth – and at the same time their old instincts had not suddenly ceased to make their demands! Only it was hard and rarely possible to gratify them: as a rule they had to look for new and, as it were, subterranean satisfactions. All instincts which do not discharge themselves outwardly *turn inwards* – this is that which I call the deepening and intensifying [*Verinnerlichung*] of man: thus it was that man first developed what he afterwards called his 'soul'. The entire inner world, originally as thin as if stretched between two membranes, grew and expanded, acquired depth, breadth, height, in the same measure as outward discharge was *hindered*. Those fearful bulwarks with which the social organization protected itself against the old instincts of freedom – punishment is the chief among them – brought it about that all those instincts of wild, free, prowling man turned backwards *against man himself*. Enmity, cruelty, joy in persecuting, in attacking, in change, in destruction – all this turned against the possessors of such instincts: *that* is the origin of the 'bad conscience' [. . .] thus was inaugurated the worst and uncanniest illness, from which man has not to the present moment recovered, man's suffering *from man, from himself*: as the consequence of a forcible sundering from his animal past, as it were a leap and plunge into new circumstances and conditions of existence, a declaration of war against the old instincts in which his strength, joy and fearsomeness had previously reposed. Let us add at once that, on the other hand, with the fact of an animal soul turned against itself, taking sides against itself, something so new, profound, unheard-of, enigmatic, contradictory *and full of future* was introduced that the aspect of the earth was thereby essentially altered. [. . .] From now on man [. . .] awakens an interest, a tension, a hope, almost a certainty, as if with him something were announcing, preparing itself, as if man were not a goal but only a way, an episode, a bridge, a great promise . . .

Among the presuppositions of this hypothesis on the origin

of the bad conscience is, firstly, that that change was not a gradual or voluntary one and represented not an organic adaptation to novel conditions but a break, a leap, a compulsion, a fatality against which there could be no resistance or even *ressentiment*. In the second place, however, it presupposes that the welding of a hitherto unrestrained and shapeless populace into a firm form, as it was originated by an act of violence, so it was completed by nothing but acts of violence – that the oldest 'state', consequently, appeared as a fearful tyranny, as a remorseless machine of oppression, and went on working until this raw material of people and semi-animals was at last not only kneaded and pliant but also *formed*. I employed the word 'state': it is self-evident what is meant – some herd of blond beasts of prey, a conqueror and master race, which, organized for war and with the ability to organize, unhesitatingly lays its terrible claws upon a population perhaps tremendously superior in numbers but still formless and nomad. That is how the 'state' began on earth [. . .] They do not know what guilt, responsibility, respect are, these born organizers [. . .] It is not in *them* that the 'bad conscience' developed, that goes without saying – but it would not have developed *without them* [. . .] it would be lacking if a tremendous quantity of freedom had not been expelled from the world, or at least been rendered invisible and made as it were *latent* under their hammer-blows. This *instinct for freedom* forcibly made latent, this instinct for freedom pushed back and made to retreat, incarcerated within, and in the end discharging and venting itself only on itself: that and that alone is, in its inception, the *bad conscience*.

One should guard against thinking lightly of this phenomenon on account of its initial painfulness and ugliness. For fundamentally it is the same active force which is at work on a grander scale in those artists in violence and organizes and builds states which here, internally [. . .] in the 'labyrinth of the breast', to use Goethe's words, creates for itself a bad conscience and builds negative ideals, it is that *instinct for freedom* (in my language: will to power); with the difference that the material upon which the form-constructing and overpowering nature of this force operates is here man himself, his entire old animal self – and *not*, as in that bigger and more obvious phenomenon, *other* men [. . .]

The bad conscience is an illness, there is no doubt about that, but an illness as pregnancy is an illness. [. . .]

[*GM 'Guilt,' 'Bad Conscience' and the Like* 16–19]

### 93

One knows my demand of philosophers that they place themselves *beyond* good and evil – that they have the illusion of moral judgement *beneath* them. This demand follows from an insight first formulated by me: *that there are no moral facts whatever*. Moral judgement has this in common with religious judgement, that it believes in realities which do not exist. Morality is only an interpretation of certain phenomena, more precisely a *mis*interpretation. Moral judgement belongs, as does religious judgement, to a level of ignorance at which even the concept of the real, the distinction between the real and the imaginary, is lacking [. . .] To this extent moral judgement is never to be taken literally: as such it never contains anything but nonsense. But as *semeiotics* it remains of incalculable value: it reveals, to the informed man at least, the most precious realities of cultures and inner worlds which did not *know* enough to 'understand' themselves. Morality is merely sign-language, merely symptomatology [. . .]

A first example, merely as an introduction. In all ages one has wanted to 'improve' men: this above all is what morality has meant. But one word can conceal the most divergent tendencies. Both the *taming* of the beast man and the *breeding* of a certain species of man has been called 'improvement': only these zoological *termini* express realities [. . .] To call the taming of an animal its 'improvement' is in our ears almost a joke. Whoever knows what goes on in menageries is doubtful whether the beasts in them are 'improved'. They are weakened, they are made less harmful, they become *sickly* beasts through the depressive emotion of fear, through pain, through injuries, through hunger. – It is no different with the tamed human being whom the priest has 'improved'. In the early Middle Ages, when the Church was in fact above all a menagerie, one everywhere hunted down the fairest specimens of the 'blond beast' – one 'improved', for example, the noble Teutons. But what did such a Teuton afterwards look like when he had been 'improved' and led into a monastery? Like a caricature of a human being, like an abortion: he had become a 'sinner', he was in a cage [. . .] There he lay now, sick, miserable, filled with ill-will towards himself; full of hatred for the impulses towards life, full of suspicion of all that was still strong and happy. In short, a 'Christian' . . . In physiological terms: in the struggle with the beast, making it sick *can* be the only means of making it weak. This the Church understood: it *corrupted* the human being, it weakened him – but it claimed to have 'improved' him . . .

Let us take the other aspect of so-called morality, the *breeding* of a definite race and species. The most grandiose example of this is provided by Indian morality, sanctioned, as the 'Law of Manu', into religion. Here the proposed task is to breed no fewer than four races simultaneously: a priestly, a warrior, and a trading and farming race, and finally a menial race, the Sudras. Here we are manifestly no longer among animal-tamers: a species of human being a hundred times more gentle and rational is presupposed even to conceive the plan of such a breeding. [. . .] But this organization too needed to be *dreadful* – this time in struggle not with the beast but with *its* antithesis, with the non-bred human being, the Chandala. And again it had no means of making him weak and harmless other than making him *sick* – it was the struggle with the 'great majority'. Perhaps there is nothing which outrages our feelings more than *these* protective measures of Indian morality. The third edict, for example (*Avadana-Shastra* I), that 'concerning unclean vegetables', ordains that the only nourishment permitted the Chandala shall be garlic and onions, in view of the fact that holy scripture forbids one to give them corn or seed-bearing fruits or *water* or fire. The same edict lays it down that the water they need must not be taken from rivers or springs or pools, but only from the entrances to swamps and holes made by the feet of animals. They are likewise forbidden to wash their clothes or to *wash themselves*, since the water allowed them as an act of charity must be used only for quenching the thirst. Finally, the Sudra women are forbidden to assist the Chandala women in childbirth, and the latter are likewise forbidden to *assist one another*.

These regulations are instructive enough: in them we find for once *Aryan* humanity, quite pure, quite primordial – we learn that the concept 'pure blood' is the opposite of a harmless concept. [. . .]

The morality of *breeding* and the morality of *taming* are, in the means they employ to attain their ends, entirely worthy of one another: we may set down as our chief proposition that to *make* morality one must have the unconditional will to the contrary. This is the great, the *uncanny* problem which I have pursued furthest: the psychology of the 'improvers' of mankind. [. . .] Expressed in a formula one might say: *every* means hitherto employed with the intention of making mankind moral has been thoroughly *immoral*. –

[T The '*Improvers*' of Mankind]

## 94

*Whether we have grown more moral.* – As was only to be expected, the whole *ferocity* of the moral stupidity which, as is well known, is considered morality as such in Germany, has launched itself against my concept 'beyond good and evil': I could tell some pretty stories about it. Above all, I was invited to reflect on the 'undeniable superiority' of our age in moral judgement, our real *advance* in this respect: compared with *us*, a Cesare Borgia was certainly not to be set up as a 'higher man', as a kind of *superman*, in the way I set him up. [. . .] by way of reply I permit myself to raise the question *whether we have really grown more moral*. That all the world believes so is already an objection to it ... We modern men, very delicate, very vulnerable and paying and receiving consideration in a hundred ways, imagine in fact that this sensitive humanity which we represent, this *achieved* unanimity in forbearance, in readiness to help, in mutual trust, is a positive advance, that with this we have gone far beyond the men of the Renaissance. But every age thinks in this way, *has* to think in this way. What is certain is that we would not dare to place ourselves in Renaissance circumstances, or even imagine ourselves in them: our nerves could not endure that reality, not to speak of our muscles. This incapacity, however, demonstrates, not an advance, but only a different, a more belated constitution, a weaker, more delicate, more vulnerable one, out of which is necessarily engendered a morality *which is full of consideration*. If we think away our delicacy and belatedness, our physiological ageing, then our morality of 'humanization' too loses its value at once – no morality has any value in itself – : we would even despise it. On the other hand, let us be in no doubt that we modern men, with our thick padding of humanity which dislikes to give the slightest offence, would provide the contemporaries of Cesare Borgia with a side-splitting comedy. [. . .] Ages are to be assessed according to their *positive forces* – and by this assessment the age of the Renaissance, so prodigal and so fateful, appears as the last *great* age, and we, we moderns with our anxious care for ourselves and love of our neighbour, with our virtues of work, of unpretentiousness, of fair play, of scientificality – acquisitive, economical, machine-minded – appear as a *weak* age ... Our virtues are conditioned, are *demanded* by our weakness. 'Equality', a certain actual rendering similar of which the theory of 'equal rights' is only the expression, belongs essentially to decline: the chasm between man and man, class and class, the multiplicity of types, the will to be oneself, to stand out – that which I call *pathos of distance* – characterizes every *strong* age. The tension, the range between extremes is today growing

less and less – the extremes themselves are finally obliterated
to the point of similarity. [. . .]

[*T Expeditions of an Untimely Man* 37]

## 95

Such a law-book as that of Manu originates as does every
good law-book: it summarizes the experience, policy and experimental morality of long centuries, it settles accounts, it
creates nothing new. The precondition for a codification of
this sort is the insight that the means of endowing with
authority a *truth* slowly and expensively acquired are fundamentally different from those by which one would demonstrate it. A law-book never tells of the utility of a law, of the
reason for it, of the casuistry which preceded it: for in that
way it would lose the imperative tone, the 'thou shalt', the
precondition of being obeyed. The problem lies precisely in
this. – At a certain point in the evolution of a people its most
enlightened, that is to say, most reflective and far-sighted
class declares the experience in accordance with which the
people is to live – that is, *can* live – to be fixed and settled.
Their objective is to bring home the richest and completest
harvest from the ages of experimentation and *bad* experience.
What, consequently, is to be prevented above all is the con-
tinuation of experimenting, the perpetuation *in infinitum* of
the fluid condition of values, tests, choices, criticism of values.
A twofold wall is erected against this: firstly *revelation*, that
is, the assertion that the reason for these laws is *not* of human
origin, was *not* sought and found slowly and with many
blunders, but, being of divine origin, is whole, perfect, without history, a gift, a miracle, merely communicated . . . Then
*tradition*, that is, the assertion that the law has already existed
from time immemorial, that it is impious, a crime against the
ancestors, to call it in question. [. . .] The higher rationale of
such a procedure lies in the intention of gradually making the
way of life recognized as correct (that is *demonstrated* by a

tremendous amount of finely-sifted experience) unconscious: so that a complete automatism of instinct is achieved – the precondition for any kind of mastery, any kind of perfection in the art of living. [. . .]

[*A* 57]

# ART AND AESTHETICS

## 96

*The artist's sense of truth.* – In regard to knowledge of truths, the artist possesses a weaker morality than the thinker; he does not wish to be deprived of the glittering, profound interpretations of life and guards against simple and sober methods and results. He appears to be fighting on behalf of the greater dignity and significance of man; in reality he refuses to give up the presuppositions which are *most efficacious* for his art, that is to say, the fantastic, mythical, uncertain, extreme, the sense for the symbolical, the overestimation of the person, the belief in something miraculous in genius: he thus considers the perpetuation of his mode of creation more important than scientific devotion to the true in any form, however plainly this may appear.

[HA 146]

## 97

*Poets as alleviators of life.* – Insofar as they want to alleviate the life of men, poets either turn their eyes away from the toilsome present or they procure for the present new colours through a light which they direct upon it from the past. To be able to do this, they themselves have to be in many respects backward-looking creatures: so that they can be employed as bridges to quite distant ages and conceptions, to dead or dying religions and cultures. They are, in fact, always and necessarily *epigones*. There are, to be sure, several things to be said against their means of alleviating life: they soothe and heal only provisionally, only for a moment; they even hinder men from working for a real improvement in their conditions by suspending and discharging in a palliative way the very passion which impels the discontented to action.

[HA 148]

# 98

*How metre beautifies.* – Metre lays a veil over reality: it effectuates a certain artificiality of speech and unclarity of thinking; by means of the shadows it throws over thoughts it now conceals, now brings into prominence. As beautification requires shadows, so clarification requires 'vagueness'. – Art makes the sight of life bearable by laying over it the veil of unclear thinking.

[HA 151]

# 99

*Art makes the thinker's heart heavy.* – How strong the metaphysical need is, and how hard nature makes it to bid it a final farewell, can be seen from the fact that even when the free spirit has divested himself of everything metaphysical the highest effects of art can easily set the metaphysical strings, which have long been silent or indeed snapped apart, vibrating in sympathy. [. . .] If he becomes aware of being in this condition he feels a profound stab in the heart and sighs for the man who will lead him back to his lost love, whether she be called religion or metaphysics. It is in such moments that his intellectual probity is put to the test.

[HA 153]

# 100

*Achilles and Homer.* – It is always as between Achilles and Homer: the one *has* the experience, the sensation, the other *describes* it. [. . .] Artists are by no means men of great passion but they often *pretend* to be, in the unconscious feeling that their painted passions will seem more believable if their own life speaks for their experience in this field. One has only to let oneself go, to abandon self-control, to give rein to one's anger or desires: at once all the world cries: how passionate he is! But deep-rooted passion, passion which gnaws at the individual and often consumes him, is a thing of some consequence: he who experiences such passion certainly does not describe it in dramas, music or novels. Artists are often *unbridled* individuals to the extent that they are not artists: but that is something else.

[*HA* 211]

## 101

*Old doubts over the effect of art.* – Are fear and pity really discharged by tragedy, as Aristotle has it, so that the auditor goes home colder and more placid? Do ghost stories make one less fearful and superstitious? It is true in the case of certain physical events, the enjoyment of love for example, that with the satisfaction of a need an alleviation and temporary relaxation of the drive occurs. But fear and pity are not in this sense needs of definite organs which want to be relieved. And in the long run a drive is, through practice in satisfying it, *intensified*, its periodical alleviation notwithstanding. It is possible that in each individual instance fear and pity are mitigated and discharged: they could nonetheless grow greater as a whole through the tragic effect in general, and Plato could still be right when he says that through tragedy one becomes generally more fearful and emotional. The tragic poet himself would then necessarily acquire a gloomy, disheartened view of the world and a soft, susceptible, tearful soul [. . .]

[*HA* 212]

## 102

*Music.* – Music is, of and in itself, not so significant for our inner world, nor so profoundly exciting, that it can be said to count as the *immediate* language of feeling; but its primeval union with poetry has deposited so much symbolism into rhythmic movement, into the varying strength and volume of musical sounds, that we now *suppose* it to speak directly *to* the inner world and to come *from* the inner world. [. . .] In itself, no music is profound or significant, it does not speak of the 'will' or of the 'thing in itself'; the intellect could suppose such a thing only in an age which had conquered for musical symbolism the entire compass of the inner life. It was the intellect itself which first *introduced* this significance into sounds: just as, in the case of architecture, it likewise introduced a significance into the relations between lines and masses which is in itself quite unknown to the laws of mechanics.

[*HA* 215]

## 103

*Stone is more stony than it used to be.* – In general we no longer understand architecture; at least we do not do so nearly as well as we understand music. We have grown out of the symbolism of lines and figures, just as we have weaned ourselves from the sound-effects of rhetoric, and no longer imbibe this kind of cultural mother's milk from the first moment of our lives. Everything in a Greek or Christian building originally signified something, and indeed something of a higher order of things: this feeling of inexhaustible significance lay about the building like a magical veil. Beauty entered this system only incidentally, without essentially encroaching upon the fundamental sense of the uncanny and exalted, of consecration by magic and the proximity of the divine; at most beauty *mitigated* the *dread* – but this dread was everywhere the presupposition. – What is the beauty of a building to us today?

The same thing as the beautiful face of a mindless woman: something mask-like.

[*HA* 218]


## 104

*The Beyond in art.* – It is not without profound sorrow that one admits to oneself that in their highest flights the artists of all ages have raised to heavenly transfiguration precisely those conceptions which we now recognize as false: they are the glorifiers of the religious and philosophical errors of mankind, and they could not have been so without believing in the absolute truth of these errors. If belief in such truth declines in general [. . .] that species of art can never flourish again which, like the *Divina Commedia*, the pictures of Raphael, the frescoes of Michelangelo, the Gothic cathedrals, presupposes not only a cosmic but also a metaphysical significance in the objects of art. A moving tale will one day be told how there once existed such an art, such an artist's faith.

[*HA* 220]


## 105

*In Gethsemane.* – The most grievous thing the thinker can say to the artists is: 'What, could ye not *watch with me* one hour?'

[*AOM* 29]


## 106

*On the morality of the stage.* – Whoever thinks that Shakespeare's theatre has a moral effect, and that the sight of Macbeth irresistibly repels one from the evil of ambition, is in error: and he is again in error if he thinks Shakespeare himself felt as he feels. He who is really possessed by raging ambition beholds

this its image with *joy*; and if the hero perishes by his passion
this precisely is the sharpest spice in the hot draught of this
joy. Can the poet have felt otherwise? How royally, and not
at all like a rogue, does his ambitious man pursue his course
from the moment of his great crime! Only from then on does
he exercise 'demonic' attraction and excite similar natures to
emulation – demonic means here: in defiance *against* life and
advantage for the sake of a drive and idea. Do you suppose
that Tristan and Isolde are preaching *against* adultery when
they both perish by it? This would be to stand the poets on
their head: they, and especially Shakespeare, are enamoured
of the passions as such and not least of their *death-welcoming*
moods – those moods in which the heart adheres to life no
more firmly than does a drop of water to a glass. It is not the
guilt and its evil outcome they have at heart, Shakespeare as
little as Sophocles (in Ajax, Philoctetes, Oedipus): as easy as it
would have been in these instances to make guilt the lever of
the drama, just as surely has this been avoided. The tragic
poet has just as little desire to take sides *against* life with his
images of life! He cries rather: 'it is the stimulant of stimulants, this exciting, changing, dangerous, gloomy and often
sun-drenched existence! It is an *adventure* to live – espouse
what party in it you will, it will always retain this character!'
– He speaks thus out of a restless, vigorous age which is half-
drunk and stupefied by its excess of blood and energy – out
of a wickeder age than ours is: which is why we need first to
*adjust* and *justify* the goal of a Shakespearean drama, that is to
say, not to understand it.

[*D* 240]

## 107

*The good and the beautiful.* – Artists continually *glorify* – they do
nothing else – : they glorify all those conditions and things
which have the reputation of making man feel for once good
or great or intoxicated or merry or wise. These *choice* things and

conditions, whose value for human *happiness* counts as esti-
mated and secure, are the artists' objects: they are always lying
in wait to uncover them and draw them across into the domain
of art. I mean to say: they are not themselves the assessors of
happiness and of what makes happy, but they always crowd
close up to these assessors with the greatest pleasure and
curiosity so as to make immediate use of their valuations.
Thus, because as well as their impatience they also possess
the lungs of heralds and the feet of runners, they will always
be among the first to glorify the *new* good, and will often
*appear* to be those who first call it and assess it as good. But
this is, as stated, an error: they are only faster and louder than
the actual assessors. – And who then are the actual assessors? –
They are the rich and idle.

[*GS* 85]

## 108

*Our ultimate reason for gratitude towards art.* – If we had not
approved of the arts and invented this kind of cult of the untrue, the insight into universal untruth and mendaciousness
now provided to us by science – the insight into illusion and
error as a condition of knowing and feeling existence – could
in no way be endured. *Honesty* would bring disgust and suicide
in its train. But now our honesty has a countervailing power
which helps us to avoid such consequences: art, as the *good*
will to appearance. [. . .] As an aesthetic phenomenon existence
is still *endurable* to us, and through art we are given eye and
hand, and above all a good conscience, to *enable* us to make
of ourselves such a phenomenon. [. . .]

[*GS* 107]

## 109

*What is romantic?* – It may perhaps be remembered, among my
friends at least, that I at first set upon this modern world with

a number of thumping errors and overestimations and in any event as a very *sanguine* person. I understood the philosophical pessimism of the nineteenth century – who knows on the basis of what personal experiences? – as the symptom of a higher power of thought, of audacious bravery, of victorious *abundance* of life, in the same way as these had been the property of the eighteenth century, the age of Hume, Kant, Condillac and the sensualists: so that the tragic outlook appeared to me as the actual *luxury* of our culture, as its most costly, noblest, most perilous kind of extravagance, but still in view of its great wealth a *permitted* luxury. Thus, too, I interpreted German music to myself as an expression of the Dionysian might of the German soul: I thought I heard in it the earthquake through which a primeval force which had been building up from of old finally found release – quite indifferent to the fact that everything else which was called culture was set trembling. It will be clear that I then misunderstood that which constitutes the real character of both philosophical pessimism and German music – their *romanticism*. What is romanticism? Every art, every philosophy may be viewed as an aid and remedy in the service of growing and striving life: they always presuppose suffering and sufferers. But there are two kinds of sufferer: firstly he who suffers from *superabundance of life*, who desires a Dionysian art and likewise a tragic view of and insight into life – and then he who suffers from *poverty of life*, who seeks in art and knowledge either rest, peace, a smooth sea, delivery from himself, or intoxication, paroxysm, stupefaction, madness. The twofold requirement of the *latter* corresponds to all romanticism in art and knowledge, it corresponded (and corresponds) to Schopenhauer and Richard Wagner, to name the two most famous and emphatic romantics which were formerly *misunderstood* by me – though *not* to their disadvantage, as should in all fairness be granted me. He who is richest in abundance of life, the Dionysian god and man, can allow himself, not only the sight of the fearsome and questionable, but even the fearsome deed and every luxury of destruction, disintegration, denial; the evil, senseless and ugly seem with him to be, as it were, permitted as a consequence of an excess of begetting, fructifying forces capable of creating out of every wilderness a luxuriant, fertile land. The most suffering man, the man poorest in life, will, on the contrary, have most need of kindness, peaceableness, goodness in thought and action, where possible a god who is quite especially a god of the sick, a 'saviour'; he will likewise have need of logic, the conceptual comprehensibility of existence – for logic tranquillizes, makes trusting – in short, a certain warm, fear-averting confinement and enclosure within optimistic horizons. It was in this light that I gradually learned to understand Epicurus, the antithesis of a Dionysian pessimist, likewise the 'Christian', who is in fact only a kind of Epicurean and, like those, essentially a romantic – and my eye became ever and ever sharper for that worst and most insidious form of *retrograde conclusion* in which most errors are committed – the retrograde conclusion from the work to the author, from the deed to the doer, from the ideal to him who has *need of it*, from every mode of thought and evaluation to the *requirement* which commands behind it. – With regard to all aesthetic values I now avail myself of this principal distinction: I ask in each individual case 'is it hunger or is it superfluity which has here become creative?' It might at first seem that another distinction is to be preferred – it is far more obvious – namely to observe whether creation has originated in the desire for motionlessness, immortalization, *being*, or in the desire for destruction, change, future, the new, *becoming*. But both kinds of desire, viewed more profoundly, prove to be ambiguous and indeed interpretable precisely according to that first and, as I think, preferable schema. The desire for *destruction*, change, becoming can be the expression of an overflowing strength pregnant with future (my *terminus* for it is, as is well known, the word 'Dionysian'), but it can also be the hatred of the ill-constituted, deprived, underprivileged, who destroy, *have* to destroy, because that which exists, indeed all existence, all being itself, provokes and enrages them – to understand this affect one should observe our anarchists from close up. The will to *immortalize* also requires a twofold interpretation. It can proceed from gratitude and love – an art of this origination will always be an art of apotheosis, dithyrambic perhaps with Rubens, happily mocking with Hafiz, bright and benevolent with Goethe, and spreading a Homeric glory and shimmer over all things. But it can also be that tyrannical will of one who suffers greatly, one who has to struggle, one who is tormented, who would like to stamp what is most personal, most individual and narrowest, the actual idiosyncrasy of his suffering as a binding law and compulsion, and, as it were, takes revenge on all things by impressing, forcing, branding *his* image, the image of *his* torment, upon them. The latter is the *romantic pessimist* in his most expressive form, whether as Schopenhauerian philosophy of will or as Wagnerian music – romantic pessimism, the last *great* event in the destiny of our culture. (That there *could* be a quite different kind of pessimism, a classical pessimism – this vision and presentiment belongs inseparably to me as my *proprium* and *ipsissimum*: except that I dislike the word 'classical', it is far too worn out, has grown far too smooth and unrecognizable. I call this pessimism of the future – for it is coming! I see it coming! – *Dionysian* pessimism.)

[*GS* 370 (1887)]

## 110

Schopenhauer makes use of the Kantian version of the aesthetic problem – although he quite certainly did not view it with Kantian eyes. Kant thought he was doing honour to art when of the predicates of the beautiful he preferred and set in the foreground those which constitute the honour of the intellect: impersonality and universality. This is not the place to consider whether this was not in its chief essentials a mistake; all I wish to underline is that, like all philosophers, instead of visualizing the aesthetic problem from the point of view of the experiences of the artist (the creator) Kant reflected on art

and the beautiful only from the point of view of the 'spectator'
and in doing so unconsciously introduced the 'spectator'
himself into the concept 'beautiful'. If the philosophers of the
beautiful had been sufficiently familiar with this 'spectator'
that at least would have been something! – familiar, that is to
say, as a great *personal* fact and experience, as an abundance of
vivid events, desires, surprises, transports in the realm of the
beautiful! But the opposite has, I fear, always been the case:
and so we get from them from the very first definitions in
which, as in the celebrated definition Kant gives of the beautiful, a lack of subtler personal experience reposes in the shape
of a fat worm of error. 'That is beautiful,' Kant said, 'which
pleases us *without interest*.' Without interest! Compare with
this definition that other provided by a real 'spectator' and
artist – Stendhal, who once called the beautiful *une promesse de
bonheur*. Here, in any event, precisely that which Kant exclusively emphasized in the aesthetic condition is *rejected* and
cancelled: *le désintéressement*. Who is right, Kant or Stendhal?
When our aestheticians never weary of maintaining, in favour
of Kant, that under the spell of beauty one can view *even* un-
draped female statues 'without interest', we may, to be sure,
laugh a little at their expense – the experiences of *artists* are in
regard to this ticklish point 'more interesting', and Pygmalion
was in any event *not* necessarily an 'unaesthetic man'. [. . .]
And here we come back to Schopenhauer, who stood much
closer to the arts than Kant did and yet failed to emerge from
the spell of the Kantian definition: why was that? The fact is
sufficiently surprising: he interpreted the expression 'without
interest' in the most personal possible fashion as a result of an
experience which must have been one of the most regularly
recurring. Of few things does Schopenhauer speak with so
much certainty as he does of the effect of aesthetic contemplation: he says of it that it operates precisely against *sexual*
'interestedness', in a similar way, that is, to lupulin and cam-
phor; he never wearied of glorifying *this* liberation from the
'will' as the great merit and utility of the aesthetic condition.
[. . .] But supposing Schopenhauer was a hundred times right

with regard to himself, what insight could that provide into the nature of the beautiful? Schopenhauer described *one* effect of the beautiful, its ability to calm the will – but is it even a regular effect? Stendhal, a no less sensual but more happily constituted nature than Schopenhauer, emphasized, as I have said, a different effect: 'the beautiful *promises* happiness' – to him the fact seems to be precisely the *arousal of the will* ('of interest') through the beautiful. And could it not in the end be urged against Schopenhauer himself that he was very much in error to regard himself as a Kantian in this matter, that he understood the Kantian definition of the beautiful in a completely un-Kantian way – that he, too, was pleased by the beautiful as a consequence of 'interest', even as a consequence of the strongest, most personal, interest: that of the tortured man who is freed from his torture? [. . .]

\*

[. . .] the sight of the beautiful obviously affected him [Schopenhauer] as a releasing stimulant to the *chief force* of his nature (the force of contemplation and penetration); so that this force then exploded and all at once became master of his consciousness. But that does not in any way exclude the possibility that that peculiar sweetness and plenitude which is characteristic of the aesthetic condition might have its origin in precisely the ingredient 'sensuality' (just as the 'idealism' characteristic of nubile girls derives from the same source) – so that, with the advent of the aesthetic condition, sensuality would have been, not abolished, as Schopenhauer believed, but only transfigured and no longer enter consciousness as sexual excitation. [. . .]

[*GM What is the Meaning of Ascetic Ideals?* 6, 8]

### III

I heard yesterday – will you believe it? – for the twentieth time *Bizet's* masterpiece. [. . .] How such a work makes perfect! In its presence one becomes almost a 'masterpiece' one-

self. – I really have fancied myself more of a philosopher, a
better philosopher, every time I have heard *Carmen*: I have
grown so patient, so happy, so Indian, so *settled* ... Five
hours of sitting: first stage of sanctity!–May I say that Bizet's
orchestral sound is almost the only one I can still endure?
That *other* orchestral sound which is now on top, the Wagnerian, at once brutal, artificial and 'innocent' and thus speaking to the three senses of the modern soul at one and the same
time–how detrimental I find this Wagnerian orchestral sound!
I call it sirocco. I break into a troublesome sweat. It is good-
bye to *my* fine weather.

This music seems to me perfect. It approaches lightly,
lithely, politely. It is amiable, it does not *sweat*. 'The good is
easy, everything god-like runs on light feet': first proposition
of my aesthetics. This music is wicked, cunning, fatalistic: it
remains at the same time popular – it possesses the *raffinement*
of a race, not of an individual. It is rich. It is precise. It con-
structs, organizes, finishes: it is therewith the antithesis of the
polyp of music, 'endless melody'. Have more painfully tragic
accents ever been heard on the stage? And how they are
attained! Without grimaces! Without false-coinage! Without
the *lie* of the grand style! – Finally: this music takes the auditor
to be intelligent, even as a musician – it is also *there*with the
antithesis of Wagner, who, whatever else he may have been,
was in any event the most *impolite* genius in the world (Wagner
takes us as if – – he repeats a thing again and again until one
is driven into despair – until one is driven into believing it).
[...]

This work too redeems; it is not only Wagner who is a
'redeemer'. With it one says farewell to the *damp* North, to all
the vapour of the Wagnerian ideal. Even the plot alone redeems one from all that. It retains from Mérimée logic in
passion, the shortest route, *harsh* necessity; above all, it has
what pertains to the hot zone, dryness of air, *limpidezza* in the
air. Here the climate has changed in every respect. Here there
speaks a different sensuality, a different sensibility, a different
kind of cheerfulness. This music is cheerful; but not with a

French or German cheerfulness. Its cheerfulness is African; a fatality hangs over it, its happiness is brief, sudden, without quarter. [...] How much good the yellow afternoons of its happiness do us! We gaze into the distance: have we ever seen the sea look *smoother*? – And how tranquil the Moorish dance makes us feel! How in its lascivious melancholy our insatiability itself for once learns satiety! – Finally, love, love translated back into *nature*! *Not* the love of a 'higher virgin'! No Senta sentimentality! But love as fate, as *fatality*, cynical, innocent, cruel – and precisely in that *nature*! Love which is in its methods warfare, in its foundations the *mortal hatred* of the sexes! [...] Such a conception of love (the only one worthy of the philosopher – ) is rare: it singles out a work of art among thousands. For on average the artists do as all the world does, they even do worse – they *misunderstand* love. Wagner, too, misunderstood it. They believe they are selfless in love because they desire the advantage of another being, often to the prejudice of their own advantage. But in exchange they want to *possess* that other being ... Even God constitutes no exception here. He is far from thinking 'what is it to you if I love you?' – he becomes terrible if he is not loved in return.

You see already how much this music *improves* me? – *Il faut méditerraniser la musique* [...] The return to nature, health, cheerfulness, youth, *virtue*! – and yet I was one of the corruptest Wagnerians ... I was capable of taking Wagner seriously ... Ah this old sorcerer! how he took us in! The first thing his art proffers us is a magnifying glass: one looks into it, one doesn't believe one's eyes – everything becomes big, *even Wagner becomes big* ... What a cunning rattlesnake! Its whole life long it rattled to us of 'devotion', of 'loyalty', of 'purity', with a commendation of chastity it withdrew from the *depraved* world! – And we believed it all. [...]

But you are not listening? You prefer even the *problem* of Wagner to that of Bizet? I, too, do not underestimate it, it has its charm. The problem of redemption is even a venerable problem. Wagner reflected on nothing so deeply as he reflected on redemption: his opera is the opera of redemption. In his works someone or other always wants to be redeemed: now a little man, now a little miss – this is *his* problem. – And how richly he varies his leading motive! What rare, what profound modulations! Who if not Wagner taught us that innocence has a preference for redeeming interesting sinners? (the case in *Tannhäuser*). Or that even the Wandering Jew is redeemed, becomes *settled*, when he gets married? (the case in the *Flying Dutchman*). Or that corrupt old women prefer to be redeemed by chaste young men? (the case of Kundry). Or that pretty girls like best to be redeemed by a knight who is a Wagnerian? (the case in the *Mastersingers*). Or that even married women are happy to be redeemed by a knight? (the case of Isolde). Or that 'the old God', having compromised himself morally in every respect, is finally redeemed by a free-spirit and immoralist? (the case in the *Ring*). Do you not particularly admire this last profundity? Do you understand it? I – take care not to understand it . . . That other teachings, too, can be extracted from the said works I would rather demonstrate than dispute. That one can be reduced to despair – *and* to virtue! – by a Wagnerian ballet (again, the case of Tannhäuser). That failure to go to bed at the right time can have the most lamentable consequences (again, the case of Lohengrin). That one ought never to know too completely who it is one is married to (for the third time the case of Lohengrin). – Tristan and Isolde glorify the perfect husband, who in a certain case has only one question: 'but why didn't you tell me that before? What could be simpler than that!' Answer:

> That I cannot tell thee;
> and what thou ask'st,
> that thou canst never know.

*Lohengrin* contains a solemn outlawing of question and inquiry. Wagner therewith became an advocate of the Christian conception 'thou shalt and must *believe*'. It is a crime against the highest and holiest to be scientific . . . *The Flying Dutchman* preaches the sublime doctrine that woman constrains even the most footloose man, in Wagnerian language 'redeems' him. Here we permit ourselves a question. Supposing this were true, would it therefore also be desirable? – What becomes of the 'Wandering Jew' when worshipped and *constrained* by a woman? He merely ceases to wander: he gets married, he no longer concerns us. – Translated into reality: the danger for artists, for geniuses – and it is they who are the 'Wandering Jews' – lies in woman: *worshipping* women are their ruin. Hardly one of them has sufficient character not to be ruined – 'redeemed', when he feels himself treated like a god – he straightway *condescends* to woman. [. . .]

What Goethe would have thought of Wagner? – Goethe once posed to himself the question what the danger was which hovered over all romantics: the romantics' fatality. His answer is: 'to choke through the repeated chewing of moral and religious absurdities'. More briefly: *Parsifal* . . .

\*

– I shall once more narrate the story of the *Ring*. It belongs here. It, too, is a story of redemption: except that this time it is Wagner who is redeemed. – For half his lifetime Wagner believed in *revolution* as only a Frenchman has ever believed in it. He sought for it in the runic writings of myth, he thought that in *Siegfried* he had found the typical revolutionary. – 'Whence comes all the evil in the world?' Wagner asked himself. From 'ancient compacts', he answered, like all revolutionary ideologists. In plain words: from customs, laws, moralities, institutions, from all that upon which the old world, the old society depends. 'How can the world be rid of evil? How can the old society be abolished?' Only by declaring war on the 'compacts' (the traditional, the moral). *That is what Siegfried does.* He starts early, very early: his beginning is already a declaration of war on morality – he comes into the world through adultery, through incest . . . It is *not* the saga but Wagner who devised this radical trait; he *corrected* the saga on this point ... Siegfried continues as he has begun: he obeys only his first impulse, he throws overboard everything traditional, all reverence, all fear. Whatever he dislikes he strikes down. Ancient deities he irreverently runs full tilt at. His chief undertaking, however, is *to emancipate woman* – 'to redeem Brünnhilde' ... Siegfried *and* Brünnhilde; the sacrament of free love; the dawn of the golden age; the twilight of the gods of the old morality – *the evil has been abolished* ... For a long time Wagner's ship sailed merrily along on *this* course. No doubt of it, Wagner sought on this course *his* highest goal. – What happened? A piece of misfortune. The ship struck a rock; Wagner was stuck. The rock was Schopenhauerian philosophy; Wagner was stuck on a *contrary* world-view. What had he set to music? Optimism. Wagner felt ashamed. An optimism, moreover, for which Schopenhauer had invented a malicious epithet – *infamous* optimism. He again felt ashamed. He pondered long, his situation seemed desperate ... Finally, a way out dawned upon him: the rock on which he had come to grief, what? suppose he interpreted it as the *goal*, as the hidden intention, as the actual meaning of his voyage? To come to grief *here* – that, too, was a goal. *Bene navigavi, cum naufragium feci* ... And he translated the *Ring* into Schopenhauerian. Everything goes wrong, everything goes to pieces, the new world is as bad as the old – *nothingness*, the Indian Circe, beckons ... Brünnhilde, who according to the earlier intention had to say farewell with a song in praise of free love, holding out to the world the hope of a socialist Utopia in which 'all will be well', now has something else to do. She first has to study Schopenhauer; she has to reduce the fourth book of the *World as Will and Idea* to verse. *Wagner was redeemed* ... In all seriousness, this *was* a redemption. It was the *philosopher of décadence* who first gave to the artist of *décadence himself* – –

To the artist of *décadence* – there is the phrase we are after. And with it I now become serious. I am far from being a harmless onlooker while this *décadent* ruins our health – and music

as well! Is Wagner a human being at all? Is he not rather a
sickness? Everything he touches he makes sick – *he has made
music sick* [. . .]

That people in Germany deceive themselves about Wagner
does not surprise me. The opposite would surprise me. The
Germans have put together for themselves a Wagner they can
reverence: they have never been psychologists, they misunderstand out of gratitude. But that people in Paris also deceive
themselves about Wagner! where people are practically nothing any more but psychologists. And in St Petersburg!
where people divine things that are not divined even in Paris.
How closely related to the whole of European *décadence* Wagner must be that it does not feel him as *décadent*! He belongs
to it: he is its protagonist, its greatest name . . . People honour
themselves when they raise *him* to the clouds. – For that people
do not defend themselves against him is itself already a sign
of *décadence*. The instincts have become enfeebled. What ought
to be avoided attracts. What drives ever more speedily into
the abyss is put to one's lips. [. . .]

This is my primary viewpoint: Wagner's art is sick. The
problems he brings on to the stage – nothing but the problems of hysterics – the convulsive nature of his emotion, his
over-excited sensibility, his taste for sharper and sharper spices,
the instability which he disguised as principles, not least his
choice of heroes and heroines viewed as physiological types
( – a gallery of invalids! – ): all this taken together represents a
syndrome that admits of no dubiety. *Wagner est une névrose.*
Nothing perhaps is better known today, at any rate nothing is
better studied, than the Proteus nature of degeneration, here
hidden within the chrysalis of art and artist. Our physicians
and physiologists possess in Wagner their most interesting
case, at least a very complete one. Precisely because nothing
is more modern than this total morbidity, this decrepitude and
over-excitability of the nervous machinery, Wagner is the
*modern artist par excellence*, the Cagliostro of modernity. In
his art there is compounded in the most seductive fashion that
which all the world has most need of today – the three great

stimulants of the exhausted, the *brutal*, the *artificial* and the *innocent* (idiotic). [. . .]

*

[. . .] I confine myself for the present to the question of *style*. – What characterizes every *literary décadence*? That life no longer resides in the whole. The word becomes sovereign and leaps out of the sentence, the sentence reaches out and obscures the meaning of the page, the page gains life at the expense of the whole - the whole is no longer a whole. But that is a metaphor for every style of *décadence*: every time anarchy of atoms, dis-gregation of will, 'freedom of the individual', morally speak-ing – expanded into a political theory '*equal* rights for all'. Life, *equal* vitality, the vibration and exuberance of life pushed back into the smallest structures, the rest *poor* in life. Every-where paralysis, toil, stiffness *or* enmity and chaos: both grow-ing ever more obvious the higher the forms of organization into which one ascends. The whole no longer possesses life at all: it is put together, calculated, artificial, an artefact. –

*

[. . .] Was Wagner a musician at all? He was in any event something other *more* than he was a musician: namely an in-comparable *historio*, the greatest mime, the most astonishing genius of the theatre the Germans have had, our *scenic artist par excellence*. He belongs elsewhere than in the history of music: he must not be confused with the great genuine musi-cians. Wagner *and* Beethoven – that is a blasphemy – and ulti-mately an injustice even to Wagner . . . As a musician, too, he was only that which he was in general: he *became* a musician, he *became* a poet, because the tyrant in him, his actor-genius, compelled him to. One understands nothing of Wagner un-less one understands his dominating instinct. [. . .]

*

A word in passing on Wagner's writings: they are among other things a school of *prudence*. The system of procedures Wagner employs can be applied to a hundred other cases - he who has ears to hear, let him hear. I shall perhaps have a claim to public recognition if I give precise expression to the three most valuable procedures.

Everything Wagner *cannot* do is reprehensible.

Wagner could do much that he does not do: but he will not, from rigorousness of principle.

Everything Wagner *can* do nobody will be able to do after him, nobody has done before him, nobody *ought* to do after him . . . Wagner is divine . . .

These three propositions are the quintessence of Wagner's literature; the rest is – 'literature'. [. . .]

\*

I have explained where Wagner belongs – *not* in the history of music. What is nonetheless his significance for the history of music? *The rise of the actor in music*: a capital event which makes one think and perhaps also makes one fear. In a formula: 'Wagner and Liszt'. – Never before has the rectitude of musicians, their 'genuineness', been put so dangerously to the test. The fact is palpable: great success, success with the masses is no longer with the genuine – one has to be an actor to achieve success! – Victor Hugo and Richard Wagner – they signify one and the same thing: that in declining cultures, that everywhere where the decision is in the hands of the masses, genuineness is superfluous, disadvantageous, a drawback. Only the actor still arouses *great* enthusiasm. [. . .]

\*

[. . .] But who can still doubt *what* it is I want – what the *three demands* are for which my anger, my solicitude, my love of art have at this time opened my mouth?

That the theatre shall not become master over the arts.
That the actor shall not become a seducer of the genuine.
That music shall not become an art of lying.

[*W* 1–5, 7, 8, 10–12]

## 112

*Fair and foul.* – Nothing is so conditional, let us say *circum-scribed*, as our feeling for the beautiful. Anyone who tried to divorce it from man's pleasure in man would at once find the ground give way beneath him. The 'beautiful in itself' is not even a concept, merely a phrase. In the beautiful man sets up himself as the standard of perfection; in select cases he worships himself in it. A species *cannot* do otherwise than affirm itself alone in this manner. Its *deepest* instinct, that of self-preservation and self-aggrandizement, is still visible in such sublimated forms. Man believes that the world itself is filled with beauty – he *forgets* that it is he who has created it. He alone has bestowed beauty upon the world – alas! only a very human, all too human beauty . . . Man really mirrors himself in things, that which gives him back his own reflection he considers beautiful: the judgement 'beautiful' is his *conceit of his species*. [. . .]

Nothing is beautiful, only man: on this piece of naviety rests all aesthetics, it is the *first* truth of aesthetics. Let us immediately add its second: nothing is ugly but *degenerate* man – the domain of aesthetic judgement is therewith defined. – Reckoned physiologically, everything ugly weakens and afflicts man. It recalls decay, danger, impotence; he actually suffers a loss of energy in its presence. The effect of the ugly can be measured with a dynamometer. Whenever man feels in any way depressed, he senses the proximity of something 'ugly'. His feeling of power, his will to power, his courage, his pride – they decline with the ugly, they increase with the beautiful . . . In the one case as in the other *we draw a conclusion*: its premises have been accumulated in the instincts in tremendous abundance. The ugly is understood as a sign and symptom of degeneration: that which recalls degeneration, however remotely, produces in us the judgement 'ugly'. Every token of exhaustion, of heaviness, of age, of weariness, every kind of unfreedom, whether convulsive or paralytic, above all the smell, colour and shape of dissolution, of decomposition, though it be attenuated to the point of being no more than a symbol – all this calls forth the same reaction, the value judgement 'ugly'. [. . .]

[*T Expeditions of an Untimely Man* 19–20]

# 113

[. . .] Schopenhauer speaks of *beauty* with a melancholy ardour – why, in the last resort? Because he sees in it a *bridge* upon which one may pass over . . . It is to him redemption from the 'will' for minutes at a time – it lures on to redemption for ever . . . He values it especially as redeemer from the 'focus of the will', from sexuality – in beauty he sees the procreative impulse *denied* . . . Singular saint! Someone contradicts you, and I fear it is nature. *To what end* is there beauty at all in the sounds, colours, odours, rhythmic movements of nature? what *makes* beauty *appear*? – Fortunately a philosopher also contradicts him. No less an authority than the divine Plato ( – so Schopenhauer himself calls him) maintains a different thesis: that all beauty incites to procreation – that precisely this is the *proprium* of its effect, from the most sensual regions up into the most spiritual . . .

[*T Expeditions of an Untimely Man* 22]

# 114

The psychology of the orgy as an overflowing feeling of life and energy within which even pain acts as a stimulus provided me with the key to the concept of the *tragic* feeling, which was misunderstood as much by Aristotle as it especially was by our pessimists. Tragedy is so far from providing evidence for pessimism among the Hellenes in Schopenhauer's sense that it has to be considered the decisive repudiation of that idea and the *counter-verdict* to it. Affirmation of life even in its strangest and sternest problems, the will to life rejoicing in its own inexhaustibility through the *sacrifice* of its highest types – *that* is what I called Dionysian, *that* is what I recognized as the bridge to the psychology of the *tragic* poet. *Not* so as to get rid of pity and terror, not so as to purify oneself of a dangerous emotion through its vehement discharge – it was thus Aristotle understood it – : but, beyond pity and terror, *to realize in oneself* the eternal joy of becoming – that joy which also encompasses *joy in destruction*. [. . .]

[*T What I Owe to the Ancients* 5]


## 115

The highest conception of the lyric poet was given me by *Heinrich Heine*. I seek in vain in all the realms of millennia for an equally sweet and passionate music. He possessed that divine malice without which I cannot imagine perfection – I assess the value of people, of races according to how necessarily they are unable to separate the god from the satyr. – And how he employs German! It will one day be said that Heine and I have been by far the first artists of the German language – at an incalculable distance from everything which mere Germans have done with it. – I must be profoundly related to *Byron's* Manfred: I discovered all these abysses in myself – I was ripe for this work at 13. [. . .] When I seek my highest formula for *Shakespeare* I find it always in that he conceived the type of Caesar. One cannot guess at things like this – one is it or one is not. The great poet creates *only* out of his own reality – to the point at which he is afterwards unable to endure his own work. [. . .] I know of no more heart-rending reading than Shakespeare: what must a man have suffered to need to be a buffoon to this extent! – Is Hamlet *understood*? It is not doubt, it is *certainty* which makes mad . . . but to feel in this way one must be profound, abyss, philosopher . . . We all *fear* truth . . . and, to confess it, I am instinctively certain that Lord Bacon is the originator, the self-tormentor of this uncanniest species of literature [. . .] We do not know nearly enough about Lord Bacon, the first realist in every great sense of the word, to know *what* he did, *what* he desired, *what* he experienced in himself ... And the devil take it! Supposing I had baptized my *Zarathustra* with another name, for example with the name of Richard Wagner, the perspicuity of two millennia would not have sufficed to divine that the author of *Human, All Too Human* is the visionary of *Zarathustra* ...

[*EH Why I am So Clever* 4]

# 116

[. . .] *What* is it I suffer from when I suffer from the destiny of music? From this: that music has been deprived of its world-transfiguring, affirmative character, that it is *décadence* music and no longer the flute of Dionysus [. . .]

[*EH The Wagner Case* 1]

PSYCHOLOGICAL OBSERVATIONS

## 117

*How appearance becomes being.* – Even when in the deepest distress, the actor ultimately cannot cease to think of the impression he and the whole scenic effect is making, even for example at the burial of his own child; he will weep over his own distress and the ways in which it expresses itself, as his own audience. The hypocrite who always plays one and the same role finally ceases to be a hypocrite; for example priests, who as young men are usually conscious or unconscious hypocrites, finally become natural and are then really priests without any affectation; or if the father fails to get that far then perhaps the son does so, employing his father's start and inheriting his habits. If someone obstinately and for a long time wants to *appear* something it is in the end hard for him to *be* anything else. The profession of almost every man, even that of the artist, begins with hypocrisy, with an imitation from without, with a copying of what is most effective. He who is always wearing the mask of a friendly countenance must finally acquire a power over benevolent moods without which the impression of friendliness cannot be obtained – and finally these acquire power over him, he *is* benevolent.

[HA 51]

## 118

*The point of honesty in deception.* – With all great deceivers there is a noteworthy occurrence to which they owe their power.

In the actual act of deception [. . .] they are overcome by *belief in themselves*; it is this which then speaks so miraculously and compellingly to those who surround them. The founders of religions are distinguished from these great deceivers by the fact that they never emerge from this state of self-deception [. . .] Self-deception has to exist if a grand *effect* is to be produced. For men believe in the truth of that which is plainly strongly believed.

[*HA* 52]

## 119

*Errors of the sufferer and the doer.* – When a rich man takes a possession from a poor one (for example, a prince robs a plebeian of his beloved) an error arises in the poor man: he thinks the rich man must be utterly infamous to take from him the little that he has. But the rich man does not feel nearly so deeply the value of a *single* possession because he is used to having many: thus he cannot transport himself into the soul of the poor man and has not committed nearly so great an injustice as the latter supposes. Both have a false idea of one another. The injustice of the powerful which arouses most indignation in history is not nearly as great as it seems. The inherited sense of being a higher type of creature with higher claims already makes such a man fairly cold and leaves his conscience at rest [. . .] Indeed, no cruel man is *so* cruel as he whom he has misused believes; the idea of pain is not the same thing as the suffering of it. The same applies to the unjust judge, to the journalist who misleads public opinion with petty untruths. Cause and effect are in all these cases surrounded by quite different groups of thoughts and sensations; while one involuntarily presupposes that doer and sufferer think and feel the same and, in accordance with this presupposition, assesses the guilt of the one by the pain of the other.

[*HA* 81]

### 120

*Sleep of virtue.* – When virtue has slept it will arise more vigorous.

[*HA* 83]

### 121

*The index of the scales.* – We praise or blame according to whether the one or the other offers a greater opportunity for our power of judgement to shine out.

[*HA* 86]

### 122

*Origin of the comic.* – If one considers that man was for many hundreds of thousands of years an animal in the highest degree accessible to fear and that everything sudden and unexpected bade him prepare to fight and perhaps to die that even later on, indeed, in social relationships all security depended on the expected and traditional in opinion and action then one cannot be surprised if whenever something sudden and unexpected in word and deed happens without occasioning danger or injury man becomes wanton, passes over into the opposite of fear: the anxious, crouching creature springs up, greatly expands – man laughs. This transition from momentary anxiety to short-lived exuberance is called the *comic*. [. . .]

[*HA* 169]

### 123

*Pleasure in nonsense.* – How can man take pleasure in nonsense? For wherever in the world there is laughter this is the case; one can say, indeed, that almost everywhere there is happiness there is pleasure in nonsense. The overturning of experience into its opposite, of the purposive into the purposeless, of the necessary into the arbitrary, but in such a way that this event causes no harm and is imagined as occasioned by high spirits, delights us, for it momentarily liberates us from the constraint of the necessary, the purposive and that which corresponds to our experience which we usually see as our inexorable masters; we play and laugh when the expected (which usually makes us fearful and tense) discharges itself harmlessly. It is the pleasure of the slave at the Saturnalia.

[HA 213]

## 124

*Preference for specific virtues.* – We do not place especial value on the possession of a virtue until we notice its total absence in our opponent.

[HA 302]

## 125

*Arrogance of the meritorious.* – Arrogance on the part of the meritorious is even more offensive to us than the arrogance of those without merit: for merit itself is offensive.

[HA 332]

## 126

*The danger in our own voice.* – Sometimes in the course of conversation the sound of our own voice disconcerts us and misleads us into making assertions which in no way correspond to our opinions.

[HA 333]

## 127

*Test of a good marriage.* – A marriage proves itself a good marriage by being able to endure an occasional 'exception'.

[*HA* 402]

## 128

*Elements of revenge.* – The word 'revenge' is said so quickly it almost seems as if it could contain no more than one conceptual and perceptional root. And so one continues to strive to discover it: just as our economists have not yet wearied of scenting a similar unity in the word 'value' and of searching after the original root-concept of the word. As if every word were not a pocket into which now this, now that, now several things at once have been put! Thus 'revenge', too, is now this, now that, now something more combined. Distinguish first of all that defensive return blow which one delivers even against lifeless objects (moving machinery, for example) which have hurt us: the sense of our counter-action is to put a stop to the injury by putting a stop to the machine. [. . .] One behaves in a similar way towards people who have harmed us when we feel the injury directly; if one wants to call this an act of revenge, so be it; only let it be considered that *self-preservation* alone has here set its clockwork of reason in motion, and that one has fundamentally been thinking, not of the person who caused the injury, but only of oneself: we act thus *without* wanting to do harm in return, but only so as *to get out* with life and limb. – One needs *time* if one is to transfer one's thoughts from oneself to one's opponent and to ask oneself how he can be hit at most grievously. This happens in the second species of revenge: its presupposition is a reflection over the other's vulnerability and capacity for suffering: one wants to hurt. To secure himself against further harm is here so far from the mind of the revenger that he almost always brings further harm upon himself and very often cold-bloodedly anticipates it. [. . .] Of what use is it to us if our opponent now suffers after we have suffered through him? It is a question of *restitution* [. . .] Perhaps we lost property, rank, friends, children through our opponent – these losses are not made good by revenge, the restitution applies only to an *attendant loss* occasioned by the other losses referred to. Restitutional revenge does not protect one from further harm, it does not make good the harm one has suffered – except in one case. If our *honour* has suffered through our opponent revenge is capable of *restoring* it. But our honour has suffered harm in every case in which someone has done us a deliberate injury: for our opponent proved thereby that he did not *fear* us. By revenging ourselves on him we prove that we do not fear him either: it is in this that the compensation, the restitution, lies. [. . .] In the first species of revenge it is precisely fear which directs the counter-blow: here, on the contrary, it is the absence of fear which, as stated, *wants to prove itself* through the counter-blow. – Nothing, therefore, could appear more different than the inner motives of these two modes of action which are called by the common word 'revenge': and yet it very often happens that the revenger is unclear as to what has really determined his action; perhaps he delivered the counter-blow out of fear and to preserve himself but afterwards, when he has had time to reflect on the motive of wounded honour, convinces himself he has exacted revenge on account of his honour: – this motive is, after all, *nobler* than the other. An essential element in this is whether he sees his honour as having been injured in the eyes of others (the world) or only in the eyes of him who injured it: in the latter case he will prefer secret revenge, in the former public. His revenge will be the more incensed or the more moderate according to how deeply or weakly he can think his way into the soul of the perpetrator and the witnesses of his injury; if he is wholly lacking in this kind of imagination he will not think of revenge at all, since the feeling of 'honour' will not be present in him and thus cannot be wounded. He will likewise not think of revenge if he *despises* the perpetrator and the witnesses: because, as people he despises, they cannot accord him any honour and consequently cannot take any honour from him either. Finally, he will refrain from revenge in the not uncommon case that he loves the perpetrator: he will thus lose honour in the perpetrator's eyes, to be sure, and will perhaps become less worthy of being loved in return. But to renounce even all claim to love in return is a sacrifice which love is prepared to make if only it does not *have to hurt* the beloved being: this would mean hurting oneself more than any sacrifice hurts. – Thus: everyone will revenge himself, except he be without honour or full of contempt or full of love for the person who has harmed and offended him. Even when he turns to the courts he desires revenge as a private person: *additionally*, however, as a forethoughtful man of society, he desires the revenge of society on one who does not *honour* it. Through judicial punishment, private honour as well as the honour of society is thus *restored*: that is to say – punishment is revenge. – Undoubtedly there is also in it those other elements of revenge already described, insofar as through punishment society serves its own *self-preservation* and delivers a counter-blow in *self-defence*. Punishment serves to prevent *further* injury, it wishes to *deter*. Two such various elements of revenge are thus actually *united* in punishment, and the main effect of this may be to sustain the confusion of concepts referred to by virtue of which the individual who takes revenge usually does not know what he really wants.

[*WS* 33]

### 129

*Pity and contempt.* – To show pity is felt as a sign of contempt because one has clearly ceased to be an object of *fear* as soon as one is pitied. [. . .]

[*WS* 50]

## 130

*Self-mastery and moderation and their ultimate motive.* – I find no more than six essentially different methods of combating the vehemence of a drive. Firstly, one can avoid opportunities for gratification of the drive, and through long and ever longer periods of non-gratification weaken it and make it wither away. Then, one can impose upon oneself strict regularity in its gratification [. . .] one has then gained intervals during which one is no longer troubled by it – and from there one can perhaps go over to the first method. Thirdly, one can deliberately give oneself over to the wild and unrestrained gratification of a drive in order to generate disgust with it and with disgust to acquire a power over the drive [. . .] Fourthly, there is the intellectual artifice of associating its gratification in general so firmly with some very painful thought that, after a little practice, the thought of its gratification is itself at once felt as very painful. [. . .] Fifthly, one brings about a dislocation of one's quanta of strength by imposing on oneself a particularly difficult and strenuous labour, or by deliberately subjecting oneself to a new stimulus and pleasure and thus directing one's thought and plays of physical forces into other channels [. . .] Finally, sixth: he who can endure it and finds it reasonable to weaken and depress his *entire* bodily and physical organization will naturally thereby also attain the goal of weakening an individual violent drive. [. . .]

[D 109]

## 131

*Feeling with others.* – To understand another person, that is, *to imitate his feelings in ourselves,* we do indeed often go back to the *reason* for his feeling thus or thus and ask for example: *why* is he troubled? – so as then for the same reason to become troubled ourselves; but it is much more usual to omit to do this and instead to produce the feeling in ourselves after the *effects* it exerts and displays on the other person by imitating with our own body the expression of his eyes, his voice, his walk, his bearing (or even their reflection in word, picture, music). Then a similar feeling arises in us in consequence of an ancient association between movement and sensation [. . .] We have brought our skill in understanding the feelings of others to a high state of perfection and in the presence of another person we are always almost involuntarily practising this skill [. . .] If we ask how we became so fluent in the imitation of the feelings of others the answer admits of no doubt: man, as the most timid of all creatures on account of his subtle and fragile nature, has in his *timidity* the instructor in that feeling with others, that quick understanding of the feelings of another (and of animals). Through long millennia he saw in everything strange and lively a danger: at the sight of it he at once imitated the expression of the features and the bearing and drew his conclusion as to the kind of evil intention behind these features and this bearing. [. . .]

[D 142]

132

*For the promotion of health.* – One has hardly begun to reflect on the physiology of the criminal, and yet one already stands before the irrefutable insight that there exists no essential difference between criminals and the insane: presupposing one *believes* that the *usual* mode of moral thinking is the mode of thinking of *spiritual health*. But no belief is still so firmly believed as this is, and so one should not hesitate to accept the consequence and treat the criminal as a mental patient [. . .] At present, to be sure, he who has been injured [by the criminal], irrespective of how this injury is to be made good, will still desire his *revenge* and will turn for it to the courts – and for the time being the courts continue to maintain our detestable criminal codes, with their shopkeeper's scales and the *desire to counterbalance guilt with punishment:* but can we not get beyond this? [. . .] Let us do away with the concept *sin* – and let us quickly send after it the concept *punishment*! [. . .]

[*D* 202]


## 133

*Night and music.* – The ear, the organ of fear, could have evolved as greatly as it has only in the night and twilight of obscure caves and woods, in accordance with the mode of life of the age of timidity, that is to say the longest human age there has ever been: in bright daylight the ear is less necessary. That is how music acquired the character of an art of night and twilight.

[*D* 250]


## 134

*Consciousness.* – Consciousness is the last and latest development of the organic and consequently also the most unfinished and weakest part of it. From consciousness there proceed countless errors which cause an animal, a man, to perish earlier than necessary [. . .] If the preservative combination of the instincts were not incomparably stronger, if it did not in general act as regulator, mankind must have perished through its perverse judgements and waking phantasies, its superficiality and credulity, in short through its consciousness [. . .]

[*GS* 11]


## 135

*Of the goal of science.* – What? The ultimate goal of science is to create for man the greatest possible amount of pleasure and the least possible amount of pain? But suppose pleasure and pain were so linked together that he who *wants* to have the greatest possible amount of the one *must* have the greatest possible amount of the other also [. . .]? And perhaps that is how things are! The Stoics, at any rate, thought so, and were consistent when they desired to have the least possible amount of pleasure in order to have the least possible amount of pain from life. [. . .] Today, too, you have the choice: either *as little pain as possible*, in short painlessness [. . .] or *as much pain as possible* as the price of an abundance of subtle joys and pleasures hitherto rarely tasted! [. . .]

[*GS* 12]


## 136

*Thoughts.* – Thoughts are the shadows of our sensations – always darker, emptier, simpler than these.

[*GS* 179]


## 137

*To laugh.* – To laugh means: to be malicious [*schadenfroh sein*] but with a good conscience.

[*GS* 200]


## 138

All psychology has hitherto remained anchored to moral prejudices and timidities: it has not ventured into the depths. To conceive it as morphology and the *development-theory of the will to power*, as I conceive it – has never yet so much as entered the mind of anyone else [. . .] A genuine physio-psychology has to struggle with unconscious resistances in the heart of the investigator, it has 'the heart' against it: even a theory of the mutual dependence of the 'good' and the 'wicked' impulses causes, as a more refined immorality, revulsion to a conscience still strong and hearty – and even more a theory of the derivation of all good impulses from wicked ones. Supposing, however, that someone goes so far as to regard the emotions of hatred, envy, covetousness, and lust for domination as life-conditioning emotions, as something which must fundamentally and essentially be present in the total economy of life, consequently must be heightened further if life is to be heightened further – he suffers from such a judgement as from sea-sickness. And yet even this hypothesis is far from being the strangest and most painful in this tremendous, still almost unexplored realm of dangerous knowledge. [. . .]

[*BGE* 23]

### 139

'I have done that,' says my memory. 'I cannot have done that' – says my pride, and remains adamant. At last – memory yields.

[*BGE* 68]

### 140

The degree and kind of a person's sexuality reaches up into the topmost summit of his spirit.

[*BGE* 75]

### 141

[. . .] One should open one's eyes and take a new look at cruelty; one should at last grow impatient, so that the kind of immodest fat errors which have, for example, been fostered about tragedy by ancient and modern philosophers should no longer go stalking virtuously and confidently about. Almost

everything we call 'higher culture' is based on the spiritualization and intensification of *cruelty* – this is my proposition [. . .]
That which constitutes the painful voluptuousness of tragedy
is cruelty; that which produces a pleasing effect in so-called
tragic pity, indeed fundamentally in everything sublime up to
the highest and most refined thrills of metaphysics, derives
its sweetness solely from the ingredient of cruelty mixed in
with it. What the Roman in the arena, the Christian in the
ecstasies of the Cross, the Spaniard watching burnings or bull-
fights, the Japanese of today crowding in to the tragedy, the
Parisian workman who has a nostalgia for bloody revolutions,
the Wagnerienne who, with will suspended, 'experiences'
*Tristan und Isolde* – what all of these enjoy and look with
secret ardour to imbibe is the spicy potion of the great Circe
'cruelty'. Here, to be sure, we must put aside the thick-witted
psychology of former times which had to teach of cruelty
only that it had its origin in the sight of the sufferings of
*others*: there is also an abundant, over-abundant enjoyment of one's own suffering, of making oneself suffer – and
wherever man allows himself to be persuaded to self-denial in
the *religious* sense, or to self-mutilation, as among Phoenicians
and ascetics, or in general to desensualization, decarnalization,
contrition, to Puritanical spasms of repentance, to conscience-
vivisection and to a Pascalian *sacrifizio dell' intelletto*, he is
secretly lured and urged onward by his cruelty, by the dangerous thrills of cruelty directed *against himself*. Consider,
finally, how even the man of knowledge, when he compels
his spirit to knowledge which is *counter* to the inclination of
his spirit and frequently also to the desires of his heart – by
saying No, that is, when he would like to affirm, love, worship – disposes as an artist in and transfigurer of cruelty;
in all taking things seriously and thoroughly, indeed there
is already a violation, a desire to hurt the fundamental will
of the spirit, which ceaselessly strives for appearance and
the superficial – in all desire to know there is already a drop
of cruelty.

[*BGE* 229]

## 142

Apart from the ascetic ideal, man, the *animal* man, hitherto had no meaning. His existence on earth contained no goal; 'why man at all?' – was a question without an answer; the *will* for man and earth was lacking; behind every great human destiny there resounded as a refrain an even greater 'In vain!' *That* is the meaning of the ascetic ideal: that something was *lacking*, that a tremendous chasm surrounded man – he did not know how to justify, to explain, to affirm himself, he *suffered* from the problem of his meaning. He also suffered otherwise, he was essentially a *sickly* animal: but it was *not* suffering itself that was his problem, it was the lack of an answer to the crying question '*Why* suffering?' [...] The meaninglessness of suffering, *not* suffering itself, was the curse which hitherto lay over mankind – *and the ascetic ideal gave it meaning!* It was hitherto the only meaning; any meaning is better than no meaning at all; the ascetic ideal has been in every respect the '*faut de mieux*' *par excellence* [...] man was *saved* by it, he had a *meaning*, he was henceforth no longer like a leaf in the wind, a plaything of meaninglessness, he could from now on *will* something – it was almost a matter of indifference what, why, with what he willed: *the will itself was saved.* One cannot conceal from oneself *what* this whole will really expresses which has acquired its direction from the ascetic ideal: this hatred for the human, even more for the animalic, even more for the material, this abhorrence of the senses, of reason itself, fear of happiness and beauty, this desire to flee from all appearance, change, becoming, death, wishing, desire itself – all this, let us dare to grasp, signifies a *will to nothingness*, a will directed against life, a rebellion against the most fundamental presuppositions of life, but it is and remains a *will* ... And [...] man will rather will *nothingness* than *not* will ...

[*GM What is the Meaning of Ascetic Ideals?* 28]

There is a time with all passions when they are merely fatalities, when they drag their victim down with the weight of their folly – and a later, very much later time when they are wedded with the spirit, when they are 'spiritualized'. Formerly, one made war on passion itself on account of the folly inherent in it: one conspired for its extermination – all the old moral monsters are unanimous that '*il faut tuer les passions*'. The most famous formula for doing this is contained in the New Testament, in the Sermon on the Mount, where [. . .] it is said, with reference to sexuality, 'if thy eye offend thee, pluck it out': fortunately, no Christian follows this prescription. To *exterminate* the passions and desires merely in order to do away with their folly and its unpleasant consequences – this itself seems to us today merely an acute form of folly. We no longer admire dentists who *pull out* the teeth to stop them hurting . . . On the other hand, it is only fair to admit that on the soil out of which Christianity grew the concept '*spiritualization* of passion' could not possibly be conceived. [. . .] The Church combats the passions with excision in every sense of the word: its practice, its 'cure' is *castration*. It never asks: 'How can one spiritualize, beautify, deify a desire?' – it has at all times laid the emphasis of its discipline on extirpation (of sensuality, of pride, of lust for power, of avarice, of revengefulness). – But to attack the passions at their roots means to attack life at its roots: the practice of the Church is *hostile to life* . . .

The same expedient – castration, extirpation – is instinctively selected in a struggle against a desire by those who are too weak-willed, too degenerate to impose moderation upon it: by those natures which need La Trappe, to speak metaphorically (and not metaphorically – ), some sort of definitive declaration of hostility, a *chasm* between themselves and a passion. It is only the degenerate who cannot do without radical expedients; weakness of will, more precisely the inability *not* to react to a stimulus, is itself merely another form of degeneration. Radical hostility, mortal hostility towards

sensuality is always a thought-provoking symptom: it justifies making certain conjectures as to the general condition of
one who is excessive in this respect. – That hostility, that hatred
reaches its height, moreover, only when such natures are no
longer sufficiently sound even for the radical cure, for the renunciation of their 'devil'. Survey the entire history of priests
and philosophers, and that of artists as well: the most virulent
utterances against the senses have *not* come from the impotent,
*nor* from ascetics, but from those who found it impossible to
be ascetics, those who stood in need of being ascetics . . .

   The spiritualization of sensuality is called *love*: it is a great
triumph over Christianity. A further triumph is our spiritualization of *enmity*. It consists in profoundly grasping the value
of having enemies [. . .] We adopt the same attitude towards
the 'enemy within': there, too, we have spiritualized enmity,
there, too, we have grasped its *value*. One is *fruitful* only at the
cost of being rich in contradictions; one remains *young* only
on condition the soul does not relax, does not long for peace
. . . Nothing has grown more alien to us than that desideratum
of former times 'peace of soul', the *Christian* desideratum;
nothing arouses less envy in us than the moral cow and the
fat contentment of the good conscience . . . One has renounced
*grand* life when one renounces war [. . .]

[T Morality as Anti-Nature 1–3]

## 144

The most general formula at the basis of every religion and
morality is: 'Do this and this, refrain from this and this – and
you will be happy! Otherwise . . .' Every morality, every religion *is* this imperative – I call it the great original sin of
reason, *immortal unreason*. In my mouth this formula is converted into its reverse – *first* example of my 'revaluation of all
values': a well-constituted human being, a 'happy one', *must*
perform certain actions and instinctively shrinks from other
actions, he transports the order of which he is the physio-

logical representative into his relations with other human beings and with things. In a formula: his virtue is the *consequence* of his happiness. [. . .] The Church and morality say: 'A race, a people perishes through vice and luxury.' My *restored* reason says: when a people is perishing, degenerating physiologically, vice and luxury (that is to say the necessity for stronger and stronger and more and more frequent stimulants, such as every exhausted nature is acquainted with) *follow* therefrom. A young man grows prematurely pale and faded. His friends say: this and that illness is to blame. I say: *that* he became ill, *that* he failed to resist the illness, was already the consequence of an impoverished life, an hereditary exhaustion. The newspaper reader says: this party will ruin itself if it makes errors like this. My *higher* politics says: a party which makes errors like this is already finished – it is no longer secure in its instincts. Every error, of whatever kind, is a consequence of degeneration of instinct, disgregation of will: one has thereby virtually defined the *bad*. Everything *good* is instinct – and consequently easy, necessary, free. Effort is an objection, the *god* is typically distinguished from the hero (in my language: *light* feet are the first attribute of divinity).

[*T The Four Great Errors* 2]

## 145

At this point I cannot absolve myself from giving an account of the psychology of 'belief', of 'believers' [. . .] It appears, if I have not misheard, that there exists among Christians a kind of criterion of truth called 'proof by potency'. 'Belief makes blessed: *therefore* it is true.' – One might here object straightaway that this making-blessed itself is not proved but only *promised*: blessedness conditional upon 'believing' – one *shall* become blessed *because* one believes . . . But *that* what the priest promises the believer for a 'Beyond' inaccessible to any control actually occurs, how could *that* be proved? – The alleged 'proof by potency' is therefore at bottom only a further belief that the effect which one promises oneself from the belief will not fail to appear. In a formula: 'I believe that belief makes blessed – consequently it is true.' – But with that we have already reached the end of the argument. This 'consequently' would be the *absurdum* itself as a criterion of truth. – But if, with no little indulgence, we suppose that the fact that belief makes blessed be regarded as proved ( – *not* merely desired, *not* merely promised by the somewhat suspect mouth of a priest): would blessedness – more technically, *pleasure* – ever be a proof of truth? So little that it provides almost the counter-proof, at any rate the strongest suspicion against 'truth' when feelings of pleasure enter into the answer to the question 'what is true?' The proof by 'pleasure' is a proof *of* pleasure – that is all: when on earth was it established that *true* judgements give more enjoyment than false ones, and in accordance with a predetermined harmony, necessarily bring pleasant feelings in their train? – The experience of all severe, all profound intellects teaches *the reverse*. Truth has had to be fought for every step of the way, almost everything else dear to our hearts, on which our love and our trust in life depend, has had to be sacrificed to it. Greatness of soul is needed for it: the service of truth is the hardest service. – For what does it mean to be *honest* in intellectual things? That one is stern towards one's heart, that one despises 'fine feelings', that one makes every Yes and No a question of conscience! – Belief makes blessed: *consequently* it lies . . .

[*A* 50]

# RELIGION

## 146

*Origin of the religious cult.* – If we transport ourselves back to the ages in which the religious life flourished most vigorously we discover a fundamental conviction which we no longer share and on account of which we see the door to the religious life once and for all closed to us: it concerns nature and our traffic with nature. In those ages one as yet knows nothing of natural laws; neither earth nor sky are constrained by any compulsion; a season, sunshine, rain can come or they can fail to come. Any conception of *natural* causality is altogether lacking. When one rows it is not the rowing which moves the ship: rowing is only a magical ceremony by means of which one compels a demon to move the ship. All illness, death itself is the result of magical influences. [. . .] The whole of nature is in the conception of religious men a sum of actions by conscious and volitional beings, a tremendous complex of *arbitrarinesses*. In regard to everything external to us no conclusion can be drawn that something *will* be thus or thus, *must* happen thus or thus; it is *we* who are the fairly secure and calculable; man is the *rule*, nature is *irregularity* – this proposition contains the fundamental conviction which dominates rude, religiously productive primitive cultures. We men of today feel precisely the opposite: the richer a man feels within himself, the more polyphonic his subjectivity is, the more powerfully is he impressed by the uniformity of nature [. . .] Formerly, the reverse was the case: if we think back to rude, primitive conditions of peoples, or if we look closely at present-day savages, we find them determined in the strongest way by the *law*, by *tradition*: the individual is tied to them almost automatically and moves with the regularity of a pendulum. To him, nature [. . .] must seem the *domain of freedom*, of caprice, of a higher power, indeed, as it were, a superhuman stage of existence, a god. But every individual living in such ages and conditions feels how his existence, his happiness, that of the family and the state, the success of any undertaking depends on these arbitrarinesses of nature: certain natural events must occur at the right time, others fail to occur. How can one exercise an influence over these terrible unknown powers, how can one fetter the domain of freedom? thus he asked himself, thus he anxiously seeks: are there then no means of regulating these powers through a tradition and law in just the way you are regulated by them? – The believer in magic and miracles reflects on how to *impose a law on nature* – : and, in brief, the religious cult is the outcome of this reflection. [. . .]

[*HA* 111]

### 147

*Christianity as antiquity.* – When on a Sunday morning we hear the bells ringing we ask ourselves: it is possible! this is going on because of a Jew crucified 2,000 years ago who said he was the son of God. The proof of such an assertion is lacking. – In the context of our age the Christian religion is certainly a piece of antiquity intruding out of distant ages past, and that the above-mentioned assertion is believed [. . .] is perhaps the most ancient piece of this inheritance. A god who begets children on a mortal woman; a sage who calls upon us no longer to work, no longer to sit in judgement, but to heed the signs of the imminent end of the world; a justice which accepts an innocent man as a substitute sacrifice; someone who bids his disciples drink his blood; prayers for miraculous interventions; sins perpetrated against a god atoned for by a god; fear of a Beyond to which death is the gateway: the figure of the Cross as a symbol in an age which no longer knows the meaning and shame of the Cross – how gruesomely all this is wafted to us, as if out of the grave of a primeval past! Can one believe that things of this sort are still believed in?

[*HA* 113]

## 148

*On the Christian need of redemption*. – Careful reflection ought to be able to yield an explanation of the occurrence in the soul of a Christian called need of redemption which is free of mythology: that is to say, a purely psychological explanation. [. . .] Man is conscious of certain actions which stand low in the customary order of rank of actions; indeed, he discovers in himself a tendency to actions of this sort which seems to him almost as immutable as his whole nature does. How much he would like to attempt that other species of actions which in the general estimation are accounted the highest, how much he would like to feel full of that good consciousness which is supposed to attend a selfless mode of thought! Unhappily he gets no further than desiring this: his discontent at his insufficiency is added to all the other kinds of discontent which his lot in life in general or the consequences of those other actions called wicked have engendered in him; so that there arises a profound depression of spirits, together with a watching-out for a physician who might be able to alleviate this condition and all its causes. – This condition would not be felt so bitterly if man compared himself only with other men: for then he would have no reason to be especially discontented with himself, since he would see he was only bearing the general burden of human dissatisfaction and imperfection. But he compares himself with a being which alone is capable of those actions called unegoistic and lives continually in the consciousness of a selfless mode of thought, with God; it is because he looks into this brilliant mirror that his own nature seems to him so dismal, so uncommonly distorted. Then again, the thought of this same being makes him fearful inso-far as it appears to his imagination as chastising justice: in all possible experiences, great and small, he believes he recog-nizes its anger and menaces, indeed that he feels already in advance the whiplash of this judge and executioner. [. . .]

Before we go on to exhibit this condition in its further con-sequences let us confess to ourselves that the man in this con-dition has got into it, not through his 'guilt' and 'sin', but through a succession of errors of reason, that it was the fault of the mirror if his nature appeared to him dark and hateful to such a degree, and that this mirror was *his* work, the very imperfect work of human imagination and judgement. Firstly, a being capable of nothing but pure unegoistic actions is more fabulous than the Phoenix; it cannot even be imagined clearly, if only because under strict examination the whole concept 'unegoistic action' vanishes into thin air. [. . .] On the other hand, a God who was *wholly* love, as is occasionally supposed, would be incapable of a single unegoistic action: in connection with which one should recall a thought of Lichtenberg's, though it was, to be sure, taken from a somewhat lower sphere: 'It is impossible, as is commonly said, for us to *feel* for others; we feel only for ourselves. The proposition sounds hard, but is not if it is correctly und_rstood. One loves neither father, nor mother, nor wife, nor child, one loves the pleasant sensations they produce in us,' or as La Rochefoucauld says: '*si on croit aimer sa maîtresse pour l'amour d'elle, on est bien trompé*'. [. . .] Further: the idea of a God is disturbing and humiliating as long as it is believed, but how it *originated* can at the present stage of comparative ethnology no longer admit of doubt; and with the insight into this origination that belief falls away. The Christian who compares his nature with that of God is like Don Quixote, who underestimated his own courage because his head was filled with the miraculous deeds of the heroes of chivalric romances: the standard of compari-son applied in both cases belongs in the domain of fable. But if the idea of God falls away, so does the feeling of 'sin' as a transgression against divine percepts, as a blemish on a creature consecrated to God. Then there probably still remains over that feeling of depression which is very much entwined with and related to fear of punishment by secular justice or the disapprobation of other men; the depression caused by the pang of conscience, the sharpest sting in the feeling of guilt, is nonetheless abolished when one sees that, although one may by one's actions have offended against human tradition, human laws and ordinances, one has not therewith endangered the 'eternal salvation of the soul' and its relationship to the divinity. If a man is, finally, able to attain to the philosophical conviction of the unconditional necessity of all actions and their complete unaccountability and to make it part of his flesh and blood, then that remainder of the pang of conscience also disappears.

Now if, as has been said, the Christian has got into the feeling of self-contempt through certain errors, that is to say, through a false, unscientific interpretation of his actions and sensations, he also notices with the highest astonishment that this condition of contempt, the pang of conscience, displeasure in general, does not persist, but that occasionally there are hours when all this is wafted away from his soul and he again feels free and valiant. What has happened is that his pleasure in himself, his contentment at his own strength, has, in concert with the weakening which every profound excitation must necessarily undergo, carried off the victory: he loves himself again, he feels it – but precisely this love, this new self-valuation seems to him incredible, he can see in it only the wholly undeserved flowing down of a radiance of mercy from on high. If he earlier believed he saw in every event warnings, menaces, punishments and every sort of sign of divine wrath, he now *interprets* divine goodness *into* his experiences [. . .] If he earlier in a condition of depression interpreted his actions falsely, now he does the same with his experiences; he conceives his mood of consolation as the effect upon him of an external power, the love with which fundamentally he loves himself appears as divine love; that which he calls mercy and the prelude to redemption is in truth self-pardon, self-redemption.

Thus: a definite false psychology, a certain kind of fantasy in the interpretation of motives and experiences is the necessary presupposition for becoming a Christian and for feeling the need of redemption. With the insight into this aberration of reason and imagination one ceases to be a Christian.

[*HA* 132–5]

## 149

'*Love.*' – The subtlest artifice which Christianity has over the other religions is a word: it spoke of *love*. Thus it became the *lyrical* religion. [. . .] There is in the word love something so ambiguous and suggestive, something which speaks to the memory and to future hope, that even the meanest intelligence and the coldest heart still feels something of the lustre of this word. The shrewdest woman and the commonest man think when they hear it of the relatively least selfish moments of their whole life, even if Eros has only paid them a passing visit; and those countless numbers who *never experience* love, of parents, or children, or lovers, especially however the men and women of sublimated sexuality, have made their find in Christianity.

[*AOM* 95]

## 150

*Balm and poison.* – This fact can never be sufficiently pondered: Christianity is the religion of antiquity grown old, its presupposition is degenerated ancient cultures; on these it could and can act as a balm. [. . .] On the other hand, for youthful, vigorous barbarians Christianity is *poison*; to implant the teaching of sinfulness and damnation into the heroic, childish and

animal soul of the ancient German, for example, is nothing
other than to poison it [. . .]

[*AOM* 224]

## 151

*What is truth?* – *Schwarzert* (Melanchthon): 'One often preaches
one's faith precisely when one has lost it and is looking for it
everywhere – and at such a time one does not preach it worst!'
– *Luther*: Thou speak'st true today like an angel, brother!
– *Schwarzert*: 'But it is thy enemies who think this thought
and they apply it to thee.' – *Luther*: Then it's a lie from the
Devil's behind.

[*WS* 66]

## 152

*Belief in the sickness as sickness.* – It was Christianity which first
painted the Devil on the world's wall; it was Christianity
which first brought sin into the world. Belief in the cure which
it offered has now been shaken to its deepest roots: but *belief
in the sickness* which it taught and propagated continues to
exist.

[*WS* 78]

## 153

*The first Christian.* – All the world still believes in the writings
of the 'Holy Ghost' or stands in the after-effect of this belief:
when one opens the Bible one does so to 'edify' oneself, to
discover a signpost of consolation in one's own personal distress, great or small – in short, one reads oneself into and out
of it. That it also contains the history of one of the most ambitious and importunate souls, of a mind as superstitious as it

was cunning, the history of the apostle Paul – who, apart from a few scholars, knows that? But without this remarkable history, without the storms and confusions of such a mind, of such a soul, there would be no Christianity; we would hardly have heard of a little Jewish sect whose master died on the cross. [. . .] That the ship of Christianity threw overboard a good part of the Jewish ballast, that it went and was able to go among the heathen – that is a consequence of the history of this one man, of a very tormented, very pitiable, very unpleasant man who also found himself unpleasant. He suffered from a fixed idea, or more clearly from a *fixed question* which was always present to him and would never rest: what is the Jewish *law* really all about? and in particular what is the *fulfilment of this law*? In his youth he had himself wanted to satisfy it, voracious for this highest distinction the Jews were able to conceive – this people which had taken the fantasy of moral sublimity higher than any other people and which alone achieved the creation of a holy God together with the idea of sin as an offence against this holiness. Paul had become at once the fanatical defender and chaperone of this God and his law and was constantly combating and on the watch for transgressors and doubters, harsh and malicious towards them and with the extremest inclination for punishment. And then he discovered in himself that he himself – fiery, sensual, melancholy, malevolent in hatred as he was – *could* not fulfil the law, he discovered indeed what seemed to him the strangest thing of all: that his extravagant lust for power was constantly provoked to transgress it and that he *had* to give way to this goad. Is it really 'carnality' which again and again makes him a transgressor? And not rather, as he later suspected, behind it the law itself, which *must* continually prove itself unfulfillable and with irresistible magic lures on to transgression? But at that time he did not yet possess this way out of his difficulty. [. . .] there were moments when he said to himself: 'It is all in vain! the torture of the unfulfilled law cannot be overcome.' Luther may have felt a similar thing when he wanted in his monastery to become the perfect man of the spiritual ideal:

and similarly to Luther, who one day began to hate the
spiritual ideal and the Pope and the saints and the whole
clergy with a more deadly hatred the less he dared to admit it
to himself – a similar thing happened to Paul. The law was the
cross to which he felt himself nailed: how he hated it! how
he had to drag it along! how he sought about for a means of
*destroying* it – and no longer to fulfil it! And at last the liber-
ating idea came to him, together with a vision, as was bound
to happen in the case of this epileptic: to him, the zealot of the
law who was inwardly tired to death of it, there appeared on
a lonely road Christ with the light of God shining in his
countenance, and Paul heard the words: 'Why persecutest
thou *me*?' What essentially happened then is however this:
his *mind* suddenly became clear: 'it is *unreasonable*,' he says to
himself, 'to persecute precisely this Christ! For here is the
way out, here is perfect revenge, here and nowhere else do I
have and hold the *destroyer of the law*!' Sick with the most
tormented pride, at a stroke he feels himself recovered, the
moral despair is as if blown away, for morality is blown away,
destroyed – that is to say, *fulfilled*, there on the Cross! Hitherto
that shameful *death* had counted with him as the principal
argument against the 'Messiahdom' of which the followers of
the new teaching spoke: but what if it were *necessary* for the
*abolition* of the law! – The tremendous consequences of this
notion, this solution of the riddle, whirl before his eyes, all at
once he is the happiest of men – the destiny of the Jews – no,
of all mankind – seems to him to be tied to this notion, to this
second of his sudden enlightenment, he possesses the idea of
ideas, the key of keys, the light of lights; henceforth history
revolves around him! For from now on he is the teacher of
the *destruction of the law*! To die to evil – that means also to die
to the law; to exist in the flesh – that means also to exist in the
law! To become one with Christ – that means also to become
with him the destroyer of the law; to have died with him –
that means also to have died to the law! Even if it is still
possible to sin, it is no longer possible to sin against the law,
'I am outside the law.' 'If I were now to accept the law again

and submit to it I should be making Christ an assistant of sin,'
for the law existed so that sins might be committed, it continually brought sin forth as a sharp juice brings forth a dis-
ease; God could never have resolved on the death of Christ
if a fulfilment of the law had been in any way possible without
this death; now ı ot only has all guilt been taken away, guilt
as such has been destroyed; now the law is dead, now the
carnality in which it dwelt is dead – or at least dying constantly
away, as though decaying. Yet but a brief time within this
decay! – that is the Christian's lot, before, become one with
Christ, he arises with Christ, participates with Christ in
divine glory and becomes a 'son of God', like Christ. – With
that the intoxication of Paul is at its height, and likewise the
importunity of his soul – with the idea of becoming one with
Christ all shame, all subordination, all bounds are taken from
it, and the intractable lust for power reveals itself as an anticipatory revelling in *divine* glories. – This is the *first Christian*,
the inventor of Christianness! Before him there were only a
few Jewish sectarians.

[*D* 68]

## 154

*Justice which punishes*. – Misfortune and guilt – Christianity has
placed these two things on a balance: so that, when misfortune
consequent on guilt is great, even now the greatness of the
guilt itself is still involuntarily measured by it. But this is not
*antique*, and that is why the Greek tragedy, which speaks so
much yet in so different a sense of misfortune and guilt, is a
great liberator of the spirit in a way in which the ancients
themselves could not feel it. They were still so innocent as
not to have established an 'adequate relationship' between
guilt and misfortune. The guilt of their tragic heroes is, indeed, the little stone over which they stumble and perhaps
break an arm or put out an eye: antique sensibility com-
mented: 'Yes, he should have gone his way a little more
cautiously and with less haughtiness!' But it was reserved for

Christianity to say: 'Here is a great misfortune and behind it there *must* lie hidden a great, *equally great* guilt, even though it may not be clearly visible! If you, unfortunate man, do not feel this you are *obdurate* – you will have to suffer worse things!' – Moreover, in antiquity there still existed actual misfortune, pure innocent misfortune; only in Christendom did everything become punishment, well-deserved punishment [...]

[*D* 78]

## 155

*Doubt as sin*. – Christianity has done its utmost to close the circle and declared even doubt to be a sin. One is supposed to be cast into belief without reason, by a miracle, and from then on to swim in it as in the brightest and least ambiguous of elements: even a glance towards land, even the thought that one perhaps exists for something else as well as swimming, even the slightest impulse of our amphibious nature – is sin! And notice that all this means that the foundation of belief and all reflection on its origin is likewise excluded as sinful. What is wanted are blindness and intoxication and an eternal song over the waves in which reason has drowned!

[*D* 89]

## 156

*Incense*. – Buddha said: 'Do not flatter your benefactor!' Repeat this saying in a Christian church – and it at once purifies the air of everything Christian.

[*GS* 142]

## 157

*Where polytheism is most useful*. – That the individual should set up his *own* ideal and derive from it his law, his joys and his rights – that has hitherto counted as perhaps the most terrible of all human aberrations and as idolatry as such; in fact the few who have dared to do this have always needed to offer an apologia to themselves, and this has usually been: 'not I!' not I! but *a god* through me!' It was the marvellous art and power to create gods – polytheism – in which this drive could discharge itself, in which it purified, perfected, ennobled itself: for originally it was a mean and vulgar drive related to obstinacy, disobedience and envy. To be *inimical* to this drive to an individual's own ideal: that was formerly the law of every morality. Then there was only one norm: '*the* human being' – and every people believed it *possessed* this one and final norm. But above and outside, in a distant supra-world, one might see a *multiplicity of norms*: the one god was not the denial of or a blasphemy against another god! It was here that the right of individuals was first honoured. The invention of gods, heroes and supermen of all kinds, together with that of fictitious fellow men and sub-men, of dwarfs, fairies, centaurs, satyrs, demons and devils, was the invaluable preparatory exercise for the justification of the selfishness and autocracy of the individual: the freedom one accorded the god in relation to other gods one at last gave oneself in relation to laws and customs and neighbour. Monotheism, on the other hand, that rigid consequence of the teaching of a standard human being – therefore the belief in a standard god beside whom other gods were no more than false and fraudulent – has been perhaps the greatest danger facing mankind hitherto: mankind was threatened with that premature inertia which, as far as we can see, other species of animals reached long ago [. . .]. Polytheism was a prefiguration of free spiritedness and multi-spiritedness: the power to create new and personal eyes for oneself and again and again new and even more personal ones: so that for man alone of all the animals there is no eternally fixed horizon and perspectives.

[*GS* 143]

## 158

*On the origin of religion.* – The metaphysical need is not the origin of religions, as Schopenhauer will have it, but only an *aftershoot* of them. Under the domination of religious notions one became accustomed to the idea of 'another (back, under, over) world' and with the destruction of religious notions felt an uncomfortable emptiness and deprivation – and out of this feeling there again grew 'another world', but this time only a metaphysical and no longer a religious one. That which in primeval times led to the assumption of 'another world' at all was, however, *not* a drive and need but an *error* in the inter-pretation of certain natural events, a confusion of intellect.

[*GS* 151]

## 159

The faith such a primitive Christianity demanded and not infre-quently obtained in the midst of a sceptical and southerly free-spirited world with a centuries-long struggle between philosophical schools behind it and in it, plus the education in tolerance provided by the *Imperium Romanum* – this faith is *not* that gruff, true-hearted liegeman's faith with which a Luther, say, or a Cromwell, or some other northern barbarian of the spirit cleaved to his God and his Christianity; it is rather that faith of Pascal which resembles in a terrible fashion a protracted suicide of reason [. . .] The Christian faith is from the beginning a sacrifice: sacrifice of all freedom, all pride, all self-confidence of the spirit, at the same time enslavement and self-mockery, self-mutilation. There is cruelty and re-ligious Phoenicianism in this faith exacted of an over-ripe, manifold and much-indulged conscience: its presupposition is that the subjection of the spirit is indescribably *painful*, that the entire past and habitude of such a spirit resists the *absur-dissimum* which 'faith' appears to it to be. Modern men, with their obtuseness to all Christian nomenclature, no longer sense the gruesome superlative which lay for an antique taste in the paradoxical formula 'god on the cross'. Never and nowhere has there hitherto been a comparable boldness in inversion, anything so fearsome, questioning and questionable, as this formula: it promised a revaluation of all antique values. – It is the orient, the *innermost* orient, it is the oriental slave who in this fashion took vengeance on Rome and its noble and frivolous tolerance, on Roman 'catholicism' of faith – and it has never been faith but always freedom from faith, that half-stoical unconcern with the seriousness of faith, that has enraged slaves in their masters and against their masters. 'Enlightenment' enrages: for the slave wants the unconditional, he understands in the domain of morality too only the tyrannical, he loves as he hates, without nuance, into the depths of him, to the point of pain, to the point of sickness – the great *hidden* suffering he feels is enraged at the noble taste which seems to *deny* suffering. Scepticism towards suffering, at bottom no more than a pose of aristocratic morality, was likewise not the least contributory cause of the last great slave revolt which began with the French Revolution.

[*BGE* 46]

## 160

The philosopher as *we* understand him, we free spirits – as the man of the most comprehensive responsibility who has the conscience for the collective evolution of mankind: this philosopher will make use of the religions for his work of education and breeding, just as he will make use of existing political and economic conditions. The influence on selection and breeding, that is to say, the destructive as well as the creative and formative influence which can be exercised with the aid of the religions, is manifold and various depending on the kind of man placed under their spell and protection. For the strong and independent prepared and predestined for command, in whom the art and reason of a ruling race is incar-

nated, religion is one more means of overcoming resistance
so as to be able to rule: as a bond that unites together ruler
and ruled and betrays and hands over to the former the consciences of the latter, all that is hidden and most intimate in
them which would like to exclude itself from obedience; and
if some natures of such noble descent incline through lofty
spirituality to a more withdrawn and meditative life and reserve to themselves only the most refined kind of rule (over
select disciples or brothers), then religion can even be used as
a means of obtaining peace from the noise and effort of cruder
modes of government, and cleanliness from the *necessary* dirt
of all politics. [. . .] religion also gives a section of the ruled
guidance and opportunity for preparing itself for future rule
and command; that is to say, those slowly rising orders and
classes in which through fortunate marriage customs the
strength and joy of the will, the will to self-mastery is always
increasing – religion presents them with sufficient instigations
and temptations to take the road to higher spirituality, to test
the feelings of great self-overcoming, of silence and solitude.
[. . .] To ordinary men, finally, to the great majority, who exist
for service and general utility and who *may* exist only for that
purpose, religion gives an invaluable contentment with their
nature and station, manifold peace of heart, an ennobling of
obedience, one piece of joy and sorrow more to share with
their fellows, and some transfiguration of the whole everyday-
ness, the whole lowliness, the whole half-bestial poverty of
their souls. [. . .]

In the end, to be sure, to present the debit side of the
account to these religions and to bring into the light of day
their uncanny perilousness – it costs dear and terribly when
religions hold sway, *not* as means of education and breeding
in the hands of the philosopher, but in their own right and as
*sovereign*, when they themselves want to be final ends and not
means beside other means. Among men, as among every
other species, there is a surplus of failures, of the sick, the
degenerate, the fragile, of those who are bound to suffer; the
successful cases are, among men too, always the exception

and, considering that man is the animal *whose nature has not yet been fixed*, the rare exception. But worse still: the higher the type of man a man represents, the greater the improbability he will *turn out well*: chance, the law of absurdity in the total economy of mankind, shows itself in its most dreadful shape in its destructive effect on higher men, whose conditions of life are subtle, manifold and difficult to compute. Now what is the attitude of the [. . .] two chief religions [Christianity and Buddhism] towards this *surplus* of unsuccessful cases? They seek to preserve, to retain in life, whatever can in any way be preserved, indeed they side with it as a matter of principle as religions *for sufferers*, they maintain that all those who suffer from life as from an illness are in the right, and would like every other feeling of life to be counted false and become impossible. However highly one may rate this kindly preservative solicitude [. . .] in the total accounting the hitherto *sovereign* religions are among the main reasons the type 'man' has been kept on a lower level – they have preserved too much of that *which ought to perish*. We have inestimable benefits to thank them for [. . .] And yet, when they gave comfort to the suffering, courage to the oppressed and despairing, a staff and stay to the irresolute, and lured those who were inwardly shattered and had become savage away from society into monasteries and houses of correction for the soul: what did they have to do in addition so as thus, with a good conscience, as a matter of principle, to work at the preservation of everything sick and suffering, which means in fact and truth at the *corruption of the European race*? Stand all evaluations *on their head* – *that* is what they had to do! And smash the strong, contaminate great hopes, cast suspicion on joy in beauty, break down everything autocratic, manly, conquering, tyrannical, all the instincts proper to the highest and most successful of the type 'man', into uncertainty, remorse of conscience, self-destruction, indeed reverse the whole love of the earth and the earthly – *that* is the task the Church set itself and had to set itself, until in its evaluation 'unworldliness', 'unsensuality', and 'higher man' were finally fused together into *one* feeling. [. . .] What I am saying is: Christianity has been the most fatal kind of self-presumption ever. Men not high or hard enough for the artistic refashioning of *mankind*; men not strong or far-sighted enough for the sublime self-constraint needed to *allow* the foreground law of thousandfold failure and perishing to prevail; men not noble enough to see the abysmal disparity in order of rank and abysm of rank between man and man – it is *such* men who, with their 'equal before God', have hitherto ruled over the destiny of Europe, until at last a shrunken, almost ludicrous species, a herd animal, something full of goodwill, sickly and mediocre has been bred, the European of today . . .

[*BGE* 61–2]

## 161

*The Peasants' Revolt of the spirit.* – We Europeans find ourselves viewing a tremendous world of ruins [. . .] The Church is this City of Destruction: we behold the religious community of Christendom shaken to its deepest foundations – belief in God has been overturned, belief in the Christian-ascetic ideal is even now fighting its last fight. Such a protracted and thoroughly constructed work as Christianity – it was the last Roman building! – could, to be sure, not be destroyed at a single blow; every kind of earthquake, every kind of under-mining and gnawing spirit had to assist in it. But the most miraculous thing is that those who strove hardest to maintain Christianity became its most effective destroyers – the Germans. It seems that the Germans do not understand the nature of a Church. Are they insufficiently spiritual? insufficiently mistrustful? The structure of the Church rests in any event on a *southerly* freedom and freemindedness of the spirit and equally on a southerly suspiciousness of nature, man and spirit – it rests on a quite different knowledge of man, experience of man, than the north has had. The Lutheran Reformation was, to speak cautiously, in its entire breadth the indignation of

simplicity at something 'manifold', a crude, philistine misunderstanding in which there is much to be forgiven – they
did not grasp the way in which a *victorious* Church expresses
itself and saw only corruption, they misunderstood the noble
scepticism and tolerance which every victorious, self-confident
power permits itself ... Today one can perceive well enough
how Luther was in every cardinal question of power inclined
to be fatefully summary, superficial, incautious, above all as a
man of the people who lacked any inheritance of a ruling
caste, any instinct for power: so that his work, his will to the
restoration of that Roman work, became without his wanting
or knowing it only the beginning of a work of destruction.
With honest wrath he untwisted and pulled together where
the ancient spider had spun longest and most carefully. He
handed the holy books over to everyman – so that at last they
got into the hands of the philologists, that is to say, the destroyers of every belief which rests on books. By rejecting belief in the inspiration of the Church Councils he destroyed the
concept 'Church': for it is only on condition that the inspirational spirit which founded the Church still lives in it, is
still building, still continues to build its house, that the concept 'Church' retains its force. He restored to the priest sexual
intercourse with woman: but three-quarters of the awe of
which the people, above all the woman of the people, is capable rests on the belief that a man who is an exception on this
point will also be an exception on other points – it was precisely here that popular belief in something superhuman in
man, in the miracle, in the redeeming God in man had its
subtlest and most insidious advocate. After he had given him
woman, Luther had to *take from* the priest the confessional:
that was psychologically correct, but fundamentally the Christian priest himself was therewith abolished, for his profoundest utility has always been that he was a sacred ear, a silent
well, a grave for secrets. 'Everyman his own priest' – behind
such formulae and their peasant cunning there was concealed
in the case of Luther the most abysmal hatred for 'higher
men' and the rule of the 'higher man' as the Church had con-

ceived him – he destroyed an ideal to which he could not attain, while he seemed to be combating and to detest the degeneration of this ideal. In reality he, who found it impossible to be a monk, struck the *rule* of the *homines religiosi* from him; he thus made within the ecclesiastical social order precisely that which in regard to the civil order he so intolerantly opposed – a 'Peasants' Revolt'. [. . .]

[*GS* 358 (1887)]

## 162

In Christianity neither morality nor religion come into contact with reality at any point. Nothing but imaginary *causes* ('God', 'soul', 'ego', 'spirit', 'free-will' – or 'unfree-will'): nothing but imaginary *effects* ('sin', 'redemption', 'grace', 'punishment', 'forgiveness of sins'). A traffic between imaginary *beings* ('God', 'spirits', 'souls'); an imaginary *natural* science (anthropocentric; complete lack of the concept of natural causes); an imaginary *psychology* (nothing but self-misunderstandings, interpretations of pleasant or unpleasant general feelings, for example the condition of the *nervus sympathicus*, with the aid of the sign-language of religio-moral idiosyncrasy – 'repentance', 'sting of conscience', 'temptation by the Devil' 'the proximity of God'); an imaginary *teleology* ('the kingdom of God', 'the Last Judgement', 'eternal life'). [. . .] Once the concept 'nature' had been devised as the concept antithetical to 'God', 'natural' had to be the word for 'reprehensible' – this entire fictional world has its roots in *hatred* of the natural (– actuality! –), it is the expression of a profound discontent with the actual . . . *But that explains everything.* Who alone has reason to *lie himself out* of actuality? He who *suffers* from it. But to suffer from actuality means to be an abortive actuality . . . The preponderance of feelings of displeasure over feelings of pleasure is the *cause* of a fictitious morality and religion: such a preponderance, however, provides the *formula* for *décadence* . . .

A critical examination of the *Christian concept of God* invites a similar conclusion. – A people which still believes in itself still also has its own God. In him it venerates the conditions through which it has prospered, its virtues -- it projects its joy in itself, its feeling of power on to a being whom one can thank for them. He who is rich wants to bestow; a proud people needs a God in order to *sacrifice* . . . Within the bounds of such presuppositions religion is a form of gratitude. One is grateful for oneself: for that one needs a God. – Such a God must be able to be both useful and harmful, both friend and foe – he is admired in good and bad alike. The *anti-natural* castration of a God into a God of the merely good would be totally undesirable here. One has as much need of the evil God as of the good God: for one does not owe one's existence to philanthropy or tolerance precisely . . . Of what consequence would be a God who knew nothing of anger, revengefulness, envy, mockery, cunning, acts of violence? to whom even the rapturous *ardeurs* of victory and destruction were unknown? One would not understand such a God: why should one have him? – To be sure: when a people is perishing; when it feels its faith in the future, its hope of freedom vanish completely; when it becomes conscious that the most profitable thing of all is submissiveness and that the virtues of submissiveness are a condition of its survival, then its God *has* to alter, too. He now becomes a dissembler, timid, modest, counsels 'peace of soul', no more hatred, forbearance, 'love' even towards friend and foe. He is continually moralizing, he creeps into the cave of every private virtue, becomes a God for everybody, becomes a private man, becomes a cosmopolitan . . . Formerly, he represented a people, the strength of a people, everything aggressive and thirsting for power in the soul of a people: now he is merely the good God . . . There is in fact no other alternative for Gods: *either* they are the will to power – and so long as they are that they will be national Gods – *or* else the impotence for power – and then they necessarily become *good* . . .

Wherever the will to power declines in any form there is

every time also a physiological regression, a *décadence*. The divinity of *décadence*, pruned of all its manliest drives and virtues, from now on necessarily becomes the God of the physiologically retarded, the weak. They do *not* call themselves the weak, they call themselves 'the good' . . . One will understand without further indication at what moment of history the dual fiction of a good and an evil God first becomes possible. The same instinct which makes the subjugated people reduce its God to the 'good in itself' makes them expunge the good qualities from the God of their conqueror; they revenge themselves on their masters by changing their masters' God into a devil. – The *good* God and the Devil: both products of *décadence*. [. . .]

The Christian conception of God [. . .] is one of the most corrupt conceptions of God arrived at on earth: perhaps it even represents the low-water mark in the descending development of the God type. God degenerated to the *contradiction of life*, instead of being its transfiguration and eternal *Yes*! In God a declaration of hostility towards life, nature, the will to life! God the formula for every calumny of 'this world', for every lie about 'the next world!' In God nothingness defied, the will to nothingness sanctified! . . .

[*A* 15–18]

## 163

I only touch on the problem of the *origin* of Christianity here. The *first* proposition towards its solution is: Christianity can be understood only by referring to the soil out of which it grew – it is *not* a counter-movement against the Jewish instinct, it is actually its logical consequence [. . .] The *second* proposition is: the psychological type of the Galilean is still recognizable – but only in a completely degenerate form (which is at once a mutilation and an overloading with foreign traits) could it serve the end to which it was put, that of being the type of a *redeemer* of mankind. –

The Jews are the most remarkable nation of world history because, faced with the question of being or not being, they preferred, with a perfectly uncanny conviction, being *at any price*: the price they had to pay was the radical *falsification* of all nature, all naturalness, all reality, the entire inner world as well as the outer. [...] they inverted religion, religious worship, morality, history, psychology one after the other in an irreparable way into the *contradiction of their natural values*. We encounter the same phenomenon again and in unutterably vaster proportions, although only as a copy – the Christian Church, in contrast to the 'nation of saints', renounces all claim to originality. For precisely this reason the Jews are the most *fateful* nation in world history: their after-effect has falsified mankind to such an extent that today the Christian is able to feel anti-Jewish without realizing he is the *ultimate consequence of the Jews*.

In my *Genealogy of Morals* I introduced for the first time the psychology of the antithetical concepts of a *noble* morality and a *ressentiment* morality, the latter deriving from a *denial* of the former: but this latter corresponds totally to Judaeo-Christian morality. To be able to reject all that represents the *ascending* movement of life, well-constitutedness, power, beauty, self-affirmation on earth, the instinct of *ressentiment* here become genius had to invent *another* world from which that *life-affirmation* would appear evil, reprehensible as such. Considered psychologically, the Jewish nation is a nation of the toughest vital energy which, placed in impossible circumstances, voluntarily, from the profoundest shrewdness in self-preservation, took the side of all *décadence* instincts – *not* as being dominated by them but because it divined in them a power by means of which one can prevail *against* 'the world'. [...]

[*A* 24]

What *I* am concerned with is the psychological type of the redeemer. [...] Precisely the opposite of all contending, of all feeling oneself in struggle has here become instinct: the incapacity for resistance here becomes morality ('resist not evil': the profoundest saying of the Gospel, its key in a certain sense), blessedness in peace, in gentleness, in the *inability* for enmity. What are the 'glad tidings'? True life, eternal life is found – it is not promised, it is here, it is *within you*: as life lived in love, in love without deduction or exclusion, without distance. Everyone is a child of God – Jesus definitely claims nothing for himself alone – as a child of God everyone is equal to everyone else. [...] We recognize a condition of morbid susceptibility of the *sense of touch* which makes it shrink back in horror from every contact, every grasping of a firm object. Translate such a physiological *habitus* into its ultimate logic – as instinctive hatred of *every* reality, as flight into the 'ungraspable', into the 'inconceivable', as antipathy towards every form, every spatial and temporal concept, towards everything firm, all that is custom, institution, Church, as being at home in a world undisturbed by reality of any kind, a merely 'inner' world, a 'real' world, an 'eternal' world ... 'The kingdom of God *is within you*' ...

*Instinctive hatred of reality*: consequence of an extreme capacity for suffering and irritation which no longer wants to be 'touched' at all because it feels every contact too deeply.

*Instinctive exclusion of all aversion, all enmity, all feeling for limitation and distancing*: consequence of an extreme capacity for suffering and irritation which already feels all resisting, all need for resistance, as an unbearable *displeasure* [...] and knows blessedness (pleasure) only in no longer resisting anyone or anything, neither the evil nor the evil-doer – love as the sole, as the last possibility of life ...

These are two *physiological realities* upon which, out of which, the doctrine of redemption has grown. I call it a sublime further evolution of hedonism on a thoroughly morbid basis. [. . .] The fear of pain, even of the infinitely small in pain – *cannot* end otherwise than in a *religion of love* . . .

*

[. . .] The 'glad tidings' are precisely that there are no more opposites; the kingdom of Heaven belongs to *children*; the faith which here finds utterance is not a faith which has been won by struggle – it is there, from the beginning, it is, as it were, a return to childishness in the spiritual domain. [. . .] Such a faith is not angry, does not censure, does not defend itself: it does not bring 'the sword' – it has no idea to what extent it could one day cause dissension. It does not prove itself, either by miracles or by rewards and promises, and certainly not 'by the Scriptures': it is every moment its own miracle, its own reward, its own proof, its own 'kingdom of God'. Neither does this faith formulate itself – it *lives*, it resists formulae. [. . .] One could, with some freedom of expression, call Jesus a 'free spirit' – he cares nothing for what is fixed: the word *killeth*, everything fixed *killeth*. The concept, the *experience* 'life' in the only form he knows it is opposed to any kind of word, formula, law, faith, dogma. He speaks only of the inmost thing: 'life' or 'truth' or 'light' is his expression for the inmost thing – everything else, the whole of reality, the whole of nature, language itself, possesses for him merely the value of a sign, a metaphor. [. . .]

[. . .] In the entire psychology of the 'Gospel' the concept guilt and punishment is lacking; likewise the concept reward. 'Sin', every kind of distancing relationship between God and man, is abolished – *precisely this is the 'glad tidings'*. Blessedness is not promised, it is not tied to any conditions: it is the *only* reality – the rest is signs for speaking of it . . .

*

[. . .] The 'kingdom of Heaven' is a condition of the heart – not something that comes 'upon the earth' or 'after death'. [. . .] The 'kingdom of God' is not something one waits for; it has no yesterday or tomorrow, it does not come 'in a thousand years' – it is an experience within a heart; it is every-where, it is nowhere . . .

\*

This 'bringer of glad tidings' died as he lived, as he *taught* – *not* to 'redeem mankind' but to demonstrate how one ought to live. What he bequeathed to mankind is his *practice*: his bearing before the judges, before the guards, before the accusers and every kind of calumny and mockery – his bearing on the *Cross*. He does not resist, he does not defend his rights, he takes no steps to avert the worst that can happen to him – more, *he provokes it* . . . And he entreats, he suffers, he loves *with* those, *in* those who are doing evil to him. His words to the *thief* on the cross contain the whole Evangel. 'That was verily a *divine* man, a child of God!' – says the thief. 'If thou feelest this' – answers the redeemer – '*thou art in Paradise*, thou art a child of God.' *Not* to defend oneself, *not* to grow angry, *not* to make responsible . . . But not to resist even the evil man – to *love* him . . .

[*A* 29, 30, 32–5]

## 165

[. . .] I shall now relate the *real* history of Christianity. – The word 'Christianity' is already a misunderstanding – in reality there has been only one Christian, and he died on the Cross. The 'Evangel' *died* on the Cross. [. . .]

It was only the death, this unexpected shameful death, only the Cross, which was in general reserved for the *canaille* alone – it was only this terrible paradox which brought the disciples face to face with the real enigma: '*who was that? what was that?*' – The feeling of being shaken and disappointed to their depths, the suspicion that such a death might be the *refutation* of their cause, the frightful question-mark 'why has this happened?' – this condition is only too understandable. Here everything *had* to be necessary, meaningful, reasonable, rea-

sonable in the highest degree; a disciple's love knows nothing
of chance. Only now did the chasm open up: '*who* killed
him? *who* was his natural enemy?' – this question came like a
flash of lightning. Answer: *ruling* Judaism, its upper class. From
this moment one felt oneself in mutiny *against* the social order,
one subsequently understood Jesus as having been *in mutiny
against the social order*. Up till then this warlike trait, this negative
trait in word and deed, was *lacking* in his image; more, he
was the contradiction of it. Clearly the little community had
*failed* to understand precisely the main thing, the exemplary
element in his manner of dying, the freedom from, the superiority *over* every feeling of *ressentiment*: – a sign of how little they
understood of him at all! [. . .] Precisely the most unevangelic
of feelings, *revengefulness*, again came uppermost. The affair
could not possibly be at an end with this death: one required
'retribution', 'judgement' (– and yet what can be more unevangelic than 'retribution', 'punishment', 'sitting in judgement'!) The popular expectation of a Messiah came once more
into the foreground; an historic moment appeared in view:
the 'kingdom of God' is coming to sit in judgement on its
enemies . . . But with this everything is misunderstood: the
'kingdom of God' as a last act, as a promise! For the Evangel
had been precisely the existence, the fulfilment, the *actuality* of
this 'kingdom'. Such a death *was* precisely this 'kingdom of
God'. Only now was all that contempt and bitterness against
Pharisee and theologian worked into the type of the Master –
one thereby *made* of him a Pharisee and theologian! On the
other hand, the enraged reverence of these utterly unhinged
souls could no longer endure that evangelic equal right of
everyone to be a child of God which Jesus had taught, and
their revenge consisted in *exalting* Jesus in an extravagant
fashion, in severing him from themselves: just as the Jews,
in revenge on their enemies, had previously separated their
God from themselves and raised him on high. The *one* God
and the *one* Son of God: both products of *ressentiment* . . .

And now an absurd problem came up: 'How *could* God
have permitted that?' For this question the deranged reason

of the little community found a downright terrifyingly absurd answer: God gave his Son for the forgiveness of sins, as a *sacrifice*. All at once it was all over with the Gospel! The *guilt sacrifice*, and that in its most repulsive, barbaric form, the sacrifice of the *innocent man* for the sins of the guilty! What atrocious paganism! [. . .] From now on there is introduced into the type of the redeemer step by step: the doctrine of a Judgement and a Second Coming, the doctrine of his death as a sacrificial death, the doctrine of the Resurrection with which the entire concept 'blessedness', the whole and sole reality of the Evangel, is juggled away – for the benefit of a state *after* death! [. . .]

One sees *what* came to an end with the death on the Cross: a new, an absolutely primary beginning to a Buddhistic peace movement, to an actual and *not* merely promised *happiness on earth*. For this remains [. . .] the basic distinction between the two *décadence* religions: Buddhism makes no promises but keeps them, Christianity makes a thousand promises but *keeps none*. – On the heels of the 'glad tidings' came the *worst of all*: those of Paul. In Paul was embodied the antithetical type to the 'bringer of glad tidings', the genius of hatred, of the vision of hatred, of the inexorable logic of hatred. *What* did this dysangelist not sacrifice to his hatred! The redeemer above all: he nailed him to *his* Cross. The life, the example, the teaching, the death, the meaning and the right of the entire Gospel – nothing was left once this hate-obsessed false-coiner had grasped what alone he could make use of. *Not* the reality, *not* the historical truth! [. . .] The type of the redeemer, the doctrine, the practice, the death, the meaning of the death, even the sequel to the death – nothing was left untouched, nothing was left bearing even the remotest resemblance to reality. [. . .]

[*A* 39–42]

# PART TWO

# NIHILISM

## 166

*Appearance and thing-in-itself.* – Philosophers are accustomed to place themselves before life and experience – before that which they call the world of appearance – as if before a painting that has been unrolled once and for all and unchangingly displays almost the same event: this event, they think, must be interpreted correctly in order to draw a conclusion as to the being which produced the painting: that is to say, as to the thing-in-itself, which is seen as the sufficient reason for the world of appearance. More rigorous logicians, on the other hand, after they had strictly established the concept of the metaphysical as that of the unconditioned, consequently also the unconditioning, denied any connection between the unconditioned (the metaphysical world) and the world known to us: so that what appears in appearance is precisely not the thing-in-itself, and any conclusion from the former to the latter is to be rejected. Both parties, however, overlook the possibility that this painting – that which we men call life and experience – has gradually *become*, is indeed still fully in process of *becoming*, and should thus not be regarded as a fixed magnitude from which one might draw a conclusion as to the originator (the sufficient reason) or even reject such a conclusion. [. . .] That which we now call the world is the result of a host of errors and fantasies which have gradually arisen in the course of the total evolution of organic nature, have become entwined with one another and are now inherited by us as the accumulated treasure of the entire past – as a treasure: for the value of our humanity depends on it. Rigorous science is in fact able to detach us from this ideational world only to a slight extent [. . .] but it can gradually and step by step illuminate the history of how this world as idea arose – and raise us above the whole thing at least for moments at a time. Perhaps we then recognize that the thing-in-itself is worthy of Homeric laughter: it *appeared* to be so much, indeed everything, and is actually empty, that is to say empty of meaning.

[*HA* 16]


## 167

*From experience.* – The irrationality of a thing is no argument against its existence, rather a condition of it.

[*HA* 515]


## 168

*Fundamental insight.* – There is no pre-established harmony between the furtherance of truth and the well-being of mankind.

[*HA* 517]


## 169

*The human lot.* – He who considers more deeply knows that, whatever his acts and judgements may be, he is always wrong.

[*HA* 518]


## 170

*The fundamental errors.* – For man to feel any sort of physical pleasure or displeasure he must be in the grip of one of these two illusions: *either* he believes in the *identity* of certain facts, certain sensations: in which case he experiences psychical pleasure or displeasure through comparing his present states with past ones and declaring them identical or not identical (as happens in all recollection); *or* he believes in *freedom of will*, for instance when he thinks 'I did not have to do this', 'this could have happened differently', and likewise gains pleasure or displeasure. Without the errors which are active in every psychical pleasure and displeasure a humanity would never have come into existence – whose fundamental feeling is and remains that man is the free being in a world of unfreedom, the eternal *miracle worker* whether he does good or ill, the astonishing exception, the superbeast and almost-god, the meaning of creation which cannot be thought away, the solution of the cosmic riddle, the mighty ruler over nature and the despiser of it, the creature which calls *its* history *world history*! – *Vanitas vanitatum homo*.

[*WS* 12]

## 171

*The new fundamental feeling: our conclusive transitoriness.* – Formerly one sought the feeling of the grandeur of man by pointing to his divine *origin*: this has now become a forbidden way, for at its portal stands the ape [. . .] One therefore now tries the opposite direction: the way mankind is *going* shall serve as proof of its grandeur and kinship with God. Alas, this, too, is vain! At the end of this way stands the funeral urn of the *last* man and gravedigger (with the inscription '*nihil humani a me alienum puto*'). However high mankind may have evolved – and perhaps at the end it will stand even lower than at the beginning! – it cannot pass over into a higher order, as little as the ant and the earwig can at the end of its 'earthly course' rise up to kinship with God and eternal life. [. . .]

[*D* 49]

## 172

*A fable.* – The Don Juan of knowledge: no philosopher or poet has yet discovered him. He does not love the things he knows, but has spirit and appetite for and enjoyment of the chase and intrigues of knowledge – up to the highest and remotest stars of knowledge! – until at last there remains to him nothing of knowledge left to hunt down except the absolutely *detrimental*; he is like the drunkard who ends by drinking absinthe and *aqua fortis*. Thus in the end he lusts after Hell – it is the last knowledge that *seduces* him. Perhaps it too proves a disillusionment, like all knowledge! And then he would have to stand to all eternity transfixed to disillusionment and himself become a stone guest, with a longing for a supper of knowledge which he will never get! – for the whole universe has not a single morsel left to give to this hungry man.

[D 327]

## 173

*Let us beware!* – Let us beware of thinking the world is a living being. Whither should it spread itself? What should it nourish itself with? How could it grow and multiply? We know indeed more or less what the organic is: and shall we interpret the unspeakably derivative, late, rare, chance phenomena which we perceive only on the surface of the earth into the essential, universal, eternal, as they do who call the universe an organism? I find that disgusting. Let us likewise beware of believing the universe is a machine; it is certainly not constructed so as to perform some operation, we do it far too great honour with the word 'machine'. Let us beware of presupposing that something so orderly as the cyclical motions of our planetary neighbours are the general and universal case; even a glance at the Milky Way gives rise to doubt whether there may not exist far more crude and contradictory motions, likewise stars with eternally straight trajectories and the like. The astral order in which we live is an exception; this order and the apparent permanence which is conditional upon it is in its turn made possible by the exception of exceptions: the formation of the organic. The total nature of the world is, on the other hand, to all eternity chaos, not in the sense that necessity is lacking but in that order, structure, form, beauty, wisdom and whatever other human aesthetic notions we may have are lacking. Judged from the viewpoint of our reason, the unsuccessful cases are far and away the rule, the exceptions are not the secret objective, and the whole contraption repeats its theme, which can never be called a melody, over and over again to eternity – and ultimately even the term 'unsuccessful case' is already a humanization which contains a reproof. But how can we venture to reprove or praise the universe! Let us beware of attributing to it heartlessness and unreason or their opposites: it is neither perfect nor beautiful nor noble, and has no desire to become any of these; it is by no means striving to imitate mankind! It is quite impervious to all our aesthetic and moral judgements! It has likewise no impulse to self-preservation or impulses of any kind; neither does it know any laws. Let us beware of saying there are laws in nature. There are only necessities: there is no one to command, no one to obey, no one to transgress. When you realize that there are no goals or objectives, then you realize, too, that there is no chance: for only in a world of objectives does the word 'chance' have any meaning. Let us beware of saying that death is the opposite of life. The living being is only a species of the dead, and a very rare species. [. . .]

[*GS* 109]

## 174

*The four errors.* – Man has been reared by his errors: first he never saw himself other than imperfectly, second he attributed to himself imaginary qualities, third he felt himself in a false order of rank with animal and nature, fourth he continually invented new tables of values and for a time took each of them to be eternal and unconditional, so that now this, now that human drive and state took first place and was, as a consequence of this evaluation, ennobled. If one deducts the effect of these four errors, one has also deducted away humanity, humaneness and 'human dignity'.

[*GS* 115]

## 175

*Life no argument.* – We have arranged for ourselves a world in which we are able to live – with the postulation of bodies, lines, surfaces, causes and effects, motion and rest, form and content: without these articles of faith nobody could now endure to live! But that does not yet mean they are something proved and demonstrated. Life is no argument; among the conditions of life could be error.

[*GS* 121]

## 176

*The madman.* – Have you not heard of that madman who lit a lantern in the bright morning hours, ran to the market-place and cried incessantly: 'I am looking for God! I am looking for God!' – As many of those who did not believe in God were standing together there he excited considerable laughter. Have you lost him then? said one. Did he lose his way like a child? said another. Or is he hiding? Is he afraid of us? Has he gone on a voyage? Or emigrated? – thus they shouted and laughed. The madman sprang into their midst and pierced them with his glances. 'Where has God gone?' he cried. 'I shall tell you. *We have killed him* – you and I. We are all his murderers. But how have we done this? How were we able to drink up the sea? Who gave us the sponge to wipe away the entire horizon? What did we do when we unchained this earth from its sun?

Whither is it moving now? Whither are we moving now? Away from all suns? Are we not perpetually falling? Backward, sideward, forward, in all directions? Is there any up or down left? Are we not straying as through an infinite nothing? Do we not feel the breath of empty space? Has it not become colder? Is more and more night not coming on all the time? Must not lanterns be lit in the morning? Do we not hear anything yet of the noise of the gravediggers who are burying God? Do we not smell anything yet of God's decomposition? – gods, too, decompose. God is dead. God remains dead. And we have killed him. How shall we, the murderers of all murderers, console ourselves? That which was holiest and mightiest of all that the world has yet possessed has bled to death under our knives – who will wipe this blood off us? With what water could we purify ourselves? What festivals of atonement, what sacred games shall we need to invent? Is not the greatness of this deed too great for us? Must we not ourselves become gods simply to seem worthy of it? There has never been a greater deed – and whoever shall be born after us, for the sake of this deed he shall be part of a higher history than all history hitherto.' Here the madman fell silent and again regarded his listeners; and they, too, were silent and stared at him in astonishment. At last he threw his lantern to the ground and it broke and went out. 'I come too early,' he said then; 'my time has not yet come. This tremendous event is still on its way, still travelling – it has not yet reached the ears of men. Lightning and thunder require time, deeds require time after they have been done before they can be seen and heard. This deed is still more distant from them than the most distant stars – *and yet they have done it themselves.'* – It has been related further that on that same day the madman entered divers churches and there sang a *requiem aeternam deo*. Led out and quieted, he is said to have retorted each time: 'What are these churches now if they are not the tombs and sepulchres of God?'

[*GS* 125]

# 177

*Ultimate scepticism.* – What then in the last resort are the truths of mankind? – They are the *irrefutable* errors of mankind.

[*GS* 265]

# 178

[. . .] Hitherto, there have been a thousand goals, for there have been a thousand peoples. Only fetters are still lacking for these thousand necks, the one goal is still lacking.

Yet tell me, my brothers: if a goal for humanity is still lacking, is there not still lacking – humanity itself?

[Z I *Of the Thousand and One Goals*]

# ANTI-NIHILISM

## 179

*We aeronauts of the spirit!* – All those brave birds which fly
out into the distance, into the farthest distance – it is certain!
somewhere or other they will be unable to go on and will
perch down on a mast or a bare cliff-face – and they will even
be thankful for this miserable accommodation! But who could
venture to infer from that, that there was *not* an immense open
space before them, that they had flown as far as one *could* fly!
All our great teachers and predecessors have at last come to
a stop [. . .] it will be the same with you and me! But what
does that matter to you and me! *Other birds will fly farther!*
This insight and faith of ours vies with them in flying up and
away; it rises above our heads and above our impotence into
the heights and from there surveys the distance and sees before
it the flocks of birds which, far stronger than we, still strive
whither we have striven, and where everything is sea, sea,
sea! – And whither then would we go? Would we *cross* the sea?
Whither does this mighty longing draw us, this longing that
is worth more to us than any pleasure? Why just in this
direction, thither where all the sums of humanity have hitherto
*gone down*? Will it perhaps be said of us one day that we too,
*steering westward, hoped to reach an India* – but that it was our
fate to be wrecked against infinity? Or, my brothers. Or? –

[D 575]

## 180

*Consciousness of appearance.* – In what a marvellous and new and at the same time terrible and ironic relationship with the totality of existence do I feel myself to stand with my knowledge! I have *discovered* for myself that the old human and animal world, indeed the entire prehistory and past of all sentient being, works on, loves on, hates on, thinks on in me – I have suddenly awoken in the midst of this dream but only to the consciousness that I am dreaming and that I *have* to go on dreaming in order not to be destroyed: as the sleep-walker has to go on dreaming in order not to fall. What is 'appearance' to me now! Certainly not the opposite of some kind of being – what can I possibly say about being of any kind that is not a predicate of its appearance! Certainly not a dead mask placed over an unknown 'x', which could, if one wished, be removed! Appearance is for me the active and living itself, which goes so far in its self-mockery as to allow me to feel that there is nothing here but appearance and will-o'-the-wisp and a flickering dance of spirits – that among all these dreamers I, too, the 'man of knowledge', dance my dance, that the man of knowledge is a means of spinning out the earthly dance and to that extent one of the masters-of-ceremonies of existence, and that the sublime consistency and unity of all knowledge is and will be perhaps the supreme means of *preserving* the universality of dreaming and the mutual intelligibility of all these dreamers, and thereby *the continuance of the dream.*

[*GS* 54]

## 181

*New struggles.* – After Buddha was dead, his shadow was for centuries still pointed out in a cave – an immense, frightful shadow. God is dead: but, men being what they are, perhaps there will for millennia still be caves in which his shadow is pointed out. – And we – we still have to conquer his shadow too!

[*GS* 108]

## 182

*Horizon: infinity.* – We have left the land and taken to our ship! We have burned our bridges – more, we have burned our land behind us! Now, little ship, take care! The ocean lies all around you; true, it is not always roaring, and sometimes it lies there as if it were silken and golden and a gentle favourable dream. But there will be times when you will know that it is infinite and that there is nothing more terrible than infinity . . . Alas, if homesickness for land should assail you, as if there were more *freedom* there – and there is no longer any 'land'!

[*GS* 124]

## 183

*Preparatory men.* – I greet all the signs that a more manly, warlike age is coming, which will, above all, bring valour again into honour! For it has to prepare the way for a yet higher age, and assemble the force which that age will one day have need of – that age which will carry heroism into knowledge and *wage war* for the sake of ideas and their consequences. To that end many brave pioneers are needed now [. . .] men who know how to be silent, solitary, resolute, [. . .] who have an innate disposition to seek in all things that which must be *overcome* in them: men to whom cheerfulness, patience, simplicity and contempt for the great vanities belong just as much as do generosity in victory and indulgence towards the little vanities of the defeated: [. . .] men with their own festivals, their own work-days, their own days of mourning, accustomed to and assured in command and equally ready to obey when necessary, equally proud in the one case as in the other, equally serving their own cause: men more imperilled, men more fruitful, happier men! For believe me! – the secret of realizing the greatest fruitfulness and the greatest enjoyment of existence is: to *live dangerously*! Build your cities on the slopes of Vesuvius! Send your ships out into uncharted seas! Live in conflict with your equals and with yourselves! Be robbers and ravagers as long as you cannot be rulers and owners, you men of knowledge! The time will soon be past when you could be content to live concealed in the woods like timid deer! [. . .]

[*GS* 283]

# 184

*On board ship!* – If one considers the effect on every individual of a philosophical total justification of his way of living and thinking – it is like a warming, scorching, fructifying sun which shines especially for him, it makes him indifferent to praise or blame, self-contented, rich, generous with happiness and benevolence, it constantly transforms evil to good, brings all his forces to blossom and ripeness and forbids the small and great weeds of anger and vexation to flourish – then one at last cries out: oh that many such new suns might be created! The evil, the unfortunate, the exceptional man too shall have his philosophy, his rights, his sunshine! It is not pity they need! [. . .] They need a new *justice*! And a new watchword! And new philosophers! The moral earth too is round! The moral earth too has its antipodes! The antipodes too have a right to exist! There is another new world to discover – and more than one! On board ship, philosophers!

[*GS* 289]

# 185

*What our cheerfulness signifies.* – The greatest recent event – that 'God is dead', that belief in the Christian God has become unbelievable – is already beginning to cast its first shadows over Europe. For the few, at least, whose eyes, the *suspicion* in whose eyes is strong and subtle enough for this spectacle, it seems as though some sun had just gone down, some ancient profound trust had been turned round into doubt: to them our old world must appear daily more crepuscular, untrust-worthy, stranger, 'older'. On the whole, however, one has to say that the event itself is much too great, too distant, too re-mote from the comprehension of many for news of it even to have *arrived* yet; not to speak of many knowing already *what* has really taken place – and what, now that this belief has been undermined, must now fall in because it was built on this be-lief, leaned on it, had grown into it: for example, our entire European morality. This protracted abundance and succession of demolition, destruction, decline, overturning which now stands before us: who today could divine enough of this to feel obliged to be the teacher and herald of this tremendous logic of terror, the prophet of a darkening and eclipse of the sun such as there has probably never yet been on earth? ... Even we born readers of riddles, who wait, as it were, on the mountains, set between today and tomorrow and yoked to the contradiction between today and tomorrow, we first-born and premature-born of the coming century, to whom the shadows which must soon envelop Europe *ought* already to have come into sight: why is it that even we lack any real participation in this darkening, above all behold its advent without any care or fear for *ourselves*? Do we perhaps still stand too much within the *immediate consequences* of this event – and these immediate consequences, its consequences for *us*, are, conversely from what one could expect, in no way sad and darkening but, rather, like a new, hard to describe kind of light, happiness, alleviation, encouragement, dawn ... We philosophers and 'free spirits' in fact feel at the news that the 'old God is dead' as if illumined by a new dawn; our heart overflows with gratitude, astonishment, presentiment, expec-tation – at last the horizon seems to us again free, even if it is not bright, at last our ships can put out again, no matter what

the danger, every daring venture of knowledge is again permitted, the sea, *our* sea again lies there open before us, perhaps
there has never yet been such an 'open sea'.

[*GS* 343 (1887)]


# 186

*The great health.* – We new, nameless, ill-understood premature-
born of a yet undemonstrated future – we need for a new goal
also a new means, namely a new health, a stronger, shrewder,
tougher, more daring, more cheerful health than any has been
hitherto. He whose soul thirsts to have experienced the whole
compass of values and desiderata hitherto and to have sailed
around every coast of this 'Middle Sea' of ideals, who wants
to know from the adventures of his own most personal experience how a conqueror and discoverer of the ideal feels, likewise how an artist, a saint, a lawgiver, a sage, a scholar, a man
of piety, a prophet, a divine hermit of the old stamp feels: he
needs one thing before all else, *great health* – a health such as
one does not merely have but has continually to win because
one has again and again to sacrifice it! ... And now, after
having been thus under way for a long time, we argonauts of
the ideal, braver perhaps than is prudent and often enough
shipwrecked and come to grief but, as said, healthier than
others would like us to be, dangerously healthy, healthy again
and again – it seems to us as if we have, as a reward, a yet undiscovered country before us whose boundaries none has ever
seen, a land beyond all known lands and corners of the ideal,
a world so over-full of the beautiful, strange, questionable,
terrible and divine that our curiosity and our thirst for possession are both beside themselves – so that nothing can any
longer satisfy us! How, after such prospects and with such a
ravenous hunger in conscience and knowledge, could we remain content with the *man of the present*? [...] Another ideal
runs ahead of us, a strange, seductive, dangerous ideal to
which we do not want to convert anyone because we do not

easily admit that anyone has a *right to it*: the ideal of a spirit who naively, that is to say, impulsively and from overflowing plenitude and power, plays with everything hitherto called holy, good, untouchable, divine; for whom the highest things by which the people reasonably enough take their standards would signify something like a danger, a corruption, a degradation, or at least a recreation, a blindness, a temporary self-forgetfulness; the ideal of a human-superhuman well-being and well-wishing which will often enough seem *inhuman*, for example when it is set beside the whole of earthly seriousness hitherto, beside every kind of solemnity in gesture, word, tone, glance, morality and task as their most corporal involuntary parody – and with which, in spite of all that, perhaps *the great seriousness* first arises, the real question-mark is first set up, the destiny of the soul veers round, the clock-hand moves on, the tragedy *begins* . . .

[*GS* 382 (1887)]

## 187

What alone can *our* teaching be? – That no one *gives* a human being his qualities: not God, not society, not his parents or ancestors, not *he himself* (– the nonsensical idea here last rejected was propounded, as 'intelligible freedom', by Kant, and perhaps also by Plato before him). *No one* is accountable for existing at all, or for being constituted as he is, or for living in the circumstances and surroundings in which he lives. The fatality of his nature cannot be disentangled from the fatality of all that which has been and will be. He is *not* the result of a special design, a will, a purpose; he is *not* the subject of an attempt to attain an 'ideal of man' or an 'ideal of happiness' or an 'ideal of morality' – it is absurd to want to *hand over* his nature to some purpose or other. *We* invented the concept 'purpose': in reality purpose is *lacking* . . . One is necessary, one is a piece of fate, one belongs to the whole, one *is* in the whole – there exists nothing which could judge, measure, compare, condemn our being, for that would be to judge, measure, condemn the whole . . . *But nothing exists apart from the whole!* – That no one is any longer made accountable, that the kind of being manifested cannot be traced back to a *causa prima*, that the world is a unity neither as sensorium nor as 'spirit', *this alone is the great liberation* – thus alone is the *innocence* of becoming restored . . . The concept 'God' has hitherto been the greatest *objection* to existence . . . We deny God; in denying God, we deny accountability: only by doing *that* do we redeem the world. –

[*T The Four Great Errors* 8]

# PART THREE

## 188

There is a *defiance of oneself* of which many forms of asceticism
are among the most sublimated expressions. For certain men
feel so great a need to exercise their strength and lust for
power that, in default of other objects or because their efforts
in other directions have always miscarried, they at last hit
upon the idea of tyrannizing over certain parts of their own
nature, over, as it were, segments or stages of themselves.
Thus some thinkers confess to views which are plainly not
calculated to increase or improve their reputation; some formally call down the disrespect of others upon themselves when
by keeping silent they could easily have remained respected
men. [. . .] Thus a man climbs on dangerous paths in the
highest mountains so as to mock at his fears and trembling
knees. [. . .] This division of oneself, this mockery of one's
own nature, this *spernere se sperni* of which the religions have
made so much, is actually a very high degree of vanity. The
entire morality of the Sermon on the Mount belongs here:
man takes a real delight in oppressing himself with excessive
claims and afterwards idolizing this tyrannically demanding
something in his soul. In every ascetic morality man worships
a part of himself as God and for that he needs to diabolize
the other part.

[*HA* 137]

## 189

*Artist's ambition.* – The Greek artists, the tragedians for example, poetized in order to conquer; their whole art cannot
be thought of apart from contest: Hesiod's good Eris, ambition, gave their genius its wings. [. . .]

[*HA* 170]

## 190

*The tyrants of the spirit.* – Only where the radiance of the myth
falls is the life of the Greeks bright; elsewhere it is gloomy.
Now, the Greek philosophers deprived themselves of precisely this myth: is it not as if they wanted to move out of the
sunshine into shadows and gloom? But no plant avoids the
light; fundamentally these philosophers were only seeking a
*brighter* sun, the myth was not pure, not lucid enough for
them. They discovered this light in their knowledge, in that
which each of them called his 'truth'. [. . .] These philosophers
possessed a firm belief in themselves and their 'truth' and
with it they overthrew all their contemporaries and predecessors; each of them was a warlike brutal *tyrant.* [. . .] They
were tyrants, that is to say, that which every Greek wanted
to be and what everyone was when he *could* be. Perhaps Solon
alone constitutes an exception; he says in his poems how he
disdained personal tyranny. But he did it for love of his work,
of his lawgiving; and to be a lawgiver is a more sublimated
form of tyranny. Parmenides also gave laws, Pythagoras and
Empedocles probably did also; Anaximander founded a city.
Plato was the incarnate desire to become the supreme philosophical lawgiver and founder of states; he appears to have
suffered terribly from the non-fulfilment of his nature, and
towards the end of his life his soul became full of the blackest
gall. [. . .]

[*HA* 261]

# 191

*What we are most subtle in.* – Because for many thousands of
years one thought that *things* (nature, tools, property of all
kinds) were also alive and animate, with the power to cause
harm and to evade human purposes, the feeling of impotence
has been much greater and much more common among men
than it would otherwise have been: for one needed to secure
oneself against things, just as against men and animals, by
force, constraint, flattering, treaties, sacrifices – and here is the
origin of most superstitious practices, that is to say, of a considerable, *perhaps preponderant* and yet wasted and useless con-
stituent of all the activity hitherto pursued by man! – But because the feeling of impotence and fear was in a state of almost continuous stimulation so strongly and for so long, the
*feeling of power* has evolved to such a degree of *subtlety* that in
this respect man is now a match for the most delicate gold-
balance. It has become his strongest propensity; the means
discovered for creating this feeling almost constitute the history of culture.

[*D* 23]

# 192

*Brahminism and Christianity.* – There are recipes for the feeling
of power, firstly for those who can control themselves and
who are thereby accustomed to a feeling of power; then for
those in whom precisely this is lacking. Brahminism has
catered for men of the former sort, Christianity for men of the
latter.

[*D* 65]

# 193

*The striving for distinction.* – The striving for distinction keeps
a constant eye on the next man and wants to know what his

feelings are: but the empathy which this drive requires for its gratification is far from being harmless or sympathetic or kind. We want, rather, to perceive or divine how the next man outwardly or inwardly *suffers* from us, how he loses control over himself and surrenders to the impressions our hand or even merely the sight of us makes upon him; and even when he who strives after distinction makes and wants to make a joyful, elevating or cheering impression, he nonetheless enjoys this success not inasmuch as he has given joy to the next man or elevated or cheered him, but inasmuch as he has *impressed* himself on the soul of the other, changed its shape and ruled over it at his own sweet will. The striving for distinction is the striving for domination over the next man, though it be a very indirect domination and only felt or even dreamed. There is a long scale of degrees of this secretly desired domination, and a complete catalogue of them would be almost the same thing as a history of culture, from the earliest, still grotesque barbarism up to the grotesqueries of over-refinement and morbid idealism. The striving for distinction brings with it *for the next man* – to name only a few steps on the ladder: torment, then blows, then terror, then fearful astonishment, then wonderment, then envy, then admiration, then elevation, then joy, then cheerfulness, then laughter, then derision, then mockery, then ridicule, then giving blows, then imposing torment: – here at the end of the ladder stands the *ascetic* and martyr, who feels the highest enjoyment by himself enduring, as a consequence of his drive for distinction, precisely that which, on the first step of the ladder, his counterpart the *barbarian* imposes on others on whom and before whom he wants to distinguish himself. The triumph of the ascetic over himself [. . .] this final tragedy of the drive for distinction in which there is only one character burning and consuming himself – this is a worthy conclusion and one appropriate to the commencement: in both cases an unspeakable happiness at the *sight of torment*! Indeed, happiness, conceived of as the liveliest feeling of power, has perhaps been nowhere greater on earth than in the souls of superstitious ascetics. [. . .] I believe that in this

whole species of inner experience we are now incompetent
novices groping after the solution of riddles: they knew more
about these infamous refinements of self-enjoyment 4,000
years ago. The creation of the world: perhaps it was then
thought of by some Indian dreamer as an ascetic operation
on the part of a god! Perhaps the god wanted to banish himself into active and moving nature as into an instrument of
torture, in order thereby to feel his bliss and power doubled!
And supposing it was a god of love: what enjoyment for such
a god to create *suffering* men, to suffer divinely and super-
humanly from the ceaseless torment of the sight of them, and
thus to tyrannize over himself! And even supposing it was
not only a god of love, but also a god of holiness and sinless-
ness: what deliriums of the divine ascetic can be imagined
when he creates sin and sinners and eternal damnation and a
vast abode of eternal affliction and eternal groaning and sigh-
ing! – It is not altogether impossible that the souls of Dante,
Paul, Calvin and their like may also once have penetrated the
gruesome secrets of such voluptuousness of power – and in
face of such souls one can ask: is the circle of striving for distinction really at an end with the ascetic? Could this circle
not be run through again from the beginning [. . .] doing hurt
to others in order thereby to hurt *oneself*, in order then to
triumph over oneself and one's pity and to revel in an ex-
tremity of power! – Excuse these extravagant reflections on all
that may have been possible on earth through the psychical
extravagance of the lust for power!

[*D* 113]

## 194

*Praise and blame.* – If a war proves unsuccessful one asks who
was to 'blame' for the war; if it ends in victory one praises its
instigator. Guilt is always sought wherever there is failure;
for failure brings with it a depression of spirits against which
the sole remedy is instinctively applied: a new excitation of

the *feeling of power* – and this is to be discovered in the *condemnation* of the 'guilty'. [. . .] To condemn oneself can also be a means of restoring the feeling of power after a defeat. [. . .]

[*D* 140]


## 195

*On grand politics.* – However much utility and vanity, those of individuals as of peoples, may play a part in *grand politics*: the strongest tide which carries them forward is the *need for the feeling of power*, which from time to time streams up out of inexhaustible wells not only in the souls of princes and the powerful but not least in the lower orders of the people. There comes again and again the hour when the masses are *ready* to stake their life, their goods, their conscience, their virtue so as to acquire that higher enjoyment and as a victorious, capriciously tyrannical nation to rule over other nations (or to think it rules). [. . .] The great conquerors have always mouthed the pathetic language of virtue: they have had around them masses in a condition of elevation who wanted to hear only the most elevated language. Strange madness of moral judgements! When man possesses the feeling of power he feels and calls himself *good*: and it is precisely then that the others upon whom he has to *discharge* his power feel and call him *evil*! [. . .]

[*D* 189]


## 196

*Danae and God in gold.* – Whence comes this immoderate impatience which nowadays turns a man into a criminal under circumstances which would be more compatible with an opposite tendency? For if one man employs false weights, another burns his house down after he has insured it for a large sum, a third counterfeits false coins, if three-quarters of the upper classes indulge in permitted fraud and have the stock exchange and speculations on their conscience: what drives them? Not actual need, for they are not so badly off, perhaps they even eat and drink without a care – but they are afflicted day and night by a fearful impatience at the slow way with which their money is accumulating and by an equally fearful pleasure in and love of accumulated money. In this impatience and this love, however, there turns up again that fanaticism of the *lust for power* which was in former times inflamed by the belief one was in possession of the truth and which bore such beautiful names that one could thenceforward venture to be inhuman *with a good conscience* (to burn Jews, heretics and good books and exterminate entire higher cultures such as those of Peru and Mexico). The means employed by the lust for power have changed, but the same volcano continues to glow, the impatience and the immoderate love demand their sacrifice: and what one formerly did 'for the sake of God' one now does for the sake of money, that is to say, for the sake of that which *now* gives the highest feeling of power and good conscience.

[*D* 204]

## 197

*The demon of power.* – Not necessity, not desire – no, the love of power is the demon of men. Let them have everything – health, food, a place to live, entertainment – they are and remain unhappy and low-spirited: for the demon waits and waits and will be satisfied. Take everything from them and satisfy this, and they are almost happy – as happy as men and demons can be. But why do I repeat this? Luther has said it already, and better than I, in the verses: 'Let them take from us our body, goods, honour, children, wife: let it all go – the kingdom [*Reich*] must yet remain to us!' Yes! Yes! The '*Reich*'!

[*D* 262]

# 198

*Effect of happiness.* – The first effect of happiness is the *feeling of power*: this wants to *express itself*, either to us ourselves, or to other men, or to ideas or imaginary beings. The most common modes of expression are: to bestow, to mock, to destroy – all three out of a common basic drive.

[*D* 356]

# 199

*No utilitarians.* – 'Power against which much ill is done and meditated is worth more than impotence which encounters only good' – thus the Greeks felt. That is to say: they valued the feeling of power more highly than any sort of utility or good reputation.

[*D* 360]

# 200

*Field-dispensary of the soul.* – What is the strongest remedy? – Victory.

[*D* 571]

# 201

*On the theory of the feeling of power.* – By doing good and doing ill one exercises one's power upon others – more one does not want! By *doing ill* upon those to whom we first have to make our power palpable [. . .] By *doing good* and well-wishing upon those who are in some way already dependent upon us [. . .] Whether we make a sacrifice in doing good or ill does not alter the ultimate value of our actions; even if we stake our life, as the martyr does for the sake of his Church – it is a sacrifice to *our* desire for power or for the purpose of preserving our feeling of power. He who feels 'I am in possession of the truth', how many possessions does he not let go in order to rescue this sensation! What does he not throw overboard in order to remain 'aloft' – that is to say, *above* others who lack the 'truth'! Certainly, the condition in which we do ill is seldom as pleasant, as unmixedly pleasant, as that in which we do good – it is a sign that we still lack power [. . .]

[*GS* 13]

### 202

Zarathustra has seen many lands and many peoples: thus he has discovered the good and evil of many peoples. Zarathustra has found no greater power on earth than good and evil.

No people could live without evaluating: but if it wishes to maintain itself it must not evaluate as its neighbour evaluates.

Much that seemed good to one people seemed shame and disgrace to another: thus I found. I found much that was called evil in one place was in another decked with purple honours.

One neighbour never understood another: his soul was always amazed at his neighbour's madness and wickedness.

A table of values hangs over every people. Behold, it is the table of its overcomings; behold, it is the voice of its will to power.

What it accounts hard it calls praiseworthy; what it accounts indispensable and hard it calls good; and that which relieves the greatest need, the rare, the hardest of all – it glorifies as holy.

Whatever causes it to rule and conquer and glitter, to the dread and envy of its neighbour, that it accounts the sublimest, the paramount, the evaluation and the meaning of all things.

Truly, my brothers, if you only knew a people's need and

land and sky and neighbour, you could surely divine the law of its overcomings, and why it is upon this ladder that it mounts towards its hope. [. . .]

[Z I *Of the Thousand and One Goals*]


## 203

What urges you on and arouses your ardour, you wisest of men, do you call it 'will to truth'?

Will to the conceivability of all being: that is what *I* call your will!

You first want to *make* all being conceivable: for, with a healthy mistrust, you doubt whether it is in fact conceivable.

But it must bend and accommodate itself to you! Thus will your will have it. It must become smooth and subject to the mind as the mind's mirror and reflection.

That is your entire will, you wisest men; it is a will to power; and that is so even when you talk of good and evil and of the assessment of values.

You want to create the world before which you can kneel: this is your ultimate hope and intoxication.

The ignorant, to be sure, the people – they are like a river down which a boat swims: and in the boat, solemn and disguised, sit the assessments of value.

You put your will and your values upon the river of becoming; what the people believe to be good and evil betrays to me an ancient will to power.

It was you, wisest men, who put such passengers in this boat and gave them splendour and proud names – you and your ruling will! [. . .]

But that you may understand my teaching about good and evil, I shall relate to you my teaching about life and about the nature of all living creatures.

I have followed the living creature, I have followed the greatest and the smallest paths, that I might understand its nature. [. . .]

But wherever I found living creatures, there, too, I heard the language of obedience. All living creatures are obeying creatures.

And this is the second thing: he who cannot obey himself will be commanded. That is the nature of living creatures.

But this is the third thing I heard: that commanding is more difficult than obeying. And not only because the commander bears the burden of all who obey, and that this burden can easily crush him.

In all commanding there appeared to me to be an experiment and a risk: and the living creature always risks himself when he commands.

Yes, even when he commands himself: then also must he make amends for his commanding. He must become judge and avenger and victim of his own law.

How has this come about? thus I asked myself. What persuades the living creature to obey and to command and to practise obedience even in commanding? [. . .] Where I found a living creature, there I found will to power: and even in the will of the servant I found the will to be master.

The will of the weaker persuades it to serve the stronger; its will wants to be master over those weaker still: this delight alone it is unwilling to forgo.

And as the lesser surrenders to the greater, that it may have delight and power over the least of all, so the greatest, too, surrenders and for the sake of power stakes – life.

The devotion of the greatest is to encounter risk and danger and play dice for death.

And where sacrifice and service and loving glances are, there, too, is will to be master. There the weaker steals by secret paths into the castle and even into the heart of the more powerful – and steals the power.

And life itself told me this secret: 'Behold,' it said, 'I am that *which must overcome itself again and again.*

'To be sure, you call it will to procreate or impulse towards a goal, towards the higher, more distant, more manifold: but all this is one and one secret.

'I would rather perish than renounce this one thing; and truly, where there is perishing and the falling of leaves, behold, there life sacrifices itself – for the sake of power!

'That I have to be struggle and becoming and goal and conflict of goals: ah, he who divines my will surely divines, too, along what *crooked* paths it has to go!

'Whatever I create and however much I love it – soon I have to oppose it and my love: thus will my will have it.

'And you too, enlightened man, are only a path and footstep of my will: truly, my will to power walks with the feet of your will to truth!

'He who shot the doctrine of "will to existence" at truth certainly did not hit the truth: this will – does not exist!

'For what does not exist cannot will; but that which is in existence, how could it still want to come into existence?

'Only where life is, there is also will: not will to life, but – so I teach you – will to power!

'The living creature values many things higher than life itself: yet out of this evaluation itself speaks – the will to power!' [...]

[Z II *Of Self-Overcoming*]


## 204

Philosophers are given to speaking of the will as if it were the best-known thing in the world; Schopenhauer, indeed, would have us understand that the will alone is truly known to us, known completely, known without deduction or addition. But it seems to me that in this case, too, Schopenhauer has done only what philosophers in general are given to doing: that he has taken up a *popular prejudice* and exaggerated it. Willing seems to me to be above all something *complicated*, something that is a unity only as a word – and it is precisely in this *one* word that the popular prejudice resides which has overborne the always inadequate caution of the philosophers. Let us therefore be more cautious for once, let us be 'unphilo-

sophical' – let us say: in all willing there is, first of all, a
plurality of sensations, namely the sensation of the condition
we *leave*, the sensation of the condition towards which we *go*,
the sensation of this 'leaving' and 'going' itself, and then also
an accompanying muscular sensation which, even without our
putting 'arms and legs' in motion, comes into play through a
kind of habit as soon as we 'will'. As feelings, and indeed
many varieties of feeling, can therefore be recognized as an
ingredient of will, so, in the second place, can thinking: in
every act of will there is a commanding thought – and do not
imagine that this thought can be separated from the 'willing',
as though will would then remain over! Thirdly, will is not
only a complex of feeling and thinking, but above all an
*emotion*: and in fact the emotion of command. What is called
'freedom of will' is essentially the emotion of superiority over
him who must obey: 'I am free, "he" must obey' – this consciousness adheres to every will, as does that tense attention,
that straight look which fixes itself exclusively on *one* thing,
that unconditional evaluation 'this and nothing else is necessary now', that inner certainty that one will be obeyed, and
whatever else pertains to the state of him who gives commands. A man who *wills* – commands something in himself
which obeys or which he believes obeys. But now observe the
strangest thing of all about the will – about this so complex
thing for which people have only *one* word: inasmuch as in
the given circumstances we at the same time command *and*
obey, and as the side which obeys knows the sensations of constraint, compulsion, pressure, resistance, motion which usually
begin immediately after the act of will; inasmuch as, on the
other hand, we are in the habit of disregarding and deceiving
ourselves over this duality by means of the synthetic concept
'I'; so a whole chain of erroneous conclusions and consequently of false evaluations of the will itself has become
attached to the will as such – so that he who wills believes
wholeheartedly that willing *suffices* for action. Because in the
great majority of cases willing takes place only where the
effect of the command, that is to say obedience, that is to say

action, was to be *expected*, the *appearance* has translated itself into the sensation, as if there were here a *necessity of effect*. Enough: he who wills believes with a tolerable degree of certainty that will and action are somehow one – he attributes the success, the carrying out of the willing, to the will itself, and thereby enjoys an increase of that sensation of power which all success brings with it. 'Freedom of will' – is the expression for that complex condition of pleasure of the person who wills, who commands and at the same time identifies himself with the executor of the command – who as such also enjoys the triumph over resistances involved but who thinks it was his will itself which overcame these resistances. He who wills adds in this way the sensations of pleasure of the successful executive agents, the serviceable 'under-wills' or under-souls – for our body is only a social structure composed of many souls – to his sensations of pleasure as commander. [. . .] In all willing it is absolutely a question of commanding and obeying, on the basis, as I have said already, of a social structure composed of many 'souls': on which account a philosopher should claim the right to include willing as such within the field of morality: that is, of morality understood as the theory of the relations of dominance under which the phenomenon 'life' arises. –

[*BGE* 19]

### 205

Granted that nothing is 'given' as real except our world of desires and passions, that we can rise or sink to no other 'reality' than the reality of our drives – for thinking is only the relationship of these drives to one another – : is it not permitted to make the experiment and ask the question whether this which is given does not *suffice* for an understanding even of the so-called mechanical (or 'material') world? I do not mean as a deception, an 'appearance', an 'idea' (in the Berkeleyan and Schopenhauerian sense), but as possessing the same degree of reality as our emotions themselves – as a more primitive form of the world of emotions in which everything still lies locked in mighty unity and then branches out and develops in the organic process [. . .]? In the end, the question is whether we really recognize will as *efficient*, whether we believe in the causality of will: if we do – and fundamentally belief in *this* is precisely our belief in causality itself – then we *have* to make the experiment of positing causality of will hypothetically as the only one. 'Will' can of course operate only on 'will' and not on 'matter' (not on 'nerves', for example): enough, one must venture the hypothesis that wherever 'effects' are recognized, will is operating upon will. – Granted finally that one succeeded in explaining our entire instinctual life as the development and ramification of *one* basic form of will – as will to power, as is *my* theory –; granted that one could trace all organic functions back to this will to power and could also find in it the solution to the problem of procreation and nourishment – they are *one* problem – one would have acquired the right to define *all* efficient force unequivocally as: *will to power*. The world seen from within, the world described and defined according to its 'intelligible character' – it would be 'will to power' and nothing else. –

[*BGE* 36]

## 206

To refrain from mutual injury, mutual violence, mutual exploitation, to equate one's own will with that of another: this may in a certain rough sense become good manners between individuals if the conditions for it are present (namely, if their strength and value standards are in fact similar and they both belong to *one* body). As soon as there is a desire to take this principle further, however, and if possible even as the *fundamental principle of society*, it at once reveals itself for what it is: as the will to the *denial* of life, as the principle of dissolution and decay. [. . .] life itself is *essentially* appropriation, injury, overpowering of the strange and weaker, suppression, severity, imposition of one's own forms, incorporation and, at the least and mildest, exploitation. [. . .] 'Exploitation' does not pertain to a corrupt or imperfect or primitive society: it pertains to the *essence* of the living thing as a fundamental organic function, it is a consequence of the intrinsic will to power which is precisely the will of life. [. . .]

[*BGE* 259]

## 207

[. . .] To want to preserve oneself is the expression of a state of distress, a limitation of the actual basic drive of life, which aims at *extension of power* and in obedience to this will often enough calls self-preservation into question and sacrifices it. [. . .] in nature the *rule* is not the state of distress, it is superfluity, prodigality, even to the point of absurdity. The struggle for existence is only an *exception*, a temporary restriction of the will of life; the struggle, great and small, everywhere turns on ascendancy, on growth and extension, in accordance with the will to power, which is precisely the will of life.

[*GS* 349 (1887)]

## 208

[. . .] the cause of the origin of a thing and that thing's final utility, its employment and disposition in a system of objectives, lie *toto coelo* apart [. . .] No matter how well one may have understood the *utility* of some physiological organ (or of a legal institution, a social custom, a political usage, a form in the arts or in the religious cult) one has not therewith understood anything in regard to its origin [. . .] all objectives, all utilities are only *signs* that a will to power has become master of something less powerful and has imprinted upon it the sense of a function; and the entire history of a 'thing', an organ, a usage can in this way be a continuing chain of signs of ever new interpretations and arrangements whose causes themselves do not have to be connected with one another but rather in some cases merely follow and replace one another by chance. [. . .] Things are no different even within an individual organism: with every essential growth of the whole the 'meaning' of the individual organs is shifted – in some cases their partial destruction or a reduction in their numbers [. . .] can be a sign of increasing strength and perfection. I mean to say: even a partial *becoming useless*, an atrophying and degeneration, a loss of meaning and purposiveness, in short death, is among the conditions of actual *progressus*; and this always appears in the form of a will and way to *greater power*, and is always carried through at the expense of numerous smaller powers. The magnitude of an 'advance' is even to be *measured* by the mass of things that had to be sacrificed to it; mankind in the mass sacrificed to the prosperity of a single *stronger* species of man – that *would* be an advance [. . .]

[*GM* '*Guilt*', '*Bad Conscience*' *and the Like* 12]

## 209

What is good? – All that heightens the feeling of power, the will to power, power itself in man.

What is bad? – All that proceeds from weakness.

What is happiness? – The feeling that power *increases* – that a resistance is overcome. [. . .]

[*A* 2]

# SUPERMAN

## 210

'*Will a self*'. – Active, successful natures act, not according to the dictum 'know thyself', but as if there hovered before them the commandment: *will* a self and thou shalt *become* a self. [. . .]

[*AOM* 366]

## 211

*A kind of cult of the passions.* – In order to raise an accusation against the whole nature of the world, you dismal philosophical blindworms speak of the *terrible character* of human passions. As if wherever there have been passions there had also been terribleness! As if this kind of terribleness was bound to persist in the world! – Through a neglect of the *small* facts, through lack of self-observation and observation of those who are to be brought up, it is you yourselves who first allowed the passions to develop into such monsters that you are overcome by fear at the word 'passion'! It was up to you, and is up to us, to *take from* the passions their terrible character and thus prevent their becoming devastating torrents. – One should not inflate one's oversights into eternal fatalities; let us rather work honestly together on the task of transforming the passions [*Leidenschaften*] of mankind one and all into joys [*Freudenschaften*].

[*WS* 37]

## 212

*Overcoming of the passions.* – The man who has overcome his passions has entered into possession of the most fertile ground; like the colonist who has mastered the forests and swamps. To *sow* the seeds of good spiritual works in the soil of the subdued passions is then the immediate urgent task. The overcoming itself is only a *means,* not a goal; if it is not so viewed, all kinds of weeds and devilish nonsense will quickly spring up in this rich soil now unoccupied, and soon there will be more rank confusion than there ever was before.

[*WS* 53]

## 213

*Those who commend work.* – In the glorification of 'work', in the unwearied talk of the 'blessing of work', I see the same covert ideas as in the praise of useful impersonal actions: that of fear of everything individual. Fundamentally, one now feels at the sight of work – one always means by work that hard industriousness from early till late – that such work is the best policeman, that it keeps everyone in bounds and can mightily hinder the development of reason, covetousness, desire for independence. For it uses up an extraordinary amount of nervous energy, which is thus denied to reflection, brooding, dreaming, worrying, loving, hating; it sets a small goal always in sight and guarantees easy and regular satisfactions. Thus a society in which there is continual hard work will have more security: and security is now worshipped as the supreme divinity. – And now! Horror! Precisely the 'worker' has become *dangerous!* The place is swarming with 'dangerous individuals'! And behind them the danger of dangers – *the* individual!

[*D* 173]

## 214

*From a possible future.* – Is a state of affairs unthinkable in which the malefactor calls himself to account and publicly dictates his own punishment, in the proud feeling that he is thus honouring the law which he himself has made, that by punishing himself he is exercising his power, the power of the lawgiver? [. . .] Such would be the criminal of a possible future, who, to be sure, also presupposes a future lawgiving – one founded on the idea 'I submit only to the law which I myself have given, in great things and in small.'

[*D* 187]

## 215

*Victory over strength.* – If we consider all that has hitherto been reverenced as 'superhuman mind', as 'genius', we come to the sad conclusion that the intellectuality of mankind must on the whole have been something very low and paltry: it has hitherto required so little mind to feel at once considerably superior to it! Oh, the cheap fame of the 'genius'! How quickly his throne is established, how quickly worship of him becomes a practice! We are still on our knees before *strength* – after the ancient custom of slaves – and yet when the degree of *worthiness to be reverenced* is fixed, only the *degree of rationality in strength* is decisive: we must assess to what extent precisely strength has been overcome by something higher, in the service of which it now stands as means and instrument! But for such an assessment there are still far too few eyes, indeed the assessment of the genius is still usually regarded as a sacrilege. And so perhaps the most beautiful still appears only in the dark, and sinks, scarcely born, into eternal night – I mean the spectacle of that strength which employs genius *not for works* but for *itself as a work*; that is, for its own constraint, for the purification of its imagination, for the imposition of order and choice upon the influx of tasks and impressions. The great

human being is still in precisely the greatest thing that demands reverence invisible like a too distant star, his *victory
over strength* remains without eyes to see it and consequently
without song and singer. The order of rank of greatness for
all past mankind has not yet been determined.

[*D* 548]

## 216

*What we are at liberty to do.* – One can dispose of one's drives
like a gardener and, though few know it, cultivate the shoots
of anger, pity, curiosity, vanity as productively and profitably
as a beautiful fruit tree on a trellis; one can do it with the good
or bad taste of a gardener and, as it were, in the French or
English or Dutch or Chinese fashion; one can also let nature
rule and only attend to a little embellishment and tidying-up
here and there; one can, finally, without paying any attention
to them at all, let the plants grow up and fight their fight out
among themselves – indeed, one can take delight in such a
wilderness, and desire precisely this delight, though it gives
one some trouble, too. All this we are at liberty to do: but
how many know we are at liberty to do it? Do the majority
not *believe* in *themselves* as in complete *fully-developed facts?*
Have the great philosophers not put their seal on this prejudice
with the doctrine of the unchangeability of character?

[*D* 560]

## 217

*What makes heroic?* – To go to meet simultaneously one's
greatest sorrow and one's greatest hope.

*What do you believe in?* – In this: that the weight of all things
must be determined anew.

*What does your conscience say?* – 'You should become him
who you are.'

235

*Where lie your greatest dangers?* – In pity.

*What do you love in others?* – My hopes.

*Whom do you call bad?* – Him who always wants to make ashamed.

*What is to you the most humane thing?* – To spare anyone shame.

*What is the seal of freedom attained?* – No longer to be ashamed of oneself.

[*GS* 268–75]

## 218

*Excelsior!* – 'You will never again pray, never again worship, never again repose in limitless trust – you deny it to yourself to remain halted before an ultimate wisdom, ultimate good, ultimate power, and there unharness your thoughts – you have no perpetual guardian and friend for your seven solitudes [. . .] there is no longer for you any rewarder and recompenser, no final corrector – there is no longer any reason in what happens, no longer any love in what happens to you – there is no longer any resting-place open to your heart where it has only to find and no longer to seek, you resist any kind of ultimate peace, you want the eternal recurrence of war and peace – man of renunciation, will you renounce in all this? Who will give you the strength for it? No one has yet possessed this strength!' – There is a lake which one day denied it to itself to flow away and threw up a dam at the place where it formerly flowed away: since then this lake has risen higher and higher. Perhaps it is precisely that renunciation which will also lend us the strength by which the renunciation itself can be endured; perhaps man will rise higher and higher from that time when he no longer *flows out* into a God.

[*GS* 285]

## 219

*One thing is needed.* – 'To give style' to one's character – a great and rare art! He exercises it who surveys all that his nature presents in strength and weakness and then moulds it to an artistic plan until everything appears as art and reason, and even the weaknesses delight the eye. Here a large amount of second nature has been added, here a piece of original nature removed – in both instances with protracted practice and daily labour. Here that which is ugly but cannot be removed is concealed, there reinterpreted into the sublime [. . .] It will be the strong, imperious natures which experience their subtlest joy in exercising such control, in such constraint and perfecting under their own law [. . .]

[*GS* 290]

## 220

[. . .] Let us therefore *limit* ourselves to the purification of our opinions and evaluations and to the *creation of our own new tables of values* [. . .] We, however, *want to be those who we are* – the new, the unique, the incomparable, those who give themselves their own law, those who create themselves! [. . .]

[*GS* 335]

## 221

When Zarathustra arrived at the nearest of the towns lying against the forest, he found in that very place many people assembled in the market square: for it had been announced that a tightrope walker would be appearing. And Zarathustra spoke thus to the people:

*I teach you the superman.* Man is something that should be overcome. What have you done to overcome him?

All creatures hitherto have created something beyond themselves: and do you want to be the ebb of this great tide, and return to the animals rather than overcome man?

What is the ape to men? A laughing-stock or a painful embarrassment. And just so shall man be to the superman: a laughing-stock or a painful embarrassment.

You have made your way from worm to man, and much in you is still worm. Once you were apes, and even now man is more of an ape than any ape.

But he who is the wisest among you, he also is only a discord and hybrid of plant and of ghost. But do I bid you become ghosts or plants?

Behold, I teach you the superman.

The superman is the meaning of the earth. Let your will say: the superman *shall be* the meaning of the earth! [. . .]

What is the greatest thing you can experience? It is the hour of the great contempt. The hour in which even your happiness grows loathsome to you, and your reason and your virtue also.

The hour when you say: 'What good is my happiness? It is poverty and dirt and a miserable ease. But my happiness should justify existence itself!'

The hour when you say: 'What good is my reason? Does it long for knowledge as the lion for its food? It is poverty and dirt and a miserable ease!'

The hour when you say: 'What good is my virtue? It has not yet driven me mad! How tired I am of my good and my evil! It is all poverty and dirt and a miserable ease!'

The hour when you say: 'What good is my justice? I do not see that I am fire and hot coals. But the just man is fire and hot coals!'

The hour when you say: 'What good is my pity? Is not pity the cross upon which he who loves man is nailed? But my pity is no crucifixion!'

Have you ever spoken thus? Have you ever cried thus? Ah, that I had heard you crying thus!

It is not your sin but your moderation that cries to heaven, your very meanness in sinning cries to heaven!

Where is the lightning to lick you with its tongue? Where is the madness with which you should be cleansed?

Behold, I teach you the superman: he is this lightning, he is this madness! [. . .]

\*

Man is a rope, fastened between animal and superman – a rope over an abyss.

A dangerous going-across, a dangerous wayfaring, a dangerous looking-back, a dangerous shuddering and staying-still.

What is great in man is that he is a bridge and not a goal; what can be loved in man is that he is a *going-across* and a *down-going*.

I love those who do not know how to live except their lives be a down-going, for they are those who are going across.

I love the great despisers, for they are the great venerators and arrows of longing for the other bank.

I love those who do not first seek beyond the stars for reasons to go down and to be sacrifices: but who sacrifice themselves to the earth, that the earth may one day belong to the superman.

I love him who lives for knowledge and who wants knowledge that one day the superman may live. And thus he wills his own downfall.

I love him who works and invents that he may build a house for the superman and prepare earth, animals and plants for him: for thus he wills his own downfall.

I love him who loves his virtue: for virtue is will to downfall and an arrow of longing.

I love him who keeps back no drop of spirit for himself, but wants to be the spirit of his virtue entirely: thus he steps as spirit over the bridge.

I love him who makes a predilection and a fate of his virtue: thus for his virtue's sake he will live or not live.

I love him who does not want too many virtues. One virtue is more virtue than two, because it is more of a knot for fate to cling to.

I love him whose soul is lavish, who neither wants nor returns thanks: for he always gives and will not preserve himself.

I love him who is ashamed when the dice fall in his favour and who then asks: Am I then a cheat? – for he wants to perish.

I love him who throws golden words in advance of his deeds and always performs more than he promised: for he wills his own downfall.

I love him who justifies the men of the future and redeems the men of the past: for he wants to perish by the men of the present.

I love him who chastises his God because he loves his God: for he must perish by the anger of his God.

I love him whose soul is deep even in its ability to be wounded, and whom even a little thing can destroy: thus he is glad to go over the bridge.

I love him whose soul is over-full, so that he forgets himself and all things are in him: thus all things become his downfall.

I love him who is of a free spirit and a free heart: thus his head is only the bowels of his heart, but his heart drives him to his downfall.

I love all those who are like heavy drops falling singly from the dark cloud that hangs over mankind: they prophesy the coming of the lightning and as prophets they perish.

Behold, I am a prophet of the lightning and a heavy drop from the cloud: but this lightning is called *superman*.

[Z I Prologue 3–4]


### 222

[. . .] Once you had passions and called them evil. But now you have only your virtues: they grew out of your passions.

You laid your highest aim in the heart of these passions: then they became your virtues and joys.

And though you came from the race of the hot-tempered or of the lustful or of the fanatical or of the vindictive:

At last all your passions have become virtues and all your devils angels.

Once you had fierce dogs in your cellar: but they changed at last into birds and sweet singers.

From your poison you brewed your balsam: you milked your cow, affliction, now you drink the sweet milk of her udder.

And henceforward nothing evil shall come out of you, except it be the evil that comes from the conflict of your virtues. [...]

[*Z* I *Of Joys and Passions*]


### 223

[...] Do you call yourself free? I want to hear your ruling idea, and not that you have escaped from a yoke.

Are you such a man as *ought* to escape a yoke? There are many who threw off their final worth when they threw off their bondage.

Free from what? Zarathustra does not care about that! But your eye should clearly tell me: free *for* what?

Can you furnish yourself with your own good and evil and hang up your own will above yourself as a law? Can you be judge of yourself and avenger of your law?

It is terrible to be alone with the judge and avenger of one's own law. It is to be like a star thrown forth into empty space and into the icy breath of solitude. [...]

[*Z* I *Of the Way of the Creator*]

## 224

The figs are falling from the trees, they are fine and sweet; and as they fall their red skins split. I am a north wind to ripe figs.

Thus, like figs, do these teachings fall to you, my friends: now drink their juice and eat their sweet flesh! It is autumn all around and clear sky and afternoon.

Behold, what abundance is around us! And it is fine to gaze out upon distant seas from the midst of superfluity.

Once you said 'God' when you gazed upon distant seas; but now I have taught you to say 'superman'.

God is a supposition; but I want your supposing to reach no further than your creating will.

Could you *create* a god? – So be silent about all gods! But you could surely create the superman. [. . .]

God is a supposition: but I want your supposing to be bounded by conceivability.

Could you *conceive* a god? – But may the will to truth mean this to you: that everything shall be transformed into the humanly-conceivable, the humanly-evident, the humanly-palpable! You should follow your own senses to the end!

And you yourselves should create what you have hitherto called the world: the world should be formed in your image by your reason, your will, and your love! And truly, it will be to your happiness, you enlightened men!

And how should you endure life without this hope, you enlightened men? Neither in the incomprehensible nor in the irrational can you be at home.

But to reveal my heart entirely to you, friends: *if* there were gods, how could I endure not to be a god! *Therefore* there are no gods.

I, indeed, drew that conclusion; but now it draws me. [. . .]

[Z II *On the Blissful Islands*]

The most cautious people ask today: 'How may man still be preserved?' Zarathustra, however, asks as the sole and first one to do so: 'How shall man be *overcome*?'

The superman lies close to my heart, *he* is my paramount and sole concern – and *not* man: not the nearest, not the poorest, not the most suffering, not the best.

O my brothers, what I can love in man is that he is a going-across and a going-down. And in you, too, there is much that makes me love and hope.

That you have despised, you higher men, that makes me hope. For the great despisers are the great reverers.

That you have despaired, there is much to honour in that. For you have not learned how to submit, you have not learned petty prudence.

For today the petty people have become lord and master: they all preach submission and acquiescence and prudence and diligence and consideration and the long *et cetera* of petty virtues.

What is womanish, what stems from slavishness and especially from the mob hotchpotch: *that* now wants to become master of mankind's entire destiny – oh disgust! disgust! disgust!

*That* questions and questions and never tires: 'How may man preserve himself best, longest, most agreeably?' With that – they are the masters of the present.

Overcome for me these masters of the present, o my brothers – these petty people: *they* are the superman's greatest danger!

Overcome, you higher men, the petty virtues, the petty prudences, the sand-grain discretion, the ant-swarm inanity, miserable ease, the 'happiness of the greatest number!' [. . .]

*

'Man is evil' – all the wisest men have told me that to comfort me. Ah, if only it be true today! For evil is man's best strength.

'Man must grow better and more evil' – thus do *I* teach. The most evil is necessary for the superman's best.

It may have been good for that preacher of the petty people to bear and suffer the sin of man. I, however, rejoice in great sin as my great *consolation.* [. . .]

\*

Timid, ashamed, awkward, like a tiger whose leap has failed: this is how I have often seen you slink aside, you higher men. A *throw* you made had failed.

But what of that, you dice-throwers! You have not learned to play and mock as a man ought to play and mock. Are we not always seated at a great table for play and mockery?

And if great things you attempted have turned out failures, does that mean you yourselves are – failures? And if you yourselves have turned out failures, does that mean – man is a failure? If man has turned out a failure, however: very well! come on!

\*

Lift up your hearts, my brothers, high! higher! And do not forget your legs! Lift up your legs, too, you fine dancers: and better still, stand on your heads! [. . .]

Be like the wind when it rushes forth from its mountain caves: it will dance to its own pipe, the seas tremble and leap under its footsteps.

That which gives wings to asses and milks lionesses, all praise to that unruly spirit that comes to all the present and all the mob like a storm-wind

– that is enemy to all thistleheads and prying noses and to all withered leaves and weeds: all praise to that wild, good, free storm spirit that dances upon swamps and afflictions as upon meadows!

That hates the wasted dogs of the mob and all the ill-constituted brood of gloom: all praise to this spirit of all free spirits, the laughing storm that blows dust in the eyes of all the dim-sighted and ulcerated.

You higher men, the worst about you is: none of you has

learned to dance as a man ought to dance – to dance beyond yourselves! What does it matter that you are failures!

How much is still possible! So *learn* to laugh beyond yourselves! Lift up your hearts, you fine dancers, high! higher! and do not forget to laugh well.

This laughter's crown, this rose-wreath crown: to you, my brothers, do I throw this crown! I have canonized laughter: you higher men, *learn* – to laugh!

[Z IV *Of the Higher Man* 3, 5, 14, 19–20]

## 226

The man of an era of dissolution which mixes the races together and who therefore contains within him the inheritance of a diversified descent, that is to say contrary and often not merely contrary drives and values which struggle with one another and rarely leave one another in peace – such a man of late cultures and broken lights will, on average, be a rather weak man: his fundamental desire is that the war which he *is* should come to an end; happiness appears to him, in accord with a sedative (for example, Epicurean or Christian) medicine and mode of thought, pre-eminently as the happiness of repose, of tranquillity, of satiety, of unity at last attained, as a 'Sabbath of Sabbaths', to quote the holy rhetorician Augustine, who was himself such a man. – If, however, the contrariety and war in such a nature should act as one *more* stimulus and enticement to life – and if, on the other hand, in addition to powerful and irreconcilable drives, there has also been inherited and cultivated a proper mastery and subtlety in conducting a war against oneself, that is to say, self-control, self-outwitting: then there arise those marvellously incomprehensible and unfathomable men, those enigmatic men predestined for victory and the seduction of others, the fairest examples of which are Alcibiades and Caesar ( – to whom I should like to add that *first* European agreeable to my taste, the Hohenstaufen Friedrich II), and among artists perhaps Leonardo da

Vinci. They appear in precisely the same ages as those in which that rather weak type with his desire for rest comes to the fore: the two types belong together and originate in the same causes.

[*BGE* 200]

## 227

[. . .] You want if possible – and there is no madder 'if possible' – *to abolish suffering*; and we? – it really does seem that *we* would rather increase it and make it worse than it has ever been! Well-being as you understand it – that is no goal, that seems to us an *end*! A state which soon renders man ludicrous and contemptible – which makes it *desirable* that he should perish! The discipline of suffering, of *great* suffering – do you not know that it is *this* discipline alone which has created every elevation of mankind hitherto? That tension of the soul in misfortune which cultivates its strength, its terror at the sight of great destruction, its inventiveness and bravery in under- going, enduring, interpreting, exploiting misfortune, and whatever of depth, mystery, mask, spirit, cunning and great- ness has been bestowed upon it – has it not been bestowed through suffering, through the discipline of great suffering? In man, *creature* and *creator* are united: in man there is matter, fragment, excess, clay, mud, madness, chaos; but in man there is also creator, sculptor, the hardness of the hammer, the divine spectator and the seventh day – do you understand this antithesis? And that *your* pity is for the 'creature in man', for that which has to be formed, broken, forged, torn, burned, annealed, refined – that which has to *suffer* and *should* suffer? [. . .]

[*BGE* 225]

## 228

The problem I raise here is not what ought to succeed man- kind in the sequence of species (– the human being is an *end* –):

but what type of human being one ought to *breed*, ought to *will*, as more valuable, more worthy of life, more certain of the future.

This more valuable type has existed often enough already: but as a lucky accident, as an exception, never as *willed*. He has rather been the most feared, he has hitherto been virtually *the* thing to be feared – and out of fear the reverse type has been willed, bred, *achieved*: the domestic animal, the herd animal, the sick animal man – the Christian . . .

\*

Mankind does *not* represent a development of the better or the stronger or the higher in the way that is believed today. 'Progress' is merely a modern idea, that is to say, a false idea. The European of today is of far less value than the European of the Renaissance; onward development is not by *any* means, by any necessity, the same thing as elevation, advance, strengthening.

In another sense there are cases of individual success constantly appearing in the most various parts of the earth and from the most various cultures in which a *higher type* does manifest itself: something which in relation to collective mankind is a sort of superman. Such chance occurrences of great success have always been possible and perhaps always will be possible. And even entire races, tribes, nations can under certain circumstances represent such a *lucky hit*.

[*A* 3–4]

### 229

[. . .] The word '*superman*' as designating a type that has turned out supremely well, in antithesis to 'modern' men, to 'good' men, to Christians and other nihilists – a word which in the mouth of a Zarathustra, the *destroyer* of morality, becomes a very thoughtful word – has been understood almost everywhere with perfect innocence in the sense of those values

whose antithesis makes its appearance in the figure of Zarathustra: that is to say, as an 'idealistic' type of higher species
of man, half 'saint', half 'genius' ... Other learned cattle
caused me on account of it to be suspected of Darwinism;
even the 'hero cult' of that unconscious and involuntary
counterfeiter Carlyle which I rejected so maliciously has been
recognized in it. He into whose ear I whispered he should
look about him for a Cesare Borgia rather than for a Parsifal
did not believe his ears. [. . .]

[*EH Why I Write Such Excellent Books* 1]

# ETERNAL RECURRENCE

## 230

*For the New Year.* – I am still living, I am still thinking: I have to go on living because I have to go on thinking. [. . .] Today everyone is permitted to express his desire and dearest thoughts: so I, too, would like to say what I have desired of myself today and what thought was the first to cross my heart this year – what thought shall be the basis, guarantee and sweetness of all my future life! I want to learn more and more to see what is necessary in things as the beautiful in them – thus I shall become one of those who make things beautiful. *Amor fati*: may that be my love from now on! I want to wage no war against the ugly. I do not want to accuse, I do not want even to accuse the accusers. May *looking away* be my only form of negation! And, all in all: I want to be at all times hereafter only an affirmer!

[*GS* 276]

## 231

*The heaviest burden.* – What if a demon crept after you one day or night in your loneliest solitude and said to you: 'This life, as you live it now and have lived it, you will have to live again and again, times without number; and there will be nothing new in it, but every pain and every joy and every thought and sigh and all the unspeakably small and great in your life must return to you, and everything in the same series and sequence – and in the same way this spider and this moonlight among the trees, and in the same way this moment and I myself. The

249

eternal hour-glass of existence will be turned again and again
– and you with it, you dust of dust!' – Would you not throw
yourself down and gnash your teeth and curse the demon who
thus spoke? Or have you experienced a tremendous moment
in which you would have answered him: 'You are a god and
never did I hear anything more divine!' If this thought gained
power over you it would, as you are now, transform and perhaps crush you; the question in all and everything: 'do you
want this again and again, times without number?' would lie
as the heaviest burden upon all your actions. Or how well
disposed towards yourself and towards life would you have
to become to have *no greater desire* than for this ultimate eternal
sanction and seal?

[*GS* 341]

### 232

To you, the bold venturers and adventurers and whoever
has embarked with cunning sails upon dreadful seas,

to you who are intoxicated by riddles, who take pleasure in
twilight, whose soul is lured with flutes to every treacherous
abyss [. . .]

to you alone do I tell this riddle that I *saw* – the vision of
the most solitary man.

Lately, I walked gloomily through a deathly-grey twilight,
gloomily and sternly with compressed lips. Not only one sun
had gone down for me.

A path that mounted defiantly through boulders and rubble,
a wicked, solitary path that bush or plant no longer cheered:
a mountain path crunched under my foot's defiance.

Striding mute over the mocking clatter of pebbles, tramp-
ling the stones that made it slip: thus my foot with effort
forced itself upward.

Upward – despite the spirit that drew it downward, drew
it towards the abyss, the Spirit of Gravity, my devil and arch-
enemy.

Upwards – although he sat upon me, half dwarf, half mole;

crippled, crippling; pouring lead-drops into my ear, leaden thoughts into my brain.

'O Zarathustra,' he said mockingly, syllable by syllable, 'you stone of wisdom! You have thrown yourself high, but every stone that is thrown must – fall! [. . .]

'Condemned by yourself and to your own stone-throwing; o Zarathustra, far indeed have you thrown your stone, but it will fall back upon *you*!' [. . .]

I climbed, I climbed, I dreamed, I thought, but everything oppressed me. I was like a sick man wearied by his sore torment and reawakened from sleep by a worse dream.

But there is something in me that I call courage: it has always destroyed every discouragement in me. This courage at last bade me stop and say: 'Dwarf! You! Or I!' [. . .]

Then something occurred which lightened me: for the dwarf jumped from my shoulder, the inquisitive dwarf! And he squatted down upon a stone in front of me. But a gateway stood just where we had halted.

'Behold this gateway, dwarf!' I went on: 'it has two aspects. Two paths come together here: no one has ever reached their end.

'This long lane behind us: it goes on for an eternity. And that long lane ahead of us – that is another eternity.

'They are in opposition to one another, these paths; they abut on one another: and it is here at this gateway that they come together. The name of the gateway is written above it: "Moment".

'But if one were to follow them further and ever further and further: do you think, dwarf, that these paths would be in eternal opposition?'

'Everything straight lies,' murmured the dwarf disdainfully. 'All truth is crooked, time itself is a circle.' [. . .]

'Behold this moment!' I went on. 'From this gateway Moment a long, eternal lane runs *back*: an eternity lies behind us.

'Must not all things that *can* run have already run along this lane? Must not all things that *can* happen *have* already happened, been done, run past?

'And if all things have been here before: what do you think of this moment, dwarf? Must not this gateway, too, have been here – before?

'And are not all things bound fast together in such a way that this moment draws after it all future things? *Therefore* – draws itself too?

'For all things that *can* run *must* also run once again forward along this long lane.

'And this slow spider that creeps along in the moonlight, and this moonlight itself, and I and you at this gateway whispering together, whispering of eternal things – must we not all have been here before?

' – and must we not return down that other lane out before us, down that long, terrible lane – must we not return eternally?' [. . .]

[Z III *Of the Vision and the Riddle*]

## 233

[. . .] 'Sing and bubble over, o Zarathustra, heal your soul with new songs, so that you may bear your great destiny, that was never yet the destiny of any man!

'For your animals well know, o Zarathustra, who you are and must become: behold, *you are the teacher of the eternal recurrence*, that is now *your* destiny!

'That you have to be the first to teach this doctrine – how should this great destiny not also be your greatest danger and sickness!

'Behold, we know what you teach: that all things recur eternally and we ourselves with them, and that we have already existed an infinite number of times before and all things with us.

'You teach that there is a great year of becoming, a colossus of a year: this year must, like an hour-glass, turn itself over again and again, so that it may run down and run out anew:

'so that all these years resemble one another, in the greatest

things and in the smallest, so that we ourselves resemble ourselves in each great year, in the greatest things and in the
smallest.

'And if you should die now, o Zarathustra: behold, we
know too what you would then say to yourself [. . .]

' "Now I die and decay," you would say, "and in an instant
I shall be nothingness. Souls are as mortal as bodies.

' "But the complex of causes in which I am entangled will
recur – it will create me again! I myself am part of these causes
of the eternal recurrence.

' "I shall return, with this sun, with this earth, with this
eagle, with this serpent – *not* to a new life or a better life or a
similar life:

' "I shall return eternally to this identical and self-same life,
in the greatest things and in the smallest, to teach once more
the eternal recurrence of all things,

' "to speak once more the teaching of the great noontide
of earth and man, to tell man of the superman once more.

' "I spoke my teaching, I broke upon my teaching: thus
my eternal fate will have it – as prophet do I perish" ' [. . .]

[Z III *The Convalescent*]

## 234

[. . .] *Come! Come! Come! Let us walk now! The hour has come:
let us walk into the night!*

*

You higher men, midnight is coming on: so I will say something in your ears, as that old bell says it in my ear,

as secretly, as fearfully, as warmly as that midnight-bell tells
it to me [. . .]

Soft! Soft! Then many a thing can be heard which may not
speak by day; but now, in the cool air, when all the clamour
of your hearts, too, has grown still,

now it speaks, now it is heard, now it creeps into nocturnal, over-wakeful souls: ah! ah! how it sighs! how in dreams it laughs!

do you not hear, how secretly, fearfully, warmly it speaks to you, the ancient, deep, deep midnight?

*O Man! Attend!*

\*

Woe is me! Where has time fled? Did I not sink into deep wells? The world is asleep –

Ah! Ah! The dog howls, the moon is shining. I will rather die, die, than tell you what my midnight-heart is now thinking.

Now I am dead. It is finished. Spider, why do you spin your web around me? Do you want blood? Ah! Ah! The dew is falling, the hour has come

– the hour which chills and freezes me, which asks and asks and asks: 'Who has heart enough for it?

' – who shall be master of the world? Who will say: Thus shall you run, you great and small streams!'

– the hour approaches: o man, you higher man, attend! this discourse is for delicate ears, for your ears – *what does deep midnight's voice contend?*

\*

I am borne away, my soul dances. The day's task! The day's task! Who shall be master of the world?

The moon is cool, the wind falls silent. Ah! Ah! Have you flown high enough? You dance: but a leg is not a wing.

You good dancers, now all joy is over: wine has become dregs, every cup has grown brittle, the graves mutter.

You have not flown high enough: now the graves mutter: 'Redeem the dead! Why is it night so long? Does the moon not intoxicate us?'

You higher men, redeem the graves, awaken the corpses! Alas, why does the worm still burrow? The hour approaches, it approaches,

the bell booms, the heart still drones, the woodworm, the heart's worm, still burrows. Alas! *The world is deep!*

\*

Sweet lyre! Sweet lyre! Your sound, your intoxicated, ominous sound, delights me! – from how long ago, from how far away does your sound come to me, from a far distance, from the pools of love!

You ancient bell, you sweet lyre! Every pain has torn at your heart, the pain of a father, the pain of our fathers, the pain of our forefathers; your speech has grown ripe,

ripe like golden autumn and afternoon, like my hermit's heart – now you say: The world itself has grown ripe, the grapes grow brown,

now they want to die, to die of happiness. You higher men, do you not smell it? An odour is secretly welling up,

a scent and odour of eternity, an odour of roseate bliss, a brown, golden wine odour of ancient happiness,

of intoxicated midnight's dying happiness, which sings: *The world is deep: deeper than day can comprehend!*

\*

Let me be! Let me be! I am too pure for you. Do not touch me! Has my world not just become perfect?

My skin is too pure for your hands. Let me be, stupid, doltish, stifling day! Is midnight not brighter?

The purest shall be master of the world; the least known, the strongest, the midnight souls, who are brighter and deeper than any day.

O day, do you grope for me? Do you feel for my happiness? Do you think me rich, solitary, a pit of treasure, a chamber of gold?

O world, do you desire me? Do you think me worldly? Do you think me spiritual? Do you think me divine? But day and world, you are too clumsy,

have cleverer hands, reach out for deeper happiness, for deeper unhappiness, reach out for some god, do not reach out for me:

my unhappiness, my happiness is deep, you strange day, but yet I am no god, no divine Hell: *deep is its woe.*

\*

God's woe is deeper, you strange world! Reach out for God's woe, not for me! What am I? An intoxicated, sweet lyre

– a midnight lyre, a croaking bell which no one understands but which *has* to speak before deaf people, you higher men! For you do not understand me!

Gone! Gone! Oh youth! Oh noontide! Oh afternoon! Now come evening and midnight; the dog howls, the wind:

is the wind not a dog? It whines, it yelps, it howls. Ah! Ah! how it sighs! how it laughs, how it rasps and gasps, the midnight hour!

How it speaks soberly, this intoxicated poet! perhaps it has overdrunk its drunkenness? perhaps it has grown over-wakeful? perhaps it ruminates?

it ruminates upon its woe in dreams, the ancient, deep midnight hour, and still more upon its joy. For joy, though woe be deep: *Joy is deeper than heart's agony.*

*

You grape-vine! Why do you praise me? For I cut you! I am cruel, you bleed: what means your praise of my intoxicated cruelty?

'What has become perfect, everything ripe – wants to die!' thus you speak. Blessed, blessed be the vine-knife! But everything unripe wants to live: alas!

Woe says: 'Fade! Be gone, woe!' But everything that suffers wants to live, that it may grow ripe and merry and passionate,

passionate for remoter, higher, brighter things. 'I want heirs,' thus speaks everything that suffers, 'I want children, I do not want *myself*.'

Joy, however, does not want heirs or children, joy wants itself, wants eternity, wants recurrence, wants everything eternally the same.

Woe says: 'Break, bleed, heart! Walk, legs! Wings, fly! Upward! Upward, pain!' Very well! Come on! my old heart: *Woe says: Fade! Go!*

*

What do you think, you higher men? Am I a prophet? A dreamer? A drunkard? An interpreter of dreams? A midnight bell?

A drop of dew? An odour and scent of eternity? Do you not hear it? Do you not smell it? My world has just become perfect, midnight is also noonday,

pain is also joy, a curse is also a blessing, the night is also a sun – be gone, or you will learn: a wise man is also a fool.

Did you ever say Yes to one joy? O my friends, then you said Yes to *all* woe as well. All things are chained and entwined together, all things are in love;

if ever you wanted one moment twice, if ever you said: 'You please me, happiness, instant, moment!' then you wanted *everything* to return!

you wanted everything anew, everything eternal, everything chained, entwined together, everything in love, oh that is how you *loved* the world,

you everlasting men, loved it eternally and for all time: and you say even to woe: 'Go, but return!' *For all joy wants – eternity!*

*

All joy wants the eternity of all things, wants honey, wants dregs, wants intoxicated midnight, wants graves, wants the consolation of graveside tears, wants gilded sunsets,

*what* does joy not want! it is thirstier, warmer, hungrier, more fearful, more secret than all woe, it wants *itself*, it bites into *itself*, the will of the ring wrestles within it,

it wants love, it wants hatred, it is superabundant, it gives, throws away, begs for someone to take it, thanks him who takes, it would like to be hated;

so rich is joy that it thirsts for woe, for Hell, for hatred, for shame, for the lame, for the *world* – for it knows, oh it knows this world!

You higher men, joy longs for you, joy the intractable, blissful – for your woe, you ill-constituted! All eternal joy longs for the ill-constituted.

For all joy wants itself, therefore it also wants heart's agony!
O happiness! O pain! Oh break, heart! You higher men,
learn this, learn that joy wants eternity,

joy wants the eternity of all things, *wants deep, deep, deep
eternity!*

\*

Have you learned my song? Have you divined what it means?
Very well! Come on! You higher men, now sing my roundelay!

Now sing yourselves the song whose name is 'Once more',
whose meaning is 'To all eternity!' – sing, you higher men,
Zarathustra's roundelay!

> O Man! Attend!
> What does deep midnight's voice contend?
> 'I slept my sleep,
> 'And now awake at dreaming's end:
> 'The world is deep,
> 'Deeper than day can comprehend.
> 'Deep is its woe,
> 'Joy – deeper than heart's agony:
> 'Woe says: Fade! Go!
> 'But all joy wants eternity,
> 'Wants deep, deep, deep eternity!'
> [*Z* IV *The Drunken Song* 2–11]

## 235

He who, prompted by some enigmatic desire, has, like me,
long endeavoured to think pessimism through to the bottom
and to redeem it from the half-Christian, half-German simplicity and narrowness with which it finally presented itself to
this century, namely in the form of the Schopenhauerian
philosophy; he who has really gazed with an Asiatic and more
than Asiatic eye down into the most world-denying of all
possible modes of thought – beyond good and evil and no

longer, like Buddha and Schopenhauer, under the spell and illusion of morality – perhaps by that very act, and without really intending to, may have had his eyes opened to the opposite ideal: to the ideal of the most exuberant, most living and most world-affirming man, who has not only learned to get on and treat with all that was and is but who wants to have it again *as it was and is* to all eternity, insatiably calling out *da capo* not only to himself but to the whole piece and play, and not only to a play but fundamentally to him who needs precisely this play – and who makes it necessary: because he needs himself again and again – and makes himself necessary. – What? And would this not be – *circulus vitiosus deus*?

[*BGE* 56]

## 236

*Goethe* – not a German event but a European one: a grand attempt to overcome the eighteenth century through a return to nature, through a going-*up* to the naturalness of the Renaissance, a kind of self-overcoming on the part of that century. – He bore within him its strongest instincts: sentimentality, nature-idolatry, the anti-historical, the idealistic, the unreal and revolutionary (– the last is only a form of the unreal). He called to his aid history, the natural sciences, antiquity, likewise Spinoza, above all practical activity; he surrounded himself with nothing but closed horizons; he did not sever himself from life, he placed himself within it; nothing could discourage him and he took as much as possible upon himself, above himself, within himself. What he aspired to was *totality*; he strove against the separation of reason, sensuality, feeling, will [. . .] he disciplined himself as a whole, he *created* himself . . . Goethe was, in an epoch disposed to the unreal, a convinced realist: he affirmed everything which was related to him in this respect – he had no greater experience than that *ens realissimum* called Napoleon. Goethe conceived of a strong, highly cultured human being, skilled in all physical accomplishments, who, keeping himself in check and having reverence for himself, dares to allow himself the whole compass and wealth of naturalness, who is strong enough for this freedom; a man of tolerance, not out of weakness, but out of strength, because he knows how to employ to his advantage what would destroy an average nature; a man to whom nothing is forbidden, except it be *weakness*, whether that weakness be called vice or virtue ... A spirit thus *emancipated* stands in the midst of the universe with a joyful and trusting fatalism, in the *faith* that only what is separate and individual may be rejected, that in the totality everything is redeemed and affirmed – *he no longer denies* ... But such a faith is the highest of all possible faiths: I have baptized it with the name *Dionysus*.

[*T Expeditions of an Untimely Man* 49]


## 237

[. . .] My formula for greatness in a human being is *amor fati*: that one wants nothing other than it is, not in the future, not in the past, not in all eternity. Not merely to endure that which happens of necessity, still less to dissemble it – all idealism is untruthfulness in the face of necessity – but to *love* it . . .

[*EH Why I Am So Clever* 10]


## 238

[. . .] I was the first to see the real antithesis – the *degenerate* instinct which turns against life with subterranean revengefulness [. . .] and a formula of *supreme affirmation* born of abundance and plenitude, an affirmation without reserve, of suffering itself, of guilt itself, of everything questionable and strange in existence [. . .] Nothing that is can be subtracted, nothing is dispensable – the sides of existence rejected by the Christians and other nihilists are even of an endlessly higher order in the order of rank of values than that which the *décadence* instinct can approve and call good. [. . .] He who does not merely understand the word 'Dionysian' but understands *himself* in the word 'Dionysian' needs no refutation of Plato or Christianity or Schopenhauer – he *smells the decomposition* . . .

*

The extent to which I therewith discovered the concept 'tragic', the final knowledge of what the psychology of tragedy is, I at length gave expression to in the *Twilight of the Idols*. 'Affirmation of life even in its strangest and sternest problems; the will to life rejoicing in its own inexhaustibility through the *sacrifice* of its highest types – *that* is what I called Dionysian, that is what I recognized as the bridge to the psychology of the tragic poet. *Not* so as to get rid of pity and terror, not so as to purify oneself of a dangerous emotion through its vehement discharge – it was thus Aristotle misunderstood it – : but, beyond pity and terror, *to realize in oneself* the eternal joy of becoming – that joy which also encompasses *joy in destruction* . . .' In this sense I have the right to understand myself as the first *tragic philosopher* – that is to say, the extreme antithesis and antipodes of a pessimistic philosopher.

[*EH The Birth of Tragedy* 2–3]

## 239

[. . .] The basic conception of this work [*Thus Spoke Zarathustra*], the *idea of eternal recurrence*, the highest formula of affirmation that can possibly be attained – belongs to the August of the year 1881: it was jotted down on a piece of paper with the inscription: '6,000 feet beyond man and time'. I was that day walking through the woods beside the lake of Silvaplana; I stopped beside a mighty pyramidal block of stone which reared itself up not far from Surlei. Then this idea came to me. [. . .]

[*EH Thus Spoke Zarathustra* 1]


## 240

Have I been understood? – *Dionysus against the Crucified* . . .
[*EH Why I Am a Destiny* 9]

# POSTSCRIPTS

# A SHORT LEXICON

## Animals

I fear that the animals regard man as a creature of their own kind which has in a highly dangerous fashion lost its healthy animal reason – as the mad animal, as the laughing animal, as the weeping animal, as the unhappy animal.

[*GS* 224]

## Boredom

The saying 'The Magyar is much too lazy to feel bored' is thought-provoking. Only the most acute and active animals are capable of boredom. – A theme for a great poet would be *God's boredom* on the seventh day of creation.

[*WS* 56]

## Death

Disregarding the demands made by religion one might well ask: why should it be more laudable for an old man who senses the decline of his powers to await his slow exhaustion and dissolution than in full consciousness to set himself a limit? Suicide is in this case a wholly natural obvious action, which as a victory for reason ought fairly to awaken reverence: and did awaken it in those ages when the heads of Greek philosophy and the most upright Roman patriots were accustomed to die by suicide. [. . .]

[*HA* 80]

The whole way in which a person thinks of death during the high tide of his life and strength bears, to be sure, very eloquent witness as to that which is called his character; but the hour of death itself, his bearing on the deathbed, hardly does so at all. The exhaustion of expiring existence, especially when old people die, the irregular or insufficient nourishment of the brain during this last period, the occasional very bad attacks of pain, the new and untried nature of the whole condition and all too often the coming and going of superstitious impressions and fears, as if dying were a very important thing and bridges of the most terrible description are here being crossed – all this does not *permit* us to employ dying as evidence as to the living. It is, moreover, not true that the dying are in general more *honest* than the living: almost everyone is, rather, tempted by the solemn bearing of the bystanders, the streams of tears and feeling held back or let flow, into a now conscious, now unconscious comedy of vanity. [. . .]

[*AOM* 88]

I derive a melancholy happiness from living in the midst of this confusion of streets, needs, voices: how much enjoyment, impatience, desire, how much thirsty life and drunkenness of life comes to the light of day every moment! And yet for all these noisy, living, life-thirsty people it will soon be so still and silent! How behind each of them stands his shadow, his dark companion! It is always like the last moment before the departure of an emigrant ship: people have more to say to one another than ever before, the hour presses, the ocean and its empty silence waits impatiently behind all the noise – so greedy, so certain of its prey! And all and everyone believes that what has been is nothing or little, the immediate future is all: and thus this haste, this clamour, this self-deafening, this self-overreaching! Everyone wants to be the first into this future – and yet death and the silence of death is the only certain thing and the thing common to all in this future! How strange that this sole certainty and common possession has almost no power at all over men and that they are at the *furthest remove* from feeling themselves as the brotherhood of death! It makes me happy to see that men are altogether disinclined to think the thought of death! I should like to do something to make the thought of life a hundred times *more worth thinking* for them.

[*GS* 278]

Many die too late and some die too early. Still the doctrine sounds strange: 'Die at the right time.' [. . .]

Everyone treats death as an important matter: but as yet death is not a festival. As yet men have not learned to consecrate the fairest festivals.

I shall show you the consummating death, which shall be a spur and promise to the living. [. . .]

I commend to you my sort of death, voluntary death that comes to me because *I* wish it.

And when shall I wish it? – He who has a goal and an heir wants death at the time most favourable to his goal and his heir.

And out of reverence for his goal and his heir he will hang up no more withered wreaths in the sanctuary of life. [. . .]

[Z I *Of Voluntary Death*]

*Democracy*
Parliamentarianism, that is to say public permission to choose between five political opinions, flatters those many who like to *appear* independent and individual and like to fight for their opinions. In the last resort, however, it is a matter of indifference whether the herd is commanded an opinion or allowed five opinions. – He who deviates from the five public opinions and steps aside always has the whole herd against him.

[*GS* 174]

*Dreams*
The brain function which is most encroached upon by sleep is the memory: not that it ceases altogether – but it is taken back to a condition of imperfection in which everyone may have possessed it in the primeval ages of mankind. Capricious and confused as it is, it continually confounds things on the

basis of the most fleeting similarity: but it was with the same
capriciousness and confusion that the peoples devised their
mythologies. [. . .] The perfect clarity of all dream images,
whose presupposition is an unconditional belief in their reality,
recalls to us states of earlier mankind, in which hallucination
was extraordinarily common and sometimes seized entire communities, entire peoples simultaneously. Thus: in sleep and
dreams we once again go through the curriculum of earlier
humanity.

[*HA* 12]

That which we sometimes do not know or feel precisely while
awake – whether we have a good or a bad conscience towards
a particular person – the dream informs us of without any
ambiguity.

[*AOM* 76]

*Europe*
Thanks to the morbid estrangement which the lunacy of
nationality has produced and continues to produce between
the peoples of Europe, thanks likewise to the short-sighted
and hasty-handed politicians who are with its aid on top today
and have not the slightest notion to what extent the politics
of disintegration they pursue must necessarily be only an inter-
lude – thanks to all this, and to much else that is altogether
unmentionable today, the most unambiguous signs are now
being overlooked, or arbitrarily and lyingly misinterpreted,
which declare that *Europe wants to become one.* In all the more
profound and comprehensive men of this century the general
tendency of the mysterious workings of their souls has really
been to prepare the way to this new *synthesis* and to anticipate
experimentally the European of the future [. . .]

[*BGE* 256]

We have Napoleon to thank [. . .] that a couple of warlike
centuries can now follow on one another which have no equal
in history, in short that we have entered the *classic age of war*

[. . .] upon which all coming centuries will look back with awe and envy as at a piece of perfection – for the national movement out of which this war glory is growing is only the counter-shock against Napoleon and without Napoleon would not exist. To him, then, it will one day be attributed that the *man* in Europe has again become master over the shopkeeper and philistine; perhaps even over 'the woman' [. . .] Napoleon [. . .] brought back an entire portion of antique nature [. . .] And who knows whether this portion of antique nature will not at last again become master over the national movement and have in an *affirmative* sense to make itself the heir and continuator of Napoleon – who wanted *one* Europe, as is well known, and this as *mistress of the earth.*

[*GS* 362]

We are [. . .] *good Europeans*, the heirs of [. . .] millennia of the European spirit: as such we have outgrown Christianity, and precisely because we have grown *out* of it, because our forefathers were Christians of the ruthless integrity of Christianity, who for the sake of their faith gladly sacrificed their goods and their blood, their station and their country. We – do the same [. . .]

[*GS* 377]

*Everyday things*
There exists a feigned disrespect for all the things which men in fact take most seriously, *for all the things closest to them.* One says, for example, 'one eats only in order to live' – which is a damned *lie*, as is that which speaks of the begetting of children as the real objective of all voluptuousness. Conversely, the high esteem in which the 'most serious things' are held is almost never quite genuine: the priests and metaphysicians, to be sure, have in these domains altogether accustomed us to a feignedly exaggerated *linguistic usage*, but they have not converted the feeling which refuses to take these most serious things as seriously as those despised closest things. – An unfortunate consequence of this twofold hypocrisy, however, is al-

ways that the closest things, for example eating, housing, clothing, social intercourse, are not made the object of constant impartial and *general* reflection and reform [. . .]

[*WS* 5]

I shall be asked why really I have narrated all these little and, according to traditional judgement, insignificant things [. . .] Answer: these little things – food, place, climate, recreation, the whole casuistry of egoism – are beyond all comparison more serious things than anything that has been taken seriously hitherto. It is precisely here that one must begin to *learn anew*. The things which humanity has hitherto earnestly pondered on are not even realities, mere figments of imagination, more strictly *lies* out of the bad instincts of sick, in the profoundest sense pernicious natures – all those concepts 'God', 'soul', 'virtue', 'sin', 'the Beyond', 'truth', 'eternal life' . . . But the greatness of human nature, its 'divinity', has been sought in these . . . Every question of politics, of the social order, of education has been falsified to the very bottom through taking the most pernicious men for great men – through teaching contempt for the 'little' things, which is to say for the fundamental affairs of life itself [. . .]

[*EH Why I Am so Clever* 10]

*Fashion*
The obvious self-contentment of the *individual* with his form excites imitation and gradually produces the form of the *many*, that is to say, fashion: the many want through fashion to attain to precisely that pleasing self-contentment with one's form and they do attain it. – If one considers how much reason every person has for anxiety and timid self-concealment, and how three-quarters of his energy and goodwill can be paralysed and made unfruitful by it, one has to be very grateful to fashion, insofar as it sets that three-quarters free and communicates self-confidence and mutual cheerful agreeableness to those who know they are all subject to its law. [. . .]

[*AOM* 209]

*Freedom*

The value of a thing sometimes lies not in what one attains with it, but in what one pays for it – what it *costs* us. I give an example. Liberal institutions immediately cease to be liberal as soon as they are attained: subsequently there is nothing more thoroughly harmful to freedom than liberal institutions. [. . .] As long as they are still being fought for, these same institutions produce quite different effects; they then in fact promote freedom mightily. Viewed more closely, it is war which produces these effects, war *for* liberal institutions which as war permits the *illiberal* instincts to endure. And war is a training in freedom. For what is freedom? That one has the will to self-responsibility. That one preserves the distance which divides us. That one has become more indifferent to hardship, toil, privation, even to life. That one is ready to sacrifice men to one's cause, oneself not excepted. Freedom means that the manly instincts that delight in war and victory have gained mastery over the other instincts – for example, over the instinct for 'happiness'. The man *who has become free* – and how much more the *mind* that has become free – spurns the contemptible sort of well-being dreamed of by shop-keepers, Christians, cows, women, Englishmen and other democrats. The free man is a *warrior*. – How is freedom measured, in individuals as in nations? By the resistance which has to be overcome, by the effort it costs to stay *aloft*. One would have to seek the highest type of free man where the greatest resistance is constantly being overcome: five steps from tyranny, near the threshold of the danger of servitude. This is true psychologically when one understands by 'tyrants' piti-less and dreadful instincts, to combat which demands the maxi-mum of authority and discipline towards oneself – finest type Julius Caesar – ; it is also true politically: one has only to look at history. The nations which were worth something, which *became* worth something, never became so under liberal insti-tutions: it was *great danger* which made of them something deserving reverence, danger which first teaches us to know our resources, our virtues, our shield and spear, our *spirit* –

which *compels* us to be strong ... *First* principle: one must need strength, otherwise one will never have it. – Those great forcing-houses for strong human beings, for the strongest kind there has ever been, the aristocratic communities of the pattern of Rome and Venice, understood freedom in precisely the sense in which I understand the word 'freedom': as something one has and does *not* have, something one *wants*, something one *conquers* ...

[*T Expeditions of an Untimely Man* 38]

*Friendship*
We were friends and have grown distant from one another. But it is right that should be so; let us not dissemble and obscure it, as if it were something to be ashamed of. We are two ships, each of which has its destination and its course; our paths can cross and we can celebrate a feast together, as we did – and then the brave ships lay so peacefully in *one* harbour and under *one* sun that it might seem they had already reached their destination and both had *one* destination. But then the almighty power of our task again drove us apart, to different seas and different climes, and perhaps we shall never see one another again – or perhaps if we do we shall not recognize one another: different seas and sun have changed us! That we had to grow distant from one another is the law *over* us [. . .] There is probably a tremendous invisible curve and star orbit within which our so different paths and destinations may be *included* as tiny stretches of the way – let us raise ourselves to this thought! But our life is too short and our power of vision too weak for us to be more than friends in the sense of that exalted possibility. – And so let us *believe* in our friendship in the stars, even if we did have to be enemies on earth.

[*GS* 279]

*History*
If genius consists, according to Schopenhauer's observation, in the connected and lively recollection of experience, then in the striving for knowledge of the entire historical past [. . .]

it may be possible to recognize a striving for the genius of mankind as a whole. History perfect and complete would be cosmic self-consciousness.

[*AOM* 185]

Because men really respect only that which was founded of old and has developed slowly, he who wants to live on after his death must take care not only of his posterity but even more of his *past*: which is why tyrants of every kind (including tyrannical artists and politicians) like to do violence to history, so that it may appear as preparation for and step-ladder to them.

[*AOM* 307]

*Money*

An exchange is honest and just only when each of those participating demands as much as his own object seems worth to him, including the effort it cost to acquire it, its rarity, the time expended, etc., together with its sentimental value. As soon as he sets the price *with reference to the need of the other* he is a subtler robber and extortioner. – If money is the exchange object it must be considered that a shilling in the hand of a rich heir, a day-labourer, a shopkeeper, a student are quite different things: according to whether he did almost nothing or a great deal to get it, each ought to receive little or a great deal in exchange for it: in reality it is, of course, the other way round. In the great world of money the shilling of the laziest rich man is more lucrative than that of the poor and industrious.

[*WS* 25]

*Solitude*

One receives as a reward for much *ennui*, despondency, boredom – such as a solitude without friends, books, duties, passions must bring with it – those quarter-hours of profoundest contemplation within oneself and nature. He who completely entrenches himself against boredom also entrenches

273

himself against himself: he will never get to drink the strongest refreshing draught from his own innermost fountain.

[*WS* 200]

## *War*

We do not wish to be spared by our best enemies, nor by those whom we love from the very heart. So let me tell you the truth!

My brothers in war! I love you from the very heart, I am and always have been of your kind. And I am also your best enemy. So let me tell you the truth!

I know the hatred and envy of your hearts. You are not great enough not to know hatred and envy. So be great enough not to be ashamed of them!

And if you cannot be saints of knowledge, at least be its warriors. They are the companions and forerunners of such sainthood. [. . .]

You should seek your enemy, you should wage your war – a war for your opinions. And if your opinion is defeated, your honesty should still cry triumph over that!

You should love peace as a means to new wars. And the short peace more than the long.

I do not exhort you to work but to battle. I do not exhort you to peace but to victory. May your work be a battle, may your peace be a victory! [. . .]

You say it is the good cause that hallows even war? I tell you: it is the good war that hallows every cause.

War and courage have done more great things than charity. Not your pity but your bravery has saved the unfortunate up to now. [. . .]

You may have enemies whom you hate, but not enemies whom you despise. You must be proud of your enemy: then the success of your enemy shall be your success too. [. . .]

[*Z* I *Of War and Warriors*]

## *Women*

If you admit to a woman that she is in the right, she cannot refrain from setting her heel triumphantly on the neck of the defeated – she has to enjoy victory to the full; while between men in such a case being in the right usually produces a feeling of embarrassment. As a consequence the man is accustomed to victory, while to the woman it comes as an exception.

[*AOM* 291]

'Stupid as a man' say the women: 'cowardly as a woman' say the men. Stupidity is in woman the *unwomanly*.

[*WS* 273]

That someone cannot defend himself, and consequently does not want to do so, does not of itself lower him in our estimation: but we rate him low who has neither the ability nor the good will to revenge – whether this person be man or woman. Would a woman be able to hold us (or as they say 'captivate' us) if we did not believe that under certain circumstances she could use the dagger (any kind of dagger) *against us*? Or against herself: which in a certain case would be the more painful revenge (Chinese revenge).

[*GS* 69]

Today as I was going my way alone, at the hour when the sun sets, a little old woman encountered me and spoke thus to my soul:
'Zarathustra has spoken much to us women, too, but he has never spoken to us about woman.' [. . .]
And I obliged the little old woman and spoke to her thus:
Everything about woman is a riddle, and everything about woman has one solution: it is called pregnancy.
For the woman, the man is a means: the end is always the child. But what is the woman for the man?
The true man wants two things: danger and play. For that reason he wants woman, as the most dangerous plaything.
Man should be trained for war and woman for the recreation of the warrior: all else is folly. [. . .]

Let man fear woman when she loves. Then she bears every sacrifice and every other thing she accounts valueless.

Let man fear woman when she hates: for man is at the bottom of his soul only wicked, but woman is base.

Whom does woman hate most? – Thus spoke the iron to the magnet: 'I hate you most, because you attract me but are not strong enough to draw me towards you.'

The man's happiness is: I will. The woman's happiness is: He will. [. . .]

Then the little old woman answered me: 'Zarathustra has said many nice things, especially for those who are young enough for them. [. . .]

'And now accept as thanks a little truth! I am certainly old enough for it!

'Wrap it up and stop its mouth: otherwise it will cry too loudly, this little truth!'

'Give me your little truth, woman!' I said. And thus spoke the little old woman:

'Are you visiting a woman? Do not forget your whip!'

[Z I *Of Old and Young Women*]

# MAXIMS AND REFLECTIONS

*Quiet fruitfulness.* – The born aristrocrats of the spirit are not too zealous: their creations appear and fall from the tree on a quiet autumn evening unprecipitately, in due time, not quickly pushed aside by something new. The desire to create continually is vulgar and betrays jealousy, envy, ambition. If one is something one really does not need to make anything – and one nonetheless does very much. There exists above the 'productive' man a yet higher species.

[*HA* 210]

*Power without victories.* – The strongest knowledge (that of the total unfreedom of the human will) is nonetheless the poorest in successes: for it always has the strongest opponent, human vanity.

[*AOM* 50]

*Making plans.* – To make plans and project designs brings with it many good sensations; and whoever had the strength to be nothing but a forger of plans his whole life long would be a very happy man: but he would occasionally have to take a rest from this activity by carrying out a plan – and then comes the vexation and the sobering up.

[*AOM* 85]

*Judicial murders.* – The two greatest judicial murders in world history are, not to mince words, disguised and well-disguised suicides. In both cases the victim *wanted* to die; in both cases he employed the hand of human injustice to drive the sword into his own breast.

[*AOM* 94]

*When asses are needed.* – You will never get the crowd to cry Hosanna until you ride into town on an ass.

[*AOM* 313]

*To one who is praised.* – So long as you are praised think only that you are not yet on your own path but on that of another.

[*AOM* 340]

*Worms.* – It says nothing against the ripeness of a spirit that it has a few worms.

[*AOM* 353]

*On spiritual order of rank.* – It ranks you far beneath him that you seek to establish the exceptions while he seeks to establish the rule.

[*AOM* 362]

*Unforgivable.* – You gave him an opportunity of showing greatness of character and he did not seize it. He will never forgive you for that.

[*AOM* 384]

*Modesty of man.* – How little pleasure most people need to make them find life good, how modest man is!

[*WS* 15]

*The modern Diogenes.* – Before one seeks men one must have found the lantern. Will it have to be the lantern of the cynic?

[*WS* 18]

*End and goal.* – Not every end is a goal. The end of a melody is not its goal; but nonetheless, if the melody had not reached its end it would not have reached its goal either. A parable.

[*WS* 204]

*Not to assert one's rights.* – To exercise power costs effort and demands courage. That is why so many fail to assert rights to which they are perfectly entitled – because a right is a kind of *power* but they are too lazy or too cowardly to exercise it. The virtues which cloak these faults are called *patience* and *forbearance*.

[*WS* 251]

*Letter*. – A letter is an unannounced visit, the postman the agent of rude surprises. One ought to reserve an hour a week for receiving letters and afterwards take a bath.

[*WS* 261]

*Great and transitory*. – It moves the observer to tears to see the admiring look of happiness with which a pretty young wife gazes up at her husband. One is filled with autumnal melancholy to think of the greatness as well as the transitoriness of human happiness.

[*WS* 271]

*Premises of the machine age*. – The press, the machine, the railway, the telegraph are premises whose thousand-year conclusion no one has yet dared to draw.

[*WS* 278]

*The most dangerous follower*. – The most dangerous follower is he whose defection would destroy the whole party: that is to say, the best follower.

[*WS* 290]

*Man!* – What is the vanity of the vainest man compared with the vanity which the most modest possesses when, in the midst of nature and the world, he feels himself to be 'man'!

[*WS* 304]

*To become a thinker*. – How can anyone become a thinker if he does not spend at least a third of the day without passions, people and books?

[*WS* 324]

*Weather prophets.* – Just as the clouds tell us the direction of the wind high above our heads, so the lightest and freest spirits are in their tendencies foretellers of the weather that is coming. The wind in the valley and the opinions of the market-place of today indicate nothing of that which is coming but only of that which has been.

[WS 330]

*To die for 'truth'.* – We would not let ourselves be burned to death for our opinions: we are not sure enough of them for that. But perhaps for the right to have our opinions and to change them.

[WS 333]

*Justice.* – Better to let yourself be robbed than have scarecrows about you – that is my taste. And it is under all circumstances a matter of taste – and no more!

[GS 184]

*A way of asking for reasons.* – There is a way of asking us for our reasons which makes us not only forget our best reasons but awakens in us a defiance of and repugnance for reasons in general – a way of asking which makes us very stupid and a typical trick of tyrannical people!

[GS 209]

*Defiance and loyalty.* – He clings firmly out of defiance to a cause which he has seen through – but he calls it 'loyalty'.

[GS 229]

*What we do.* – What we do is never understood but always merely praised and blamed.

[GS 264]

Objection, evasion, happy distrust, pleasure in mockery are signs of health: everything unconditional belongs in pathology.

[BGE 154]

*From the military school of life.* – What does not kill me makes me stronger.

[*T Maxims and Arrows* 8]

Formula of my happiness: a Yes, a No, a straight line, a *goal* . . .

[*T Maxims and Arrows* 44]

[. . .] Early in the morning, at break of day, in all the freshness and dawn of one's strength, to read a *book* – I call that vicious!

[*EH Why I Am so Clever* 8]

## 'THE GENIUS OF THE HEART...'

The genius of the heart as it is possessed by that great hidden one, the tempter god and born pied piper of consciences whose voice knows how to descend into the underworld of every soul, who says no word and gives no glance in which there lies no touch of enticement, to whose mastery belongs knowing how to seem – not what he is but what to those who follow him is one constraint *more* to press ever closer to him, to follow him ever more inwardly and thoroughly – the genius of the heart who makes everything loud and self-satisfied fall silent and teaches it to listen, who smooths rough souls and gives them a new desire to savour – the desire to lie still as a mirror, that the deep sky may mirror itself in them – ; the genius of the heart who teaches the stupid and hasty hand to hesitate and grasp more delicately; who divines the hidden and forgotten treasure, the drop of goodness and sweet spirituality under thick and opaque ice, and is a divining-rod for every grain of gold which has lain long in the prison of much mud and sand; the genius of the heart from whose touch everyone goes away richer, not favoured and surprised, not as if blessed and oppressed with the goods of others, but richer in himself, newer to himself than before, broken open, blown upon and sounded out by a thawing wind, more uncertain perhaps, more delicate, more fragile, more broken, but full of hopes that as yet have no names, full of new will and current, full of new ill-will and counter-current . . . but what am I doing, my friends? Of whom am I speaking to you? Have I so far forgot myself that I have not even told you his name? Unless you have already yourselves divined who this questionable god and spirit is who wants to be *praised* in such a fashion. For, as

282

happens to everyone who has always been on the move and in foreign lands from his childhood up, so many a strange and not undangerous spirit has crossed my path, too, but above all he of whom I was just speaking, and he again and again, no less a personage in fact than the god *Dionysus*, that great ambiguous and tempter god to whom, as you know, once I brought in all secrecy and reverence my first-born – being, as it seems to me, the last to have brought him a *sacrifice*: for I have found no one who could have understood what I was then doing. Meanwhile, I have learned much, all too much more about the philosophy of this god and, as I have said, from mouth to mouth – I, the last disciple and initiate of the god Dionysus: and perhaps I might at last begin to give you, my friends, a little taste of this philosophy, insofar as I am permitted to? In a hushed voice, as is only proper: for it involves much that is secret, new, unfamiliar, strange, uncanny. The very fact that Dionysus is a philosopher, and that gods, too, therefore philosophize, seems a by no means harmless novelty and one calculated to excite suspicion precisely among philosophers – among you, my friends, it will meet with a friendlier reception, unless it comes too late and not at the right time: for, as I have discovered, you no longer like to believe in God and gods now. Perhaps I shall also have to go further in the frankness of my story than may always be agreeable to the habits of your ears? Certainly the above-named god went further, very much further, in conversations of this sort, and was always many steps ahead of me ... Indeed, if it were permitted to follow the human custom of applying to him the beautiful, solemn titles of pomp and virtue, I would have to extol his courage as investigator and discoverer, his daring honesty, truthfulness and love of wisdom. But such a god has nothing to do with all this venerable lumber and pomp. 'Keep that,' he would say, 'for yourself and your like and for anyone else who needs it! I – have no reason to cover my nakedness!' – One will see that this species of divinity and philosopher is perhaps lacking in shame? – Thus he once said: 'Under certain circumstances I love mankind' –

alluding to Ariadne, who was present – : 'Man is to me an agreeable, brave, ingenious animal without equal on earth, he knows how to make his way through every labyrinth. I like him: I often ponder how I might advance him and make him stronger, more evil and more profound than he is.' – 'Stronger, more evil and more profound?' I asked in alarm. 'Yes,' he repeated, 'stronger, more evil and more profound; also more beautiful' – and as he said that the tempter god smiled his halcyon smile, as though he had just paid a charming compliment. Here one will also see that this divinity is lacking not only in shame – ; and there is in general good reason to suppose that in several respects the gods could all benefit from instruction by us human beings. We humans are – more humane.

[*BGE* 295]

# BIBLIOGRAPHY

All the books drawn on for the *Nietzsche Reader* are available in English translation. *The Complete Works of Friedrich Nietzsche*, edited by Oscar Levy (London and New York, 1909–13), reprinted by Russell and Russell, New York, in 1964, naturally includes them, but the quality of translation is very uneven and often unreliable. The reader without German is therefore advised to go to more recent translations where these are available, as they are in the following cases:

*The Gay Science*, translated by Walter Kaufmann (Random House, New York, 1974)

*Thus Spoke Zarathustra*, translated by R. J. Hollingdale (Penguin Books, Harmondsworth, 1961)

*Thus Spoke Zarathustra*, translated by Walter Kaufmann (in *The Portable Nietzsche*, Viking Press, New York, 1954)

*Beyond Good and Evil*, translated by R. J. Hollingdale (Penguin Books, Harmondsworth, 1973)

*Beyond Good and Evil*, translated by Walter Kaufmann (in *Basic Writings of Nietzsche*, Modern Library Giants, New York, 1968)

*On the Genealogy of Morals*, translated by Francis Golffing (Doubleday, New York, 1956)

*On the Genealogy of Morals*, translated by Walter Kaufmann and R. J. Hollingdale (in *Basic Writings*)

*The Wagner Case*, translated by Walter Kaufmann (in *Basic Writings*)

*Twilight of the Idols*, translated by R. J. Hollingdale (Penguin Books, Harmondsworth, 1969)

*Twilight of the Idols*, translated by Walter Kaufmann (in *Portable*)

*The Anti-Christ*, translated by R. J. Hollingdale (Penguin Books, Harmondsworth, 1969)

*The Anti-Christ*, translated by Walter Kaufmann (in *Portable*)

*Ecce Homo*, translated by Walter Kaufmann (in *Basic Writings*)

The original texts are again of course to be found in any collected edition: the easiest to obtain is the *Werke in drei Bänden*, herausgegeben von Karl Schlechta (Munich, 3rd edn 1965, plus index vol) or the reprints in *Kröners Taschenausgabe* (Stuttgart, 1952 ff).

The most complete collected edition is the *Gesamtausgabe in Grossoktav* (Leipzig, 1901–13); but this will in due course be superseded by *Werke. Kritische Gesamtausgabe*, herausgegeben von Giorgio Colli und Mazzino Montinari (Berlin, Paris and Milan), now in course of publication, which is intended to be the first truly complete edition of all Nietzsche's works and MSS.

# CHRONOLOGY

1844    15 October. Friedrich Wilhelm Nietzsche born in the parsonage at Röcken, near Lützen, Germany, the first of three children of Karl Ludwig, the village pastor, and Fraziska Nietzsche, daughter of the pastor of a nearby village.

1849    27 July. Nietzsche's father dies.

1850    The Nietzsche family moves to Naumberg, in Thuringia, in April. Arthur Schopenhauer publishes *Essays, Aphorisms and Maxims*.

1856    Birth of Freud.

1858    The family moves to No. 18 Weingarten. Nietzsche wins a place at the prestigious Pforta grammar school.

1860    Forms a literary society, 'Germania', with two Naumberg friends. Jacob Burckhardt publishes *The Civilization of the Renaissance in Italy*.

1864    Enters Bonn University as a student of theology and philology.

1865    At Easter, Nietzsche abandons the study of theology having lost his Christian belief. Leaves Bonn for Leipzig, following his former tutor of philology, Friedrich Ritschl. Begins to read Schopenhauer.

1867    First publication, 'Zur Geschichte der Theognideischen Spruchsammlung' (The History of the Theognidia Collection) in the *Rheinische Museum für Philiogie*. Begins military service.

1868    Discharged from the army. Meets Richard Wagner.

1869    Appointed to the chair of classical philology at Basle University having been recommended by Ritschl. Awarded a doctorate by Leipzig. Regular visitor at Wagners' home in Tribschen.

1870    Delivers public lectures on 'The Greek Music Drama' and 'Socrates and Tragedy'. Serves as a medical orderly with the Prussian army where he is taken ill with diphtheria.

1871    Applies unsuccessfully for the chair of philology at Basle. His health deteriorates. Takes leave to recover and works on *The Birth of Tragedy*.

1872    *The Birth of Tragedy* published (January). Public lectures 'On the Future of our Educational Institutions'.

1873    *Untimely Meditations I: David Strauss* published.

1874    *Untimely Meditations II: On the Use and Disadvantage of History for*

*Life* and *III: Schopenhauer as Educator* published.

1875 Meets Peter Gast, who is to become his earliest 'disciple'. Suffers from ill-health leading to a general collapse at Christmas.

1876 Granted a long absence from Basle due to continuing ill-health. Proposes marriage to Mathilde Trampedach but is rejected. *Untimely Meditations IV: Richard Wagner in Bayreuth* published. Travels to Italy.

1878 *Human, All Too Human* published. His friendship with the Wagners comes to an end.

1879 *Assorted Opinions and Maxims* published. Retires on a pension from Basle due to sickness.

1880 *The Wanderer and his Shadow* and *Human, All Too Human* II published.

1881 *Dawn* published.

1882 *The Gay Science* published. Proposes to Lou Andreas Salomé and is rejected.

1883 13 February. Wagner dies in Venice. *Thus Spoke Zarathustra* I and II published.

1884 *Thus Spoke Zarathustra* III published.

1885 *Zarathustra* IV privately printed.

1886 *Beyond Good and Evil* published.

1887 *On the Genealogy of Morals* published.

1888 *The Wagner Case* published. First review of his work as a whole published in the Bern *Bund.* Experiences some improvement in health but this is short-lived.

1889 Suffers mental collapse in Turin and is admitted to a psychiatric clinic at the University of Jena. *Twilight of the Idols* published and *Nietzsche contra Wagner* privately printed.

1890 Nietzsche returns to his mother's home.

1891 *Dithyrambs of Dionysus* published.

1894 *The Anti-Christ* published. The 'Nietzsche Archive' founded by his sister, Elisabeth.

1895 *Nietzsche contra Wagner* published.

1897 20 April. Nietzsche's mother dies; and Elisabeth moves Nietzsche to Weimar.

1900 25 August. Nietzsche dies. Freud publishes *Interpretation of Dreams*.

1901 Publication of *The Will to Power*, papers selected by Elisabeth and Peter Gast.

1908 *Ecce Homo* published.